PRO/CON VOLUME 19

WORLD POLITICS

Published 2005 by Grolier,
an imprint of Scholastic Library Publishing
Old Sherman Turnpike
Danbury, Connecticut 06816

Library of Congress Cataloging-in-Publication Data
Pro/con
   p. cm
 Includes bibliographical references and index.
  Contents: v. 19. World Politics – v. 20 Religion and Morality – v. 21. U.S.
Judiciary – v. 22. International Law – v. 23. Poverty and Wealth – v. 24. Work and
the Workplace.
  ISBN 0-7172-5950-1 (set : alk. paper) – ISBN 0-7172-5951–X (vol. 19 : alk. paper) –
ISBN 0-7172-5952-8 (vol. 20 : alk. paper) – ISBN 0-7172-5953-6 (vol. 21 : alk. paper)
 – ISBN 0-7172-5954-4 (vol. 22 : alk. paper) – ISBN 0-7172-5955-2 (vol. 23 : alk.
paper) – ISBN 0-7172-5956-0 (vol. 24 : alk. paper)
  1. Social problems. I. Scholastic Publishing Ltd Grolier (Firm)

HN17.5 P756 2002
361.1–dc22

                                                              2001053234

Printed and bound in Singapore

SET ISBN 0-7172-5950-1
VOLUME ISBN 0-7172-5951-X

For The Brown Reference Group plc
Project Editors: Aruna Vasudevan, Claire Chandler
Editors: Fiona Plowman, Chris Marshall
Consultant Editor: Ron Lee, Chairman, Social Studies Department
at Keith Country Day School, Rockford, Illinois
Designer: Sarah Williams
Picture Research and Permissions: Clare Newman, Susy Forbes
Set Index: Kay Ollerenshaw

Senior Managing Editor: Tim Cooke
Art Director: Dave Goodman
Production Director: Alastair Gourlay

GENERAL PREFACE

"All that is necessary for evil to triumph is for good men to do nothing."
—Edmund Burke, 18th-century English political philosopher

Decisions

Life is full of choices and decisions. Some are more important than others. Some affect only your daily life—the route you take to school, for example, or what you prefer to eat for supper—while others are more abstract and concern questions of right and wrong rather than practicality. That does not mean that your choice of presidential candidate or your views on abortion are necessarily more important than your answers to purely personal questions. But it is likely that those wider questions are more complex and subtle and that you therefore will need to know more information about the subject before you can try to answer them. They are also likely to be questions about which you might have to justify your views to other people. In order to do that, you need to be able to make informed decisions, be able to analyze every fact at your disposal, and evaluate them in an unbiased manner.

What Is *Pro/Con*?

Pro/Con is a collection of debates that presents conflicting views on some of the more complex and general issues facing Americans today. By bringing together extracts from a wide range of sources—mainstream newspapers and magazines, books, famous speeches, legal judgments, religious tracts, government surveys—the set reflects current informed attitudes toward dilemmas that range from the best way to feed the world's growing population to gay rights, from the connection between political freedom and capitalism to the fate of Napster.

The people whose arguments make up the set are for the most part acknowledged experts in their fields, making the vast differences in their points of view even more remarkable. The arguments are presented in the form of debates for and against various propositions, such as "Do extradition treaties violate human rights?" or "Should companies be allowed to relocate abroad?" This question format reflects the way in which ideas often occur in daily life: in the classroom, on TV shows, in business meetings, or even in state or federal politics.

The contents

The subjects of the six volumes of *Pro/Con 4—World Politics, Religion and Morality, U.S. Judiciary, International Law, Poverty and Wealth,* and *Work and the Workplace—* are issues on which it is preferable that people's opinions be based on information rather than personal bias.

Special boxes throughout *Pro/Con* comment on the debates as you are reading them, pointing out facts, explaining terms, or analyzing arguments to help you think about what is being said.

Introductions and summaries also provide background information that might help you reach your own conclusions. There are also tips about how to structure an argument that you can apply on an everyday basis to any debate or conversation, learning how to present your point of view as effectively and persuasively as possible.

VOLUME PREFACE
World Politics

The modern word "political" derives from the Greek *politikos*, meaning of or pertaining to the *polis* (city-state). For centuries experts have studied politics: The Greek philosopher Aristotle considered it the most authoratitive science—a practical science concerned with noble action and the happiness of citizens. Others, however, view politics less favorably.

Why politics is important

Much has been written about world politics over the years in books, journals, and newspapers, but a lot of the information people receive is contradictory and therefore confusing. Today the media and new technology have also meant that increasing numbers of people can learn about events happening even in the most remote regions of the world almost as soon as they occur. However, this also makes it all the more important for us to be able to comprehend what we are seeing, hearing, or reading, to make sure that we are properly and accurately informed, are able to question the information we are given in order to make clear and unbiased judgments, and understand that even events in remote and seemingly small countries can have longlasting effects on how we live. For example, events in the Middle East may affect not only the countries immediately concerned but also the economies of nation-states in other parts of the world: Terrorism can destablize stock-market prices, while politically unstable oil-producing countries can affect the price of oil and other goods globally.

The United States

The United States has become increasingly influential in world politics over the last century. As an extremely powerful democracy and economic power, it plays a unique role in world affairs. Its political and economic strength is such that it is often the deciding voice in key international agreements such as the Kyoto Protocol. The United States has, however, also received criticism for its interference in other nation-states' affairs, particularly in Southeast Asia and Latin America during the 20th century, and more recently in Afghanistan and Iraq as part of the Bush administration's War on Terrorism. Others argue that America is acting responsibly in using its position to help bring about political change in those countries unable to do so for themselves. U.S.-related issues are among those examined in this book.

Critical thinking

Knowledge of world politics can both stimulate interesting and lively discussion and challenge existing ideas and prejudices. To form a balanced judgment about issues, it is important to have accurate information from reliable sources, such as journalists, writers, or academics.

World Politics features for-and-against arguments from reprinted sources on 16 key questions that look at the viability of competing political systems, trade, human rights, and other issues central to understanding politics in the 21st century.

HOW TO USE THIS BOOK

Each volume of *Pro/Con* is divided into sections, each of which has an introduction that examines its theme. Within each section are a series of debates that present arguments for and against a proposition, such as whether or not the death penalty should be abolished. An introduction to each debate puts it into its wider context, and a summary and key map (see below) highlight the main points of the debate clearly and concisely. Each debate has marginal boxes that focus on particular points, give tips on how to present an argument, or help question the writer's case. The summary page to the debates contains supplementary material to help you do further research.

Boxes and other materials provide additional background information. There are also special spreads on how to improve your debating and writing skills. At the end of each book is a glossary and an index. The glossary provides explanations of key words in the volume. The index covers all 24 books; it will help you find topics throughout this set and previous ones.

background information
Frequent text boxes provide background information on important concepts and key individuals or events.

summary boxes
Summary boxes are useful reminders of both sides of the argument.

further information
Further Reading lists for each debate direct you to related books, articles, and websites so you can do your own research.

other articles in the *Pro/Con* series
This box lists related debates throughout the *Pro/Con* series.

marginal boxes
Margin boxes highlight key points of the argument, give extra information, or help you question the author's meaning.

key map
Key maps provide a graphic representation of the central points of the debate.

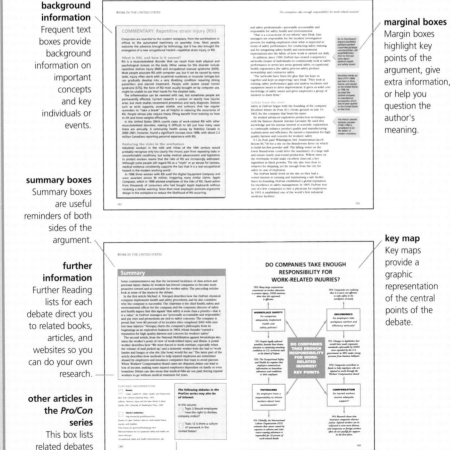

CONTENTS

PART 4:
THE UNITED STATES AND THE WORLD 164

PART 1
CONTROVERSIES IN WORLD POLITICS

Politics is the art or science of government. It involves ethical decisions that have to do with the regulation and government of a country or state, the protection of civil liberties, the moral behavior of citizens, the preservation of security, the augmentation of its strength and resources, and relations with other countries. Politics has been studied by theorists for centuries: The topics in this book include some of the current debates in world politics.

Learning from mistakes

In 2002 the president of the European Commission, Romano Prodi (1939-), stated, "We can no longer look to politics to teach and impose moral behavior. Terrible crimes were committed over the last century in the name of values and morality. But nor can we allow politics to be devalued, through skepticism, pragmatism, or nihilism. For that would signal indifference to the future of mankind and of organized society."

Prodi's comments reflect the opinion of many experts concerned that governments are failing to act in the best interests of either their citizens or the world community. Critics claim that many political leaders are driven by their own cultural, religious, or economic ambitions.

The postwar world

After World War II (1939-1945) world politics was shaped by the ideological struggle between western states led by the United States and communist states led by the Soviet Union. Much of this conflict occurred outside these two camps, in poor and politically unstable states. Competing for position in the Third World, the two superpowers often supported and advised opposing factions in civil wars, such as the conflict in Vietnam in the 1960s and early 1970s.

The toppling of the Berlin Wall in 1989 symbolized the end of the Cold War division of Europe, and Germany formally reunified in 1990. The disintegration of the Soviet Union in 1991 brought an end to the bipolar struggle that had dominated world politics for half a century, ushering in a moment unique in modern history— the unrivaled political, economic, and military supremacy of a single country—the United States.

Post-Cold War challenges

The decline in importance of communism in the last 15 years has led to an increased emphasis on democracy, specifically liberal democracy, as the most viable political system. Liberal democracy is characterized by government through representatives elected by the people and a respect for individual rights and the rule of law.

The 20th century saw a dramatic increase in democratically elected governments; by 2000 some 120 nations out of 192 had democratic systems in place. Critics believe that many of the world's problems— conflict, poverty, ethnic tensions, and

notably in parts of Asia. At the same time, there are also noticeably increasing disparities between the rich and the poor, both globally and within nations (see Volume 23 *Poverty and Wealth*). While international organizations such as the World Trade Organization (WTO) promote trade liberalization as a means to help poor nations develop and deal with their

---

"Not only is the Cold War over, the post-Cold War period is also over."

—COLIN POWELL, SECRETARY OF STATE (2001–)

---

terrorism—have originated in failed states, and that as more nations embrace democracy, many of these issues will disappear. Advocates of this viewpoint include George W. Bush, 43rd U. S. president. This has led some to claim that the U.S.-led War on Terrorism has been waged to impose democracy on resistant states. Others argue that it is a crusade against Islam or a war waged for economic gain.

Trade and globalization

Among the factors that have great influence on global relationships are economics and trade. Nations have bandied together to form beneficial trade alliances, and trade sanctions have been imposed against nations to help improve human rights and also affect political change.

In the post-Cold War period many countries have integrated into a world market, sometimes with mixed consequences. The expansion of free-market competition and global trade have resulted in economic growth, most

own problems, others argue that they actually exacerbate existing inequalities: Many trade agreements benefit countries like the United States rather than poor nations, critics claim.

Opponents of globalization include many civil and environmental rights groups, which object to the increasing power of the United States and also that of transnational corporations. Critics claim that both have contributed to the erosion of human and environmental rights, and local culture. Globalization has also had such far-reaching effects on the economies, cultures, and politics of countries that some observers have predicted the end of the nation-state itself—for centuries the world's dominant form of political organization.

Topics 1 to 4 examine democracy and globalization. They examine liberal democracy as the most viable system, if globalization and the nation-state are compatible, whether religion-based politics undermine democracy, and if Russian democracy is under threat respectively.

Topic 1
IS LIBERAL DEMOCRACY THE ONLY VIABLE POLITICAL SYSTEM?

YES
"HISTORY IS STILL GOING OUR WAY"
THE WALL STREET JOURNAL, OCTOBER 5, 2001
FRANCIS FUKUYAMA

NO
"THE END OF THE END OF HISTORY"
NEWSWEEK, SEPTEMBER 24, 2001
FAREED ZAKARIA

INTRODUCTION

Liberal democracies are political systems that are based on power, legitimacy, justice, and freedom. A written constitution usually acts to define and limit power, and a legitimate government, elected by the majority of citizens, is crucial to the democratic process. Citizens live in societies governed by justice, where they are treated equally and with respect. The rule of law protects their rights and allows them the freedom to make informed political, social, economic, religious, and cultural decisions.

Liberal democracy is the dominant political system in the western world and in many other parts of the globe. Its advocates claim that it is the ideal political system. They believe that alternative systems, such as communism or fascism, are flawed and inefficient, and that they deny citizens certain fundamental rights and freedoms. Totalitarian regimes also have a reputation for aggression.

Historians often view the 20th century as a long and epic ideological struggle of liberal democracy against competing political systems during two world wars and the long rivalry between the United States and the Soviet Union, known as the Cold War. Some see the abandonment of communism, the end of the Cold War, and the dismantling of totalitarian regimes—particularly in the former Soviet Union and eastern Europe—as the ultimate triumph of liberal democracy. They also believe that the rapid growth in democratic nations—from around 40 in 1970 to 120 in 2000—in Africa, Asia, and Russia, for example, proves that liberal democracy is the only viable political system.

As the Cold War drew to a close, Francis Fukuyama, a U.S. academic, expanded on this idea in an essay called "The End of History." Writing in 1989, Fukuyama, then deputy director of the U.S. State Department's Policy

Planning Staff, claimed that the recent collapse of communism marked "the end point of mankind's evolution and the universalization of western liberal democracy as the final form of human government." In many ways what Fukuyama was saying was not new. The German philosopher Georg Wilhelm Friedrich Hegel (1770-1831), for example, had previously believed that the perfect political and economic system had been achieved during his lifetime.

Although Fukuyama's ideas attracted attention, he was also criticized—most famously by Samuel P. Huntington, professor of government at Harvard University. While accepting that world politics had changed, Huntington rejected the notion that it would mean the end of traditional rivalries between nations. "The clash of civilizations will dominate global politics," he claimed.

> *"The spirit of democracy cannot be imposed from without. It has to come from within."*
> —MOHANDAS K. GANDHI, INDIAN CIVIL RIGHTS LEADER (1869–1948)

Advocates believe this "clash" has already occurred: The increase in ethnic and religious conflict and terrorist action, particularly in the closing decades of the 20th century and culminating in the terrorist action against the United States on September 11, 2001, prove this. Others, however, believe that violence against the United States in particular—the standard-bearer of liberal democracy—is just confirmation that there are substantial numbers of people that do not want to embrace liberal democracy. Some critics even argue that Islam, for example, is incompatible with liberal democracy since the latter operates from a western ideological premise that is not necessarily compatible with certain religious and cultural practices. But even if this is true, some commentators believe that nations may be forced to toe the liberal democratic line through economic and political pressure.

In November 2003 President George W. Bush made a speech to the National Endowment for Democracy, a Washington, D.C.-based nonprofit agency. He called the undemocratic countries of Cuba, Burma, North Korea, and Zimbabwe "outposts of oppression." Focusing on the Middle East, Bush said, "the establishment of a free Iraq at the heart of the Middle East will be a watershed event in the global democratic nation." His words were welcomed by the "neocons" (neoconservatives), who believe that the United States should not be ashamed to use its power to impose its values, especially democracy, on other nations—by force if necessary. Critics, however, believe that this will only lead to a backlash against liberal democracy and resentment toward America. They have criticized the decision of some western nations to base aid decisions on the adoption of good governance by poor nations: One of the essential factors of good governance is a fair and democratic system of government.

Francis Fukuyama and journalist Fareed Zakaria discuss the issue further in the articles that follow.

HISTORY IS STILL GOING OUR WAY
Francis Fukuyama

Francis Fukuyama (1952–) is a U.S. academic. In 1992 he published The End of History and the Last Man. Although his work received international attention, George F. Will, a Pulitzer prize-winning political commentator, and Fareed Zakaria were among his critics.

The Harvard political theorist Samuel Huntington challenged Fukuyama's theory in an article called "The Clash of Civilizations" (Foreign Affairs, 1993). He turned his thesis into a book of the same name in 1998. Huntington argued that interaction between the seven or eight great civilizations would determine world affairs (Western, Confucian, Japanese, Islamic, Hindu, Slavic-Orthodox, Latin American, and possibly African civilizations). He wrote, "For the relevant future, there will be ... a world of different civilizations, each of which will have to learn to coexist with the others."

YES

A stream of commentators have been asserting that the tragedy of Sept. 11 proves that I was utterly wrong to have said more than a decade ago that we had reached the end of history. The chorus began almost immediately, with George Will asserting that history had returned from vacation, and Fareed Zakaria [see pages 16–19] declaring the end of the end of history.

It is on the face of it nonsensical and insulting to the memory of those who died on Sept. 11 to declare that this unprecedented attack did not rise to the level of a historical event. But the way in which I used the word *history*, or rather History, was different: It referred to the progress of mankind over the centuries toward modernity, characterized by institutions like liberal democracy and capitalism.

Collapse of communism

My observation, made back in 1989 on the eve of the collapse of communism, was that this evolutionary process did seem to be bringing ever larger parts of the world toward modernity. And if we looked beyond liberal democracy and markets, there was nothing else towards which we could expect to evolve; hence the end of history. While there were retrograde areas that resisted that process, it was hard to find a viable alternative type of civilization that people actually wanted to live in after the discrediting of socialism, monarchy, fascism, and other types of authoritarian rule.

This view has been challenged by many people, and perhaps most articulately by Samuel Huntington. He argued that rather than progressing toward a single global system, the world remained mired in a "clash of civilizations" in which six or seven major cultural groups would coexist without converging and constitute the new fracture lines of global conflict. Since the successful attack on the center of global capitalism was evidently perpetrated by Islamic extremists unhappy with the very existence of Western civilization, observers have been handicapping the Huntington "clash" view over my own "end of history" hypothesis rather heavily.

I believe that in the end I remain right: Modernity is a very powerful freight train that will not be derailed by recent events, however painful and unprecedented. Democracy and free markets will continue to expand over time as the dominant organizing principles for much of the world. But it is worthwhile thinking about what the true scope of the present challenge is.

Having analyzed the criticism he has received in the past, the author states clearly that he believes he is still right to hold his opinion. Is he convincing?

It has always been my belief that modernity has a cultural basis. Liberal democracy and free markets do not work at all times and everywhere. They work best in societies with certain values whose origins may not be entirely rational. It is not an accident that modern liberal democracy emerged first in the Christian West, since the universalism of democratic rights can be seen in many ways as a secular form of Christian universalism.

Beyond the West

The central question raised by Samuel Huntington is whether institutions of modernity such as liberal democracy and free markets will work only in the West, or whether there is something broader in their appeal that will allow them to make headway in non-Western societies. I believe there is. The proof lies in the progress that democracy and free markets have made in regions like East Asia, Latin America, Orthodox Europe, South Asia and even Africa. Proof lies also in the millions of Third World immigrants who vote with their feet every year to live in Western societies and eventually assimilate to Western values. The flow of people moving in the opposite direction, and the number who want to blow up what they can of the West, is by contrast negligible.

Voting with one's feet is a metaphor meaning when someone chooses to walk away from a situation or lifestyle they do not like or enjoy.

But there does seem to be something about Islam, or at least the fundamentalist versions of Islam that have been dominant in recent years, that makes Muslim societies particularly resistant to modernity. Of all contemporary cultural systems, the Islamic world has the fewest democracies (Turkey alone qualifies), and contains no countries that have made the transition from Third to First World status in the manner of South Korea or Singapore.

There are plenty of non-Western people who prefer the economic and technological part of modernity and hope to have it without having to accept democratic politics or Western cultural values as well (e.g., China or Singapore). There are others who like both the economic and political versions of modernity, but just can't figure out how to make it happen (Russia is an example). For them, transition

See Topic 4 Is democracy under threat in Russia?

to Western-style modernity may be long and painful. But there are no insuperable cultural barriers likely to prevent them from eventually getting there, and they constitute about four-fifth's of the world's people.

Rejection of modernity

Islam, by contrast, is the only cultural system that seems regularly to produce people, like Osama Bin Laden or the Taliban, who reject modernity lock, stock and barrel. This raises the question of how representative such people are of the larger Muslim community, and whether this rejection is somehow inherent in Islam. For if the rejectionists are more than a lunatic fringe, then Mr. Huntington is right that we are in for a protracted conflict made dangerous by virtue of their technological empowerment.

The answer that politicians East and West have been putting out since Sept. 11 is that those sympathetic with the terrorists are a "tiny minority" of Muslims, and that the vast majority are appalled by what happened. It is important for them to say this to prevent Muslims as a group from becoming targets of hatred. The problem is that dislike and hatred of America and what it stands for are clearly much more widespread than that.

Certainly the group of people willing to go on suicide missions and actively conspire against the U.S. is tiny. But sympathy may be manifest in nothing more than initial feelings of *Schadenfreude* at the sight of the collapsing towers, an immediate sense of satisfaction that the U.S. was getting what it deserved, to be followed only later by pro forma expressions of disapproval. By this standard, sympathy for the terrorists is characteristic of much more than a "tiny minority" of Muslims, extending from the middle classes in countries like Egypt to immigrants in the West.

Delving for explanations

This broader dislike and hatred would seem to represent something much deeper than mere opposition to American policies like support for Israel or the Iraq embargo, encompassing a hatred of the underlying society. After all, many people around the world, including many Americans, disagree with U.S. policies, but this does not send them into paroxysms of anger and violence. Nor is it necessarily a matter of ignorance about the quality of life in the West. The suicide hijacker Mohamed Atta was a well-educated man from a well-to-do Egyptian family who lived and studied in Germany and the U.S. for several years. Perhaps, as many

---

The author asserts that politicians have stated that only a minority of Muslims support terrorism in order to prevent hate crime. What other reasons could there be?

"Schadenfreude" means taking a malicious satisfaction in the misfortune of others. Do you think it is appropriate in this context?

Some people believe that U.S. interventionist foreign policy may have contributed to 9/11. Does this seem a more likely explanation than the one given here?

Mohamed Atta was the suspected leader of the 9/11 suicide bombers. Go to http://observer.guardian.co.uk for more information.

commentators have speculated, the hatred is born out of a resentment of Western success and Muslim failure.

But rather than psychologize the Muslim world, it makes more sense to ask whether radical Islam constitutes a serious alternative to Western liberal democracy for Muslims themselves. (It goes without saying that, unlike communism, radical Islam has virtually no appeal in the contemporary world apart from those who are culturally Islamic to begin with.)

For Muslims themselves, political Islam has proven much more appealing in the abstract than in reality. After 23 years of rule by fundamentalist clerics, most Iranians, and in particular nearly everyone under 30, would like to live in a far more liberal society. Afghans who have experienced Taliban rule have much the same feelings. All of the anti-American hatred that has been drummed up does not translate into a viable political program for Muslim societies to follow in the years ahead.

The end of history

We remain at the end of history because there is only one system that will continue to dominate world politics, that of the liberal-democratic West. This does not imply a world free from conflict, nor the disappearance of culture as a distinguishing characteristic of societies. (In my original article, I noted that the posthistorical world would continue to see terrorism and wars of national liberation.)

But the struggle we face is not the clash of several distinct and equal cultures struggling amongst one another like the great powers of 19th-century Europe. The clash consists of a series of rearguard actions from societies whose traditional existence is indeed threatened by modernization. The strength of the backlash reflects the severity of this threat. But time and resources are on the side of modernity, and I see no lack of a will to prevail in the United States today.

According to www.islamweb.com, in the last 50 years the numbers of Muslims increased by 235 percent; in comparison Christians grew by 47 percent. Around 34,000 Americans also converted to Islam after 9/11.

This is the central thesis of Fukuyama's argument. Is it convincing? Is democracy suitable for every nation? What are the alternatives? Go to www.cnn.com and www.bbc.co.uk to do your research.

THE END OF THE END OF HISTORY
Fareed Zakaria

Named by Esquire *magazine as one of the 21 most influential people of the 21st century, Fareed Zakaria is editor of Newsweek International. This article was published on September 24, 2001, in the wake of the 9/11 terrorist action.*

NO

Historians will surely say, "This was the week that America changed." In the midst of jagged emotions of the moment—horror, rage, grief—we can all sense that the country has crossed a watershed. But we don't quite know what that means. Accustomed as we are to whipping up a froth of hysteria about trivia, we are struck silent by honest-to-goodness history.

Or History. This is surely the End of the End of History— the notion that after the cold war, ideological or political tussles were dead and life would be spent managing the economy and worrying about consumerism. In his brilliant essay, Francis Fukuyama actually considered the threat of radical Islam but pointed out correctly that, unlike communism, it has no ideological appeal beyond the borders of the Muslim world. Radical Islam as an ideology, in other words, posed no threat to the West. But we pose a threat to it, one its followers feel with blinding intensity. It turns out it takes only one side to restart History.

The author states that the West poses a threat to the Muslim world. What do you think he means by this?

This is also the end of the triumph of economics. That's not to say that the economy will not remain central to our society. But the idea that politics was unimportant and that government didn't matter seems almost absurd in the light of last week's events. (And not just government and the highest levels. Who can look at the extraordinary sacrifices made by the firefighters and policemen of New York City and still believe that making a million dollars is the meaning of life?) When asked whether the administration's $40 billion request to rebuild New York and combat terrorism would bust the budget, the president's spokesman brushed it off, saying simply, "National security comes first."

According to http://www. september11news. com, out of the 3,030 people who died during the 9/11 attacks, 343 were firefighters, and 75 were members of the police.

Around the world we will see governments become more powerful, more intrusive and more important. This may not please civil libertarians and human-rights activists, but it will not matter. The state is back, and for the oldest Hobbesian reason in the book—the provision of security.

"Hobbesian" comes from the English political theorist and intellectual Thomas Hobbes. See page 17.

For Americans, security has seemed a birthright. As a result, for much of the past century America has felt that foreign policy was a matter of choice, not necessity. We have been deeply involved in the world, but we have also withdrawn

COMMENTARY: Thomas Hobbes (1588–1679)

Since the terrorist action of September 11, 2001, governments around the world have insisted that national security must be maintained at all costs, even when some of the laws that have been introduced infringe on citizen rights. The work of English political theorist Thomas Hobbes has often been cited to justify why governments have a responsibility to act in whatever way they consider necessary to protect national security. However, some commentators have questioned how the theories of a man who lived over 400 years ago can possibly still be applied to 21st-century politics.

Background and influences

Born in Malmesbury on April 5, 1588, and educated at Oxford University, Hobbes lived in a time of great political turmoil and social upheaval—much of his political writing reflects his fear of political chaos. He was influenced by some of the greatest thinkers of the time, including the Italian astronomer Galileo Galilei (1564–1642), through whom he came to believe that scientific principles could be used to explain human behavior. In 1628 Hobbes published an English translation of the work of the Ancient Greek writer Thucydides, partly to warn his peers of the dangers of democracy. He later published *De Cive*, in which he theorized about the nature of civil power and the relationship between church and state. Fearing that his writing had made him unpopular, Hobbes fled to Paris after the outbreak of civil war in England. In 1651 he published *Leviathan*, one of his best known and arguably most influential works.

State of nature vs. artificial society

Hobbes was a materialist. Taking his cue from natural science, he argued that human beings were nothing more than matter in motion. He claimed that people were essentially selfish beings, motivated by self-promotion and self-preservation. Left in this brutish "state of nature," humans would compete and collude with each other in order to achieve whatever was in their own best interest: This would inevitably lead to conflict and chaos since there was no right or wrong and no justice or injustice. To prevent this happening, Hobbes believed that it was necessary to create an "artificial" society governed by a greater political authority—either one person or an assembly of people. This authority would make sure that citizens adhered to certain social contracts by enforcing laws and codes of conduct. It would also have the right to use whatever means or force necessary to protect its citizens both from each other and from outside parties. He believed states could best defend themselves when citizens surrendered their liberty—"their right to all things." Some people have used his ideas to justify greater state control and the use of liberty-curbing laws, but critics claim that his theories are incompatible with democracy.

A group of people in Karachi, Pakistan, demonstrate their support for Osama Bin Laden and protest against U.S. air strikes in Afghanistan, 2002.

from it when we wished. In our diplomacy and alliances, we assumed that the world needed us more than we needed them. No more. Of course we should and will strike alone when necessary.

The Afghan government's responsibility

Well-placed sources have told me that the administration is convinced that the Afghan government knows where Osama Bin Laden is. He may even be under its protection. We should make clear to the governments of Afghanistan and Pakistan that unless they hand him over they will pay a terrible price. But that price would be greater still if we get

NATO and Russia to join with us. Even more importantly, the real war against terrorism is going to be a war of police work, intelligence and covert actions. We cannot do this alone. We will need the active support of other governments to cooperate, share information, close down safe houses, confiscate assets and make arrests. For the first time, we need them as much as they need us.

Do you think this is a fair assessment of the U.S. role in international affairs? Is Zakaria suggesting that the United States has been exploited by other nations?

The real end of the Cold War?

Some have said that this is also, finally, the end of the Cold War. Our military, for example, will now properly refocus itself around this new threat. Yes, but in another sense, the Cold War is back. The long twilight struggle we face, like that against communism, is both military and political. The first is crucial: just as the nuclear buildup and proxy battles were at the center of the Cold War, so military strikes and covert operations will be at the core of this one. But [just] as important was the political struggle we waged across the world. From the start, America realized one of its chief missions was to discredit communism and lessen its appeal around the world. Our task now is to make sure that radical Islam is not seen as an attractive option around the Muslim world. We can do this in various ways, but most significantly by supporting Muslim moderates and secularists. No matter how successful the military strategy, ultimately this war will be won or lost on these political grounds.

What kind of support do you think the author is referring to?

For America, this is the end of unilateralism. And for the rest of the world it is the end of the free ride. People are now going to realize just how much they enjoyed the benefits of globalization; the peace and prosperity; the ease of trade and travel, the information and entertainment. They watched the movies, listened to the music, read the magazines, vacationed in America and sent their children to college here. But none of this required them actively to support the United States or affirm its values. They could denounce America by day and consume its bounties by night. But all these countries—in Europe and Asia and Latin America—must recognize that the world they have gotten used to will not survive if America is crippled. The United States is the pivot that makes today's globalization go round. If other countries believe in individual liberty, in free enterprise and free trade, in religious freedom, in democracy, then they are eating the fruits of the American order. And this order can be truly secure only when all those who benefit from it stand in its defense. Those abroad who love liberty cannot watch this war as if it were a horror movie, wondering how it will end. This is your struggle, too.

Some people have mixed feelings about globalization. Go to http://globalization.about.com/ to find out more about how globalization has affected the world. Compare the articles on that site with the ones found at www.newint.org— the site of the left-wing magazine the New Internationalist.

The author uses rousing language to convince the reader that his views are right. Is he successful?

Summary

In the first article Francis Fukuyama defends the theory he originally cited in his 1989 article called "The End of History?" While he admits that some criticisms of his work—particularly those made by academic Samuel P. Huntington—appear valid in the light of the 9/11 terrorist attacks on the United States, he maintains that the tide of events is still proceeding in the direction he originally mapped out. Fukuyama claims that although the people who disapprove of or oppose liberal democracy have achieved a high profile through their terrorist activities, they are very few in number. The spread of liberal democracy will not be halted by fundamentalist Arabs because Islam appeals only to Muslims—it lacks the universal attractions of capitalism and liberal democracy.

Fareed Zakaria agrees with Fukuyama that Islam poses no ideological threat to liberal democracy and could never defeat it, but argues that Muslim fundamentalists believe that they are threatened by the West. For as long as such people mistrust the United States, they will oppose it—even though Americans believe that there is nothing to oppose. In the aftermath of 9/11, he asserts, it has become imperative for the United States to ensure that fundamentalism does not broaden its appeal among Arabs. Until anti-American terrorism has been defeated, there can be no further progress toward liberal democracy—the state must step in, and civil liberties must be restricted in the interests of national security. In the meantime, as Zakaria puts it, "the state is back," and, for the forseeable future at least, we have come to "the end of the end of history."

FURTHER INFORMATION:

 Books:

Carter, April, and Geoffrey Stokes (eds.), *Liberal Democracy and Its Critics*. London: Polity Press, 1998.
Fukuyama, Francis, *The End of History and the Last Man*. New York: Free Press, 1992.
Hobbes, Thomas, *Leviathan*. New York: Penguin Classics, 1982.

Useful websites:

www.fareedzakaria.com
Fareed Zakaria's site, including articles, books, and biographical information.
http://www.sais-jhu.edu/fukuyama/
Francis Fukuyama's homepage, featuring articles and biographical information.
http://theatlantic.com/issues/93feb/lewis.htm
"Islam and Liberal Democracy" by Bernard Lewis.

The following debates in the Pro/Con series may also be of interest:

In this volume:
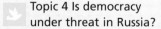 Topic 3 Do religion-based politics undermine democracy?

Topic 4 Is democracy under threat in Russia?

In *Commerce and Trade:*
Part 2: Globalization and its effects

IS LIBERAL DEMOCRACY THE ONLY VIABLE POLITICAL SYSTEM?

YES: Globalization has meant that liberal democracy is the most attractive option for every nation

YES: Communism has failed; nations can prosper only in a free market

REALPOLITIK
Has the end of the Cold War left liberal democracy as the only possible political system?

ECONOMICS
Is capitalism the only political system that works?

NO: The events of 9/11 have meant the "state is back"

NO: State ownership can work if the people agree to pay for it through taxes

IS LIBERAL DEMOCRACY THE ONLY VIABLE POLITICAL SYSTEM?

KEY POINTS

YES: Hobbes was a man of his time; he wrote during a period of great turmoil and political upheaval over 400 years ago. Political systems have developed substantially since then.

YES: 9/11 was carried out by extremists fired up by views held by a minority of Muslims. This does not signify a "clash of civilizations."

HOBBES
Is Hobbesian philosophy irrelevant in the 21st century?

CLASH OF CIVILIZATIONS
Is it wrong to think of 9/11 as an inevitable "clash of civilizations"?

NO: His writings are very relevant in the post 9/11 world: The state must make decisions to protect national security, even if its actions infringe on certain individual rights, otherwise there will be chaos

NO: 9/11 illustrated how much Islam clashes with the modern world. It also showed the level of resistance to liberal democracy in the Arab world.

Topic 2

IS THE NATION-STATE CONSISTENT WITH THE IDEA OF GLOBALIZATION?

YES

FROM "WILL THE NATION-STATE SURVIVE GLOBALIZATION?"
FOREIGN AFFAIRS, VOL. 80, NO. 1, JANUARY/FEBRUARY 2001
MARTIN WOLF

NO

FROM "THE AGE OF SOVEREIGNTY HAS COME TO AN END"
USA TODAY MAGAZINE, SEPTEMBER 1998
LLEWELLYN D. HOWELL

INTRODUCTION

The term "globalization" is used to describe the increased mobility of goods, services, labor, and capital across national borders. The phenomenon has generated much debate in recent years. One issue is whether the nation-state—what we would call a "country," the world's dominant form of political organization—is losing control of the global forces that affect it and gradually declining in importance.

The modern nation-state system was established in Europe in 1648 by the Peace of Westphalia, a series of treaties that recognized the full sovereignty of German principalities within the Holy Roman Empire. A sovereign state is completely autonomous. Its authority, which is vested in a government with the power to control its domestic and foreign affairs, is limited by the physical boundaries of the state's territory. In theory, interference in the internal affairs of one state by another is considered a violation of sovereignty.

In practice, however, some critics claim that absolute sovereignty rarely exists. Strong states such as the United States have always influenced the affairs of weaker ones, which may be willing to forfeit some of their independence in order to benefit from increased security or wealth.

Some commentators also point out that nation-states are accustomed to sharing the political stage with nonstate actors such as intergovernmental organizations. The European Union is one example of how states transfer a degree of decision-making power to a supranational body because they derive economic advantage from membership.

It is the role played by other nonstate actors—transnational corporations (TNCs)—that worries many opponents of globalization. Half of the world's 100 largest economies are TNCs—they are richer and more powerful than many of the states that try to regulate them. Some critics argue that TNCs threaten national sovereignty by influencing the politics of both their home and host countries. For example, developing nations may be reluctant to enforce environmental, social, and labor laws for fear of losing foreign investment. Those who view TNCs more favorably argue that the economic growth they bring to host countries reinforces political stability rather than undermines it.

> *"We are witnessing the end of the supremacy of the nation-state"*
>
> —ZBIGNIEW BRZEZINSKI, FORMER NATIONAL SECURITY ADVISER

Globalization is not a new trend. Some 200 years ago the philosopher Immanuel Kant (1724–1804) predicted that economic interdependence would prove stronger than nation-states. He was writing during the early Industrial Revolution, when the advent of mass production increased economic ties across political borders. Today the pace of integration has been speeded up by telecommunications. As recently as 1990 it would have been difficult for a U.S. company to buy goods from a supplier in, for example, parts of Asia; today anyone with Internet access can buy goods online from around the world. Transactions that do not involve physical goods—for example, if someone downloads music—are difficult to tax. Some people argue that such transactions challenge the survival of the state because a government is unsustainable without tax revenue. Others say that these are exaggerated

fears because most states derive the bulk of their national revenue from income and sales taxes.

The impact of more and more people moving between nation-states prompts further debate. Some commentators predict that language and cultural barriers will always act as a natural check on immigration. They point out that many states also have strict policies on immigration. However, figures show that the number of people living outside their country of origin rose from 120 million in 1990 to more than 160 million in 2002. While opponents of globalization often emphasize the negative economic consequences of increased labor mobility—the loss of trained workers from home countries, their potential to drive down wages in host countries, for example—it is the social impact that arguably poses the greater threat to the nation-state. A "nation" can be described as a group of people bound together by ethnic, linguistic, and cultural ties. Many states are made up of different nations, but some critics claim that governments find it difficult to meet the demands of increasingly diverse populations. Furthermore, they argue that people often place great value on their cultural heritage. Whereas some welcome globalization because it provides them with goods that they otherwise would not have, others view brands such as Starbucks and McDonald's as a form of cultural imperialism. They say that globalization blurs the boundaries of nation-states by homogenizing their cultural identities.

In the following extracts Martin Wolf says that governments use globalization to promote the interests of the nation-state. Llewellyn D. Howell counters that state sovereignty is disappearing.

WILL THE NATION-STATE SURVIVE GLOBALIZATION?
Martin Wolf

YES

The author uses words associated with hunting — "predatory" and "beasts of prey"— to open his argument on the survival of the nation-state. Imagery can be an effective way of making a point.

A spectre is haunting the world's governments—the spectre of globalization. Some argue that predatory market forces make it impossible for benevolent governments to shield their populations from the beasts of prey that lurk beyond their borders. Others counter that benign market forces actually prevent predatory governments from fleecing their citizens. Although the two sides see different villains, they draw one common conclusion: omnipotent markets mean impotent politicians....

But is it true that governments have become weaker and less relevant than ever before? And does globalization, by definition, have to be the nemesis of national government? Globalization is a journey. But it is a journey toward an unreachable destination—"the globalized world." A "globalized" economy could be defined as one in which neither distance nor national borders impede economic transactions. This would be a world where the costs of transport and communications were zero and the barriers created by differing national jurisdictions had vanished. Needless to say, we do not live in anything even close to such a world. And since many of the things we transport (including ourselves) are physical, we never will....

An "odyssey" is a long voyage or quest that is often characterized by many reversals of fortunes. Homer (ninth or eighth century B.C.) wrote the Odyssey, an epic poem about Odysseus, a hero of ancient Greek mythology, who spends 10 years returning home from war.

Past experience

This globalizing journey is not a new one. Over the past five centuries, technological change has progressively reduced the barriers to international integration.... Yet states have become neither weaker nor less important during this odyssey. On the contrary, in the countries with the most advanced and internationally integrated economies, governments' ability to tax and redistribute incomes, regulate the economy, and monitor the activity of their citizens has increased beyond all recognition. This has been especially true over the past century.

The question that remains, however, is whether today's form of globalization is likely to have a different impact from that of the past. Indeed, it may well, for numerous factors distinguish today's globalizing journey from past ones and could produce a different outcome. These distinctions include more rapid communications, market liberalization, and global integration of the production of goods and services. Yet contrary to one common assumption, the modern form of globalization will not spell the end of the modern nation-state....

So why do so many people believe that something unique is happening today? The answer lies with the two forces driving contemporary economic change: falling costs of transport and communications on the one hand, and liberalizing economic policies on the other.

The technological revolution

Advances in technology and infrastructure substantially and continuously reduced the costs of transport and communications throughout the nineteenth and early twentieth centuries. The first transatlantic telegraph cable was laid in 1866. By the turn of the century, the entire world was connected by telegraph, and communication times fell from months to minutes. The cost of a three-minute telephone call from New York to London in current prices dropped from about $250 in 1930 to a few cents today.... The number of Internet hosts has risen from 5,000 in 1986 to more than 30 million now....

The "infrastructure" of a country or state refers to its system of public works, such as its transportation, energy supply, and communications networks.

This article was published in early 2001. A survey by Internet Systems Consortium, Inc. (http://www.isc.org/index.pl?/ops/ds/) gave the number of Internet hosts in January 2004 as 233,101,481.

But these massive improvements in communications, however important, simply continue the trends begun with the first submarine cables laid in the last century. Furthermore, distances still impose transport and communications costs that continue to make geography matter in economic terms. Certain important services still cannot be delivered from afar.

Diminishing costs of communications and transport were nevertheless pointing toward greater integration throughout the last century. But if historical experience demonstrates anything, it is that integration is not technologically determined. If it were, integration would have gone smoothly forward over the past two centuries. On the contrary ... integration actually reversed course....

If transport and communications innovations were moving toward global economic integration throughout the last century and a half, policy was not—and that made all the difference. For this reason, the growth in the potential for economic integration has greatly outpaced the growth of integration itself ... Globalization has much further to run, if it is allowed to do so....

Globalization is not destined, it is chosen. It is a choice made to enhance a nation's economic well-being … But if integration is a deliberate choice, rather than an ineluctable destiny, it cannot render states impotent. Their potency lies in the choices they make.…

Globalization is often perceived as destroying governments' capacities to do what they want or need, particularly in the key areas of taxation, public spending for income redistribution, and macroeconomic policy. But how true is this perception? In fact, no evidence supports the conclusion that states can no longer raise taxes. On the contrary: in 1999, EU governments spent or redistributed an average of 47% of their GDPS.…

Macroeconomics is the study of the economy as a whole—Gross Domestic Product (GDP), inflation, unemployment— rather than particular markets or industries.

The international mobility of people and goods is unlikely ever to come close to the kind of mobility that exists between states in the United States. Legal, linguistic, and cultural barriers will keep levels of cross-border migration far lower than levels of movement within any given country. Since taxes on labour income and spending are the predominant source of national revenue, the modern country's income base seems quite safe.…

Purely Internet-based transactions—downloading of films, software, or music—are hard to tax. But when the Internet is used to buy tangible goods, governments can impose taxes, provided that the suppliers cooperate with the fiscal authorities of their corresponding jurisdictions. To the extent that these suppliers are large shareholder-owned companies, which they usually are, this cooperation may not be as hard to obtain as is often supposed.…

Meanwhile, governments can continue the practice of income redistribution to the extent that the most highly taxed citizens and firms cannot—or do not wish to—evade taxation.… The constraint is not globalization, but the willingness of the electorate to tolerate high taxation.

"Fiscal deficit" means the amount a government spends each year in excess of what taxes bring in.

Last but not least, some observers argue that globalization limits governments' ability to run fiscal deficits and pursue inflationary monetary policy. But macroeconomic policy is always vulnerable to the reaction of the private sector, regardless of whether the capital market is internationally integrated.…

The continuing importance of states

The proposition that globalization makes states unnecessary is even less credible than the idea that it makes states impotent. If anything, the exact opposite is true, for at least three reasons.

First, the ability of a society to take advantage of the opportunities offered by international economic integration depends on the quality of public goods, … an honest civil service, personal security, and basic education. Without an appropriate legal framework, in particular, the web of potentially rewarding contracts is vastly reduced.…

Second, the state normally defines identity. A sense of belonging is part of the people's sense of security, and one that most people would not want to give up … It is perhaps not surprising that some of the most successfully integrated economies are small, homogeneous countries with a strong sense of collective identity.

Third, international governance rests on the ability of individual states to provide and guarantee stability. The bedrock of international order is the territorial state with its monopoly on coercive power within its jurisdiction.… Globalization does not make states unnecessary. On the contrary, for people to be successful in exploiting the opportunities afforded by international integration, they need states at both ends of their transactions. Failed states, disorderly states, weak states, and corrupt states are shunned as the black holes of the global economic system.

Do you agree that people need a sense of belonging in order to feel secure? Do you think this is still true of people who migrate to another country to find a better way of life?

Do you think that global terrorism can be countered by reliance on the territorial state?

What, then, does globalization mean for states?

1. First, policy ultimately determines the pace and depth of international economic integration. For each country, globalization is at least as much a choice as a destiny.
2. Second, in important respects—notably a country's monetary regime, capital account, and above all, labour mobility—the policy underpinnings of integration are less complete than they were a century ago.
3. Third, countries choose integration because they see its benefits.

Once chosen, any specific degree of international integration imposes constraints on the ability of governments to tax, redistribute income, and influence macroeconomic conditions. But those constraints must not be exaggerated, and their effects are often beneficial.…

[A]s the world economy continues to integrate … global governance must be improved. Global governance will come not at the expense of the state but rather as an expression of the interests that the state embodies. As the source of order and basis of governance, the state will remain in the future as effective, and will be as essential, as it has ever been.

THE AGE OF SOVEREIGNTY HAS COME TO AN END
Llewellyn D. Howell

Llewellyn D. Howell is a professor at Thunderbird— The American Graduate School of International Management, Glendale, Arizona, and international affairs editor for USA Today magazine, where this article was first published in 1998.

NO

It's the end of the sovereignty century. The 19th century was strongly represented in its expression of imperialism and colonialism, repression of tribal affinities, and structuring according to the rules of state. Political rulers, as distinct from religious leaders, mobilized larger armies and navies. Economics rather than theology became the basis for societal organization, and civil politics became the source of organization to meet economic objectives.

The 20th century has seen the rise of the European state as the epitome of political organization. The contained nation-state with fixed borders replaced the systems of unbordered feudal dominance and vassalage that were common in most of the non-European world. The nation-state gave way to the multination-state as colonial powers imported labor to the entities they controlled or as they drew European lines around Asian and African territories under their power, often disregarding racial and cultural dispersions.

The result? Of the roughly 200 states that exist today, just a handful can be considered to be ethnically homogenous, and many, like the U.S., will sometime in the 21st century have only pluralities, not majorities, of racial, ethnic, or linguistic groups. Yet, powerful racial and religious bonds will continue to cross state borders.

What difference do you think it will make when the United States does not have a majority group?

Asian influences

What has been made clear in the Asian financial crisis is that the Chinese of east and southeast Asia form a union that is perhaps already more powerful than some of the region's political states. During this year's rioting in Indonesia, many of that country's Chinese citizens sought refuge and financial sanctuary in Chinese-run Singapore. Movement of capital through family structures but across borders (often without government involvement) already strongly characterizes the underpinnings of many Asian economies. The sense of what is happening is captured in the theme of Joel Kotkin's 1993 book, *Tribes: How Race, Religion and Identity Determine Success in the New Global Economy.*

In May 1998 protests in Jakarta against economic conditions and the regime of President Suharto (1921–) developed into anti-Chinese riots. About six million Chinese live in Indonesia, and they play an important role in the country's economy.

The 21st century will see the end of state sovereignty as we have known it. Sovereignty is an assumption of within-border integrity and independence from internal interference by other sovereign states. It is an assumption and an objective that is a *de jure*, rather than a *de facto*, characteristic of the way governments operate. And it is becoming more and more of a myth.

The Cold War was fought primarily in efforts of the U.S. and the Soviet Union to penetrate each other's systems and those of third parties. Monies channeled across borders to labor unions or political candidates already were common practices in undermining the sovereignty of opponents. While the Cold War is off, the "Hot Competition" is now on as populations continue to grow and resources and simple space continue to diminish.

The communications revolution has promoted the dissolution of the sovereign state. E-mail, the Internet, and satellite dishes, each with their cross-border networks, herald the end of cultural sanctity. Even when a sense of nation remains, the demonstration effect of socioeconomic success and evidence of simple freedom impels populations toward the locus of achievement—and across borders. The thirst for emigration drives growing dilution of nation-states and the political allegiances that are necessary to sustain them.

Population growth

Growing populations themselves provide a source for the limits of governance and the ability to protect and maintain sovereignty. Just because a government can rule 50,000,000 people, does that mean it can rule … 500,000,000 equally well? Both India and China, with their billions of citizens, represent the failure of macro-governments to resolve micro-problems, or even address them.

In part because of increases in populations, the power of domestic actors—both local governments and individuals—has risen since the end of the Cold War. Just as national foreign policy behavior is more directed at internal circumstances and actors, many of those same actors—such as state and local governments in the U.S.—are acting in the international arena on their own toward national governments and other internal actors, as in sister city arrangements. Can national governments control or even monitor every city's foreign policy? What about the foreign policies of multinational corporations and banks? Jane Fonda's or Jesse Jackson's foreign policy? These are not factors so far and are unlikely to be so in the future.

De jure *and de* facto *are Latin terms;* de jure *means "by right";* de facto *means* "in actual fact," *or "in reality."*

See Volume 11, Family and Society, Topic 16 Should government policy dictate the size of families?

According to the United Nations, the population of China in mid-2000 was 1,277,558,000; the population of India was 1,013,662,000. It took 33 and 34 years for their respective populations to increase from 500 million to 1 billion persons.

Jane Fonda (1937–) is a U.S. actor and political activist. Jesse Jackson (1941–) is an African American political and civil rights leader who twice sought nomination as the Democratic presidential candidate in the 1980s.

COMMENTARY: Monarchy

Monarchy is a form of government in which sovereignty—that is, supreme authority—rests with a single individual called a monarch. The word originates from the Greek *monarchia*, meaning "the rule of one." There are between 20 and 30 monarchies today in Europe, Asia, and Africa. Most modern monarchs inherit their title. In the past, however, there have been elected monarchies. For example, the emperors of Holy Roman Empire, who ruled much of western and central Europe from the 10th century until 1806, were elected by a council of nobles—although after 1438 the electors almost always chose a member of the Austrian Hapsburg dynasty. Elected monarchies exist today only in Malaysia and the Vatican City.

Absolute vs. constitutional monarchy

During the 17th century absolute monarchy—the idea that the monarch is above the law and not subject to any checks on his or her authority— assumed great importance. It was supported by the divine right of kings, a doctrine that claimed that monarchs derived their power directly from God. King Louis XIV (1643–1715) of France famously gave expression to this theory with his exclamation "L'état, c'est moi" ("I am the state"). Absolute monarchy was instrumental in the development of the modern nation-state because it provided the centralized power necessary to maintain law and order, to put an end to rival centers of power among the aristocracy, and to protect a state against its enemies. The political theorist Thomas Hobbes (1588–1679; see page 17) advocated in his book *Leviathan* (1651) that power in this absolute form was essential to keep a society together.

The notion of absolute monarchy began to decline after 1689, when the English Bill of Rights handed supreme power from the monarch to the parliament. The French Revolution (1789) established a republic; when the French monarchy was restored for short periods during the 19th century, its authority was much restricted. The monarchies of central Europe—Austria-Hungary, Germany, and Russia—did not survive the social and political upheaval of World War I (1914–1918). Those monarchies that remain are mostly constitutional monarchies—that is, the national constitution specifies that governing power belongs to the parliament, while the monarch is the symbolic head of state. Swaziland is one of the few surviving absolute monarchies in the world. Its king, Mswati III (1968–), keeps tight control of the media. Many Swazis fear political change because they think it would threaten their traditional way of life. Monarchs in Islamic states—for example, Brunei and Saudi Arabia—reign with near-absolute power. And in 2003 the electorate of the tiny European principality of Liechtenstein, which lies between Austria and Switzerland, voted to give the crown prince, Hans Adam II (1945–), sweeping new executive powers, making him, in effect, an absolute monarch.

The global system itself compels an end to sovereignty. International stability no longer is a matter of military security in the face of national armies, but, rather, is economic security, both for the U.S. in the international system and for ethnic groups in places such as Bosnia, Malaysia, and the Congo. In gauging what needs to be done with foreign policy behavior, national governments have increasingly less influence over the course of economic events, which are the bulk of both domestic and international activity in the age of privatization.

Interdependence works both ways

The manifestations of the end of sovereignty are all around us. Does an American president have a proper role in criticizing China or Myanmar [Burma] on human rights matters? Of course he does, if they want to sell products manufactured with exploited or even prison labor in the U.S. market. Can Malays or Vietnamese demand that foreign investors bow to local culture in bringing capital and technical know-how into their systems? Of course not! Those economic benefits will flow to more hospitable climes. Interdependence works both ways. Can Americans be outraged at the thought of Indonesian contributors to U.S. political campaigns? How absurd! We've been interfering with the political processes in numerous other countries for decades. Why shouldn't they have an opportunity to have a say in ours? The time to huff and puff about sovereignty has come to an end—for everyone.

Foreign nationals are banned from contributing to U.S. electoral campaigns at federal, state, and local level. Do you think that this is fair?

Summary

Is the concept of the nation-state consistent with the idea of globalization? In the first article Martin Wolf attempts to demolish the popular idea that as the power of market forces increases, the power of government is reduced. He argues that a totally globalized world—with no transport or communications costs or barriers created by different jurisdictions—is an impossibility. He insists that states choose globalization through the policies they develop rather than have it forced on them. Wolf further suggests that the benefits that international economic integration brings can only be exploited by strong nation-states that provide public goods. Even in an age of globalization, he says, people do not want to sacrifice the sense of belonging and identity that the state offers them.

In the second article Llewellyn D. Howell asserts that the 21st century will herald the end of sovereign states. He regards migration, population growth, and the communications revolution to be the key contributors to this change. Howell points out that state and local governments and multinational corporations are also playing an increasingly important role on the worldwide stage. International stability, he says, no longer depends on military might; instead, it is determined by economic security. National governments have limited influence over this area. Howell emphasizes how far the erosion of sovereignty has already advanced. Americans have no right to be outraged at the thought of foreigners having a say in how the United States should be governed, he concludes, because America has been interfering in the politics of other countries for many years.

FURTHER INFORMATION:

 Books:

Holton, Robert J., *Globalization and the Nation-State*. New York: St. Martin's Press, 1998.

Kotkin, Joel, *Tribes: How Race, Religion, and Identity Determine Success in the New Global Economy*. New York: Random House, 1993.

 Useful websites:

www.theglobalist.com

Online magazine that looks at the global economy, politics, and culture.

www.globalization101.org

A student's guide to globalization from the Center for Strategic and International Studies.

http://www1.worldbank.org/economicpolicy/globalization/

Introduction to a range of issues concerning globalization, with general articles and current statistics.

The following debates in the Pro/Con series may also be of interest:

In this volume:
Topic 10 Is a United States of Europe possible?

In *Economics*:
Topic 9 Is globalization inevitable?

In *Commerce and Trade*:
Topic 8 Do transnational corporations have more influence on the world economy than national governments?

IS THE NATION-STATE CONSISTENT WITH THE IDEA OF GLOBALIZATION?

YES: The world will never be a completely integrated market because there will always be transport costs involved. Cultural barriers prevent labor mobility to a certain extent.

YES: Nation-states are used to sharing the political stage with intergovernmental organizations. They are willing to forego a degree of sovereignty for the benefits they derive from these nonstate actors.

THE WORLD IS SHRINKING
Are improved transport and communications consistent with national sovereignty?

THE IMPACT OF NONSTATE ACTORS
Are nonstate actors beneficial to nation-states?

NO: Freedom of movement and commerce have made national boundaries obsolete

NO: Transnational corporations can negatively influence or even undermine the government policies of nation-states

IS THE NATION-STATE CONSISTENT WITH THE IDEA OF GLOBALIZATION?
KEY POINTS

YES: Globalization is not an unstoppable force; it is a policy chosen by governments to further the interests of the nation-state

YES: Globalization is not a new trend; it is a continuation of a process that began when humans started to trade with one another

MUTUAL COMPATIBILITY
Can the nation-state and globalization coexist?

NO: Globalization reduces the ability of the state to regulate the economy through taxation and income redistribution; as its revenue decreases, so does the power of the state

NO: The pace of globalization has increased so much in recent years, with the advent of new technology, that the nation-state is losing control of global economic and social forces

Topic 3

DO RELIGION-BASED POLITICS UNDERMINE DEMOCRACY?

YES

FROM "THEN: VIOLENCE—NOW: GENOCIDE"
CLAMOR MAGAZINE, ISSUE 23, NOVEMBER/DECEMBER 2003
PRIYA LAL

NO

"SECULARISM IS NO ANSWER FOR THE MUSLIM WORLD"
THE AGE, OCTOBER 28, 2002
AMIR BUTLER

INTRODUCTION

During the 2000 U.S. presidential election George W. Bush stated that he had "recommitted his life to Christ," and Al Gore told the media that the purpose of his life was "to glorify God." While it has become increasingly more common for political candidates to speak openly about their personal faith and how it affects decision-making processes, the degree that religion and politics can work together remains the focus of heated debate.

Political leaders—such as George W. Bush—are insistent that liberal democracy is the only legitimate political system, especially since the War on Terrorism began. Many of the principles of liberal democracy are based on the ideas of the English political theorist John Locke (1632–1704), including the protection of the right of individuals to worship freely. For the sake of this liberty, Locke believed, government must support religion in general; but for the sake of

civil peace it must favor no particular religion. These views influenced the Framers of the U.S. Constitution. The First Amendment bans laws "respecting an establishment of religion, or prohibiting the free exercise thereof."

Although some democratic countries, such as England, have a state religion, many democracies support the separation of church and state. Some commentators believe that it is important to maintain this distance in order to prevent the persecution, bigotry, and extremism often seen in nations that allow or encourage a closer relationship. A 2002 survey by the U.S.-based Pew Forum and Pew Research Center for the People and Press, for example, found that Americans want their political candidates to be "generically religious but not to express their religious views in any specific terms." Some proponents believe this attitude is a response to the rise of theocracies (literally "rule by the deity")—political regimes that claim to represent the divine on earth both directly and immediately. Many people associate theocracies with negative values, such as extremism, prejudice, abuse, inequality, and terrorism. They believe that the system undermines democratic principles.

Historically the ancient Hebrews and Egyptians lived in theocracies. The papal states under various popes and the New England colonies under the Puritans in the 17th century also acted as theocracies. Today, however, theocracies are most associated with extremist Islamic groups that have established such systems in countries like Iran. In theory, there is no reason why a theocracy and a democratic form of government are incompatible, but in most cases theocracies are ruled by a theologically trained elite that interprets, implements, and enforces divine laws rigidly. Ultimate political authority lies in the hands of religious leaders and a fundamentalist regime whose purpose is to organize society according to religious law.

"Islam—the faith of one-fifth of humanity—is consistent with democratic rule."

—GEORGE W. BUSH,

43RD PRESIDENT (2001–)

Some opponents claim that theocracies are doomed to failure since clerics may be trained in religious dogma but are rarely conversant with modern economics. Religious laws may seem arbitrary, unfair, or overly strict,

and security forces are often brutal in enforcing the law. Such measures undermine the legitimacy of the regime both domestically and abroad. The international community also responds badly to theocracies, fearing the effects of religious extremism and a backlash against more liberal democratic nations, such as the United States, which have resulted more and more frequently in violence and terrorism.

Scott Ritter, UN Chief Inspector in Iraq from 1991 to 1998, refers to the "theocracy of evil" pervading U.S. politics—a faith-based value system that embraces a "good versus evil" opposition. This, Ritter argues, has led to an "ends justifies the means" mentality, which he believes may be fatal to democratic principles.

George W. Bush has also been criticized for his religion-based politics, in particular his program to expand the work of religious organizations. An article in *The Atlantic Monthly* (June, 2003) claimed that "There's hardly a place where Bush hasn't increased both the presence and the potency of religion in American government. In the process, the Bush administration lavishly caters to the very religious-right groups that gave us the dubious Christian-nation concept."

In Europe, however, Christian democratic parties helped nations such as Germany, Italy, and Norway become stable after World War II (1939–1945). Similarly, in Turkey the Islamist-based Justice and Development Party introduced democratic reforms after it won the 2002 parliamentary election. Thus, some commentators argue, religion-based politics is not necessarily incompatible with democracy.

The following two articles examine this debate in greater detail.

THEN: VIOLENCE—NOW: GENOCIDE
Priya Lal

Priya Lal is a journalist. This article was published in Clamor, an online journal aimed at disseminating alternative views and "new perspectives on politics, culture, media and life."

India has the second-largest population in the world (see sidebar on page 29). China is more populous, but it is a communist state, not a democracy.

Mohandas Karamchand Gandhi (1869–1948) led India's struggle for independence from Britain. He believed that nonviolent protest was the only way to achieve progress. Indians called him Mahatma, "Great Soul."

YES

While George W. Bush sells Americans a ubiquitous stream of careless denunciations of "evil" Muslims in the Middle East and the rest of the world is distracted by the United States' inept war-mongering, a deadly mixture of religious bigotry and ruthless political instrumentalism is brewing in another distant pocket of the world.

Faith-based facism

This venomous brand of Hindu nationalism, a movement that relies on the all-purpose scapegoating of Muslim and other minorities' culture and even celebrates the literal extermination of Indian Muslims themselves, has been increasing in momentum in South Asia for over a decade now. While the hot, lethal winds of Hindu fundamentalism blow harder and faster across the subcontinent, the United States continues to celebrate India, the world's largest "democracy", as a stable base in a potentially turbulent region, and continues to ignore what is rapidly becoming a regime founded on the principles of faith-based fascism.

"The days of Mahatma Gandhi and his philosophy of non-violence are gone." So spoke Praveen Togadia, head of India's Vishwa Hindu Parishad (World Hindu Council), earlier this year, addressing a crowd on the one-year anniversary of the tragic immolation of the passenger train Sabarmati Express in the Western Indian city of Godhra.

Togadia's matter-of-fact renunciation of Gandhi's peaceful idealism echoes the aggressive, sinister, and vaguely apocalyptic rhetoric of India's increasingly powerful Hindu nationalist movement as a whole, and particularly reflects the escalation of communal tensions in the region over the past year.

The event that triggered India's recent downward spiral into the depths of religious violence was precisely the incident to which Togadia was alluding to—the burning of the Sabarmati Express in February of 2002. The train carriage carried a large contingent of the Hindu nationalist informal army (kar-sevaks) returning from a pilgrimage to Ayodhya. The carriage was set aflame in a Godhra railway station, killing some 58 people. Immediately, large-scale anti-Muslim pogroms erupted in the city of Godhra and throughout the larger state of Gujarat, fueled by official denunciations of the act of arson and the Muslims who had committed it…. Within 72 hours, mobs of outraged Hindus took to the streets and slaughtered some 2000 Gujarati Muslims with knives, guns, clubs, even swords—and more fire.

A report issued by Human Rights Watch in the wake of the killings notes that "much of the violence was planned well in advance of the Godhra attack and was carried out with state approval and orchestration" and that "state officials and the police were directly involved in the violence." [Gujarat Chief Minister Narendra] Modi and his fellow members of the BJP (Bharati Janata Party, the Hindu nationalist, right-wing party currently leading India's parliamentary coalition) flatly denied their involvement in the pogroms. Rather, they chose to characterize the violence as a spontaneous people's movement, the latest manifestation of a sort of primordial hatred that has existed between Hindus and Muslims since time immemorial. Of course, all of this rhetoric came with the implicit assumption that Hindus were justified in hating Muslims—that Hindus were defending themselves against Muslim aggression and protecting their culture from pollution by India's immoral and evil Islamic elements.

Partition as precedent for violence

This attitude, in short, sums up the platform of India's Hindu nationalist movement. The movement is not, in fact, new, and neither is the larger ideological struggle between defining the Indian nation in secular and religious terms. In the decades leading up to the independence of British India in 1947, the indigenous political leadership split into two camps—the secularists, whose philosophies were embodied in the kind of democratic, peaceful inclusiveness that Gandhi symbolized; and the proponents of a divided subcontinent based on religious identity. The result was an awkward partition of the former colony into Muslim Pakistan and what was to be a predominantly Hindu India. The 1947 partition of the subcontinent was washed in blood—astronomical numbers of Hindus fleeing Pakistan and Muslims fleeing India were massacred by methods that bear too close resemblance to those employed by angry mobs in Gujarat last year.

Since the nightmares of Partition … a tenuous cease-fire has largely allowed Muslims (12 percent of the national population) and Hindus (81 percent of the population), as well as the country's many other smaller religious groups, to coexist in relative peace. That is, however, until the rise to

> *"Pogrom" is a Russian word that means "destruction." It is applied in particular to the attacks on Russian Jews that took place in the late 19th and early 20th centuries.*

> *Go to http://hrw.org/reports/2003/india0703/ to read the Human Rights Watch report "Compounding Injustice."*

See the commentary box on page 42 for information on the partition of the Indian subcontinent.

Atal Bihari Vajpayee (1926–), a moderate within the BJP, first became prime minister of India in 1996, but he was forced to resign days later due to his party's lack of a parliamentary majority. He was prime minister of a coalition government from 1998 to 2004.

Lal Krishna Advani (1929–) was India's deputy prime minister during Vajpayee's coalition government (1998–2004). He is known for his hard-line nationalist views; he was accused of inciting Hindu–Muslim violence in 1992. Hindu militants destroyed the Babri mosque in Ayodhya, Uttar Pradesh, and demanded the restoration of the Hindu temple there. Weeks of rioting left between 2,000 and 3,000 people dead.

power of the current government—led by BJP leaders—in the early 1990s. The BJP comprises merely the political arm of the larger network of organizations and individuals that make up the Sangh Parivar (Family of Societies), the vanguard of India's Hindu nationalist movement.

And now this. Perhaps the most frightening aspect of the recent events in Gujarat revealed itself in the aftermath of the violence. Not only did India's BJP Prime Minister, Atal Bihari Vajpayee, fail to condemn Modi and the Gujarati state government for their role in organizing the Muslim pogroms; not only was Modi not brought to any kind of justice in front of a judge or jury—but Modi was re-elected this past December as State Minister in a BJP sweep of the Gujarati elections. During his campaign, Modi failed to offer even a single acknowledgement of regret or personal responsibility regarding the year's earlier violence. In fact, encouraged by other BJP leaders including Vajpayee and Advani, his rhetoric became increasingly inflammatory as he employed campaigning techniques that explicitly drew upon Muslim scapegoating and reactionary Hindu ethnocentrism....

Hard-liners such as Modi and Advani want to see the BJP adopt an openly communal (i.e. openly anti-Muslim) party line at the national level, and plan to start by staging Modi-style BJP sweeps of other state governments in upcoming elections.... All of this, of course, is taking place under the aegis of supposedly democratic, legitimately elected national leaders such as Prime Minister Vajpayee.

An unpardonable sin

As an Indian-American, I don't know who to be more ashamed of or angry with—the power-grabbing Indian politicians who commit unspeakable acts of violence in the name of my family's religion; or American leaders who ignore the obvious parroting of democratic norms and the disgusting sanctioning of ethnic cleansing by these officials. Indeed, in the context of the post September 11 U.S. bombing of Afghanistan and the current War on Terror, Bush has chosen to embrace Vajpayee's government as an ideological ally of sorts—painting India as a democratic paragon in opposition to the primitive theocracies of Muslim "fundamentalist" countries. In attempting to corral "fundamentalism" (also known as the appropriation of religious philosophy or rhetoric for power-seeking political purposes) into the same exclusive arena as Islam, Bush is both grossly distorting the public understanding of anti-democratic political movements that employ faith as a tool, as well as committing the unpardonable sin of eliding over equally insidious demonstrations of violent "fundamentalism" by non-Muslims, in countries such as India.

They're all the same

In reality, Hindu fundamentalism, Muslim fundamentalism in the Middle East, Zionist fundamentalism in Israel, and right-wing Christian Fundamentalism in our own country are all sides of the same coin. Once we choose to recognize the BJP's circus-like antics conducted in the ostensible name of a "pure" Hinduism as what they really constitute, it becomes clear that Hindu nationalism, when stripped to its core, is merely a case of naked political instrumentalism....

"Political instrumentalism" is the theory that politics serves simply as a neutral instrument through which nonpolitical concerns are put into effect.

But there is a particular urgency to the Indian case. Hindu–Muslim violence in the region, whether during Partition, in Kashmir, or more recently in Godhra, has always been characterized by what I'll call the "reprisal effect"—one act of violence begets another act of revenge begets another, and so on.... Gandhi's famous proclamation that "an eye for an eye leaves the whole world blind" has never rung truer than now, as we witness the dangerous effects of individuals like Togadia blatantly placing the concept of revenge at the center of their demagoguery.

India and Pakistan have been engaged in a dispute over Kashmir since partition. The territory is divided between both countries, with India controling the larger part (in the state of Jammu and Kashmir). Since 1989 Muslim militants have been fighting for independence. India has accused Pakistan of supporting the separatists.

As Americans, we need to look beyond the simplistic Manichean rhetoric our leaders shell out regarding the domestic politics of our national enemies and allies, and remember that fascism and "fundamentalism" are not so far away from what our government celebrates as their alternatives. And we can do more. The Sangh Parivar has effectively globalized its appalling movement by mobilizing many of the funds necessary to fuel communal activities in India from international networks of rich Hindus in the diaspora—from the U.S. and Canada to Mauritius and Malaysia. Against this globalization of hate we can work towards a globalization of awareness of the atrocities committed in the name of Hindu nationalism, and thus enrich the efforts of domestic Indian dissenters to overcome such hateful political instrumentalism. For, in fact, our acceptance of the gross distortions of "democracy" that we are witnessing in India today threatens the futures of more meaningful, socially just visions of the word for the entire rest of the world. And it is these collective visions of possible alternatives, better futures—and our dedication to working for them—that will ultimately sustain the fight against faith-based bigotry in India.

"Diaspora" is a Greek word meaning "dispersion."

SECULARISM IS NO ANSWER FOR THE MUSLIM WORLD
Amir Butler

NO

Two consistent themes in much of the contemporary analysis of world affairs have been the impending clash of civilisations and the need for the secularisation of the Muslim world.

Secularism seeks to make the temporal rather than spiritual the basis for all laws. It arose in response to a uniquely European Christian problem—the excesses of the church, the antagonism between the church and science, and the intra-Christian wars being fought at the time. The separation of church and state was a logical solution.

Islam as a force for knowledge and democracy

In contrast, the periods of Muslim caliphate, particularly between 622 and 1492, were marked as periods of growth, intellectual advancement and social justice. The rights of minorities were protected, human rights were enshrined not just in law but in scripture, and a knowledge-centred society was fostered that was the intellectual well from which all of Europe came to drink.

Contrary to popular opinion, Islam, in its political manifestation, is democratic—if democracy means that people choose their own leaders and laws are passed through discussion and deliberation.

The Prophet Muhammad (peace be upon him) himself refrained from appointing a successor, instead allowing people to choose the next ruler of the fledgling Islamic state. Umar, the second Caliph (ruler), said that the ruler can be chosen only through the consultative approval of the people.

Islamic vs. secular democracy

However, Islamic democracy differs from secular democracy in that the right of the people to legislate is limited by what they believe to be a higher law, to which human law is subordinate. There is no axiom that states that a democracy must be secular, in the same way that there is no axiom that states that a secular system is intrinsically democratic.

The above image shows Muhammad being escorted to Paradise by the angel Gabriel. It is taken from a 15-century Persian Uigur manuscript of the life of the Prophet.

The subordination of law-making to the Koran and Sunnah (traditions of the Prophet Muhammad, peace be upon him) made Muslim society immune to absolute tyranny and dictatorship.

Such emphasis also prevented absolute tyranny by giving Islamic scholars more legislative power than the ruler. It was their word that was final on many matters. If the ruler made a decision that was contrary to that of the ulema (people of knowledge), his decision was to be rejected.

The Koran, or Qur'an, is the sacred book of Islam. Muslims believe that it contains the words of God (Allah) as revealed to Muhammad. Sunnah is the body of Islamic customary practice that is based on Muhammad's words and actions.

Islamic states today

There is a stark contrast between past glories and current reality.

Whereas once the Muslim world was ruled by a single caliphate, its post-colonial manifestation is a collection of weak, mostly secular, nation-states. Termed "bunker regimes" by Samuel Huntington, their guns face their own people, ruthlessly repressing dissent and committing some of the worst violations of human rights.

"Bunker regimes" refer to Middle Eastern states with repressive military dictatorships.

COMMENTARY: Religion and partition of India

The British maintained a presence in India for almost 350 years. The East India Company first founded trading posts on the subcontinent in the early 17th century; by the time the British government took control of the company's lands in 1858, it directly governed about 60 percent of India's territory. The rest was in the hands of princely rulers who pledged loyalty to the British monarch in return for a degree of autonomy. During the 19th century there were growing demands for the British to withdraw from India. Upper-caste Hindus formed the administrative elite and comprised the majority of representatives of the Indian National Congress, the dominant nationalist political party established in 1885. Mohandas Karamchand Gandhi (1869–1948) became leader of Congress in the 1920s. He mobilized support for Congress at home and abroad through his doctrine of civil disobedience and passive resistance to British rule. Gandhi was a Hindu, but he preached religious tolerance. Muslims, however, became increasingly worried about being marginalized by the Hindu-dominated Congress—many turned to the Muslim League, established in 1906 to further Muslim rights.

The road to partition

Congress adopted a neutral stance when World War II broke out in 1939. It later tried to negotiate with the British, promising support in exchange for independence. The British responded by banning Congress. The Muslim League supported the war effort. In 1940, however, its leader Mohammed Ali Jinnah (1876–1948) began to push for a separate state for Muslims—"Pakistan," or "land of the pure." Congress adopted a "Quit India" resolution in 1942 demanding immediate independence, but its leaders continued to negotiate with Jinnah: Gandhi in particular did not want British withdrawal to lead to the partition of India. In 1946 Congress offered Jinnah a deal in which Muslims could have regional autonomy in the provinces in which they were dominant, but Jinnah rejected the plan. As tensions grew, Hindus and Muslims clashed with increasing frequency.

In 1947 the British sent Lord Louis Mountbatten (1900–1979) to negotiate independence: The final plan created a separate Pakistan from the predominantly Muslim (but geographically divided) regions of northwest India (West Pakistan) and eastern Bengal (East Pakistan). The princely states were allowed to choose which nation they wished to join. But the creation of a new Islamic nation involved not just the transfer of land but also that of people. When India achieved independence and Pakistan came into being on August 15, 1947, violence escalated. About 1 million people died, and within a year some 13 million refugees had moved from one country to the other. Religion remains a very sensitive issue in both countries, and there have been periodic bouts of communal violence and terrorist activity.

It is a sad irony that in many cases, Muslims have more freedom to practice their religion in the secular democracies of the West than in the secular dictatorships of the Middle East.

In Islam, there is no conflict between theology and science, between the demands of the spiritual and the temporal. However, one can draw parallels between Christian Europe before Enlightenment, and the intellectual stagnation, reactionary impulses and conflict that characterises the Muslim world today. Yet, what is required is not a wholesale adoption of secular democracy, but a uniquely Islamic reformation.

The Enlightenment was an 18th-century intellectual movement that took place in Europe and America. Its followers attempted to understand the world through the use of reason rather than religious belief.

The future of Islam

Is it then unreasonable that Muslims, who have their own culture, values and history, can be allowed to choose their own future? Those who advocate Western secularism as a universal panacea, are akin to the child with the hammer who thinks every problem is a nail.

"Panacea," derived from Greek, means a remedy for all ills.

Indeed, the call to secularise Islam as a means of averting a clash of civilisations is really the first salvo in such a clash. Huntington wrote that the problem for Islam is not the CIA nor the US Department of Defence. It is the West, a different civilisation whose people are convinced of the universality of their culture, and believe that their superior, if declining, power imposes on them the obligation to extend that culture throughout the world. These are the basic ingredients that fuel conflict between Islam and the West.

What is needed today is a revival of the tremendous energy that propelled Muslims forward in history; the energy that comes from a clear sense of purpose and direction.

Muslim society must subject itself to critical self-evaluation, recognising the principles that made it great in the past, as well as drawing on the positive aspects of the West and other societies, adapting and improving upon them.

From this may spring a profound sense of empowerment and a realisation that Muslims can make their own future.

The call to modernise Islam thus becomes a call to Islamisize modernity.

Summary

Do religion-based politics undermine democracy? In the first article Priya Lal examines the political climate in India, the most populous democracy in the world. Lal argues that the United States is wrong to direct global attention to the situation in the Middle East and to focus on Islam because, she says, the threat to stability in India is coming from Hindu fundamentalism. Lal details the communal violence that has taken place between Hindus and Muslims in Gujarat state in recent years and accuses the ruling Bharati Janata Party of sanctioning "ethnic cleansing." She argues that all types of fundamentalism— whether Hindu, Muslim, Zionist, or Christian—amount to antidemocratic political movements built on "faith-based bigotry."

In the second article Amir Butler refutes the need to secularize Muslim countries as the only means of preventing conflict between Islam and the West. Butler does not dispute that the separation of church and state works in a Christian context, but he also points out that there is no rule stating that a democracy has to be secular. "Islamic democracy," he argues, "differs from secular democracy in that the right of the people to legislate is limited by what they believe to be a higher law." Butler finds it ironic that Muslims today have more religious freedom in the West than in parts of the Middle East, but he anticipates a revitalized Islam that draws inspiration both from its past and from "positive aspects" of the West.

FURTHER INFORMATION:

Books:

Tamimi, Azzam, and John L. Esposito (eds.), *Islam and Secularism in the Middle East*. New York: New York University Press, 2000.

Wald, Kenneth D., *Religion and Politics in the United States*. Lanham, MD: Rowman and Littlefield, 2004.

Useful websites:

http://www.bostonreview.net/BR28.2/abou.html
"Islam and the Challenge of Democracy" by Khaled Abou El Fadl.
http://www.ceip.org/files/projects/drl/drl_home.ASP
Articles from the Democracy and Rule of Law Project by the Carnegie Endowment for International Peace.
http://www.freedomhouse.org/religion/publications/India/summary.htm
"The Rise of Hindu Extremism" by the Center for Religious Freedom.
http://www.policyreview.org/oct03/etzioni.html
"Mosque and State in Iraq" by Amitai Etzioni.

The following debates in the Pro/Con series may also be of interest:

In this volume:
Topic 1 Is liberal democracy the only viable political system?

In *U.S. Foreign Policy*:
Topic 3 Should the United States have relations with fundamentalist regimes?

In *Religion and Morality*:
Topic 14 Is the separation between church and state still necessary?

DO RELIGION-BASED POLITICS UNDERMINE DEMOCRACY?

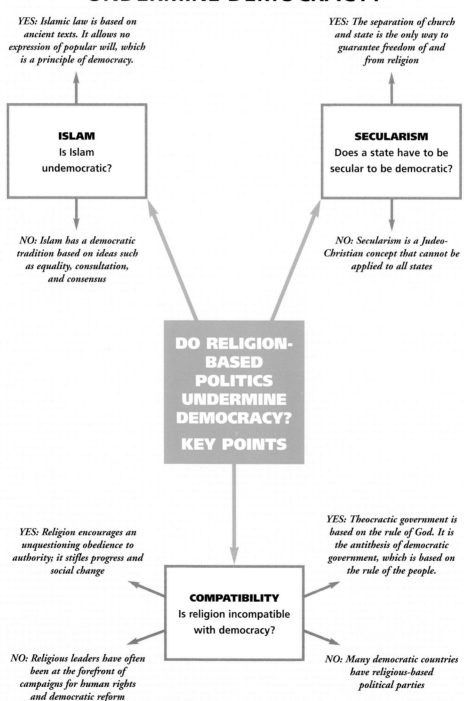

YES: Islamic law is based on ancient texts. It allows no expression of popular will, which is a principle of democracy.

YES: The separation of church and state is the only way to guarantee freedom of and from religion

ISLAM
Is Islam undemocratic?

SECULARISM
Does a state have to be secular to be democratic?

NO: Islam has a democratic tradition based on ideas such as equality, consultation, and consensus

NO: Secularism is a Judeo-Christian concept that cannot be applied to all states

DO RELIGION-BASED POLITICS UNDERMINE DEMOCRACY?

KEY POINTS

YES: Religion encourages an unquestioning obedience to authority; it stifles progress and social change

YES: Theocratic government is based on the rule of God. It is the antithesis of democratic government, which is based on the rule of the people.

COMPATIBILITY
Is religion incompatible with democracy?

NO: Religious leaders have often been at the forefront of campaigns for human rights and democratic reform

NO: Many democratic countries have religious-based political parties

Topic 4

IS DEMOCRACY UNDER THREAT IN RUSSIA?

YES

"THE ERA OF LIBERALISM VERSUS COMMUNISM IN RUSSIA IS OVER"
CARNEGIE ENDOWMENT FOR NATIONAL PEACE,
RUSSIAN AND EURASIAN AFFAIRS PROGRAM, 2003
MICHAEL MCFAUL

NO

"THE AWFUL TRUTH"
THE GUARDIAN, DECEMBER 10, 2003
JONATHAN STEELE

INTRODUCTION

In the 1990s Russia experienced great change. The collapse of communism led to the end of the Cold War; the subsequent disintegration of the Soviet Union resulted in Russia regaining its national status. Successive Russian presidents began to extol the merits of a democratic, free society. Open elections were held, and Boris Yeltsin became the first democratically elected president in June 1991. Russia became a market economy, and prices and trade were liberalized. Despite these factors, however, critics claim that Russia is not democratic. They believe that evidence such as restrictions on press freedom, the rising power of the oligarchs (businessmen and entrepreneurs), President Vladimir V. Putin's dismissal of his government less than four weeks before the 2004 presidential elections, and the generally flawed electoral procedures prove that democracy in Russia is in crisis.

A democracy is a system in which the supreme power is vested in the citizens. They enjoy certain rights and freedoms, usually written down in a constitution, such as the right to free speech and the freedom to form political parties. Officials are supposed to represent the people's best interests both domestically and abroad; citizens elect them by exercising their right to vote in free and open elections. Although countries such as the United States have espoused democracy for centuries, Russia has no such tradition. Before the 1917 Russian Revolution occurred, the country was ruled by czars or emperors; afterward, the Communist Party controlled the Soviet Union until 1991. It operated a planned economy, regulating everything from food supply to industrial output.

Although supporters argued that communism offered a fairer system of distribution of wealth and resources, critics countered that the state was secretive, repressive, and inefficient. The overly bureaucratic economy was plagued by corruption and lagged behind that of many western democracies. Some people believe that Russia's situation in the 21st century is not that different.

Soviet President Mikhail Gorbachev (1990–1991) used *glasnost* (openness) and *perestroika* (reconstruction) to introduce change from 1985 to 1991. While Gorbachev has been criticized for not going far enough, historians, such as Robert Service, argue that he was a genuine advocate of democratization—unlike his successors Boris Yeltsin (1991–1999) or Vladimir V. Putin (2000–), who have been "agents of rapacious authoritarianism."

"It is our common task to prove that democracy in Russia … is here for good."

—PRESIDENT VLADIMIR

V. PUTIN (2001)

When Yeltsin came to power, the constitutional order of the Russian Federation fell between that of the Soviet era and Gorbachev's reforms, meaning that both president and parliament had to be elected. Yeltsin, who lacked the support of of his parliament, dissolved it in 1993. The old guard barricaded themselves in the Russian White House, but Yeltsin ordered the army to open fire on them.

In 1993 Yeltsin introduced a new constitution that established a nationally elected president and a federal assembly for passing laws and approving policies. Supporters claim that this was a popular move, voted for by the majority of Russians. Critics argue that there was a poor referendum turnout—only 32 percent of the electorate voted—and that the new constitution was far from fair. It greatly enlarged the powers of the president, while constricting those of parliament.

From the beginning Yeltsin adopted policies to radically reshape the economy. By 1994, 70 percent of the economy had been privatized, but inflation was in three figures, and output was falling. Accusations of government corruption abounded. The Russian currency collapsed—it was 0.6 rubles per dollar in 1988 and more than 1,000 rubles per dollar in 1993. Yeltsin still had the support of the international community, however, which backed him against his parliament and offered Russia a $10 billion loan in 1996. At the end of 2000 one-third of the country was living below the poverty line of $38 per month. Meanwhile, reports surfaced in the late 1990s that Russian politicians had embezzled western aid.

When Yeltsin resigned at the end of 1999, Vladimir V. Putin, Yeltsin's prime minister, became acting president; he was formally elected in 2000. Supporters of Putin describe his style of government as a "managed democracy." They claim that Russia will eventually become a fully democratic state. At present, however, it has to act in whatever way it feels best to protect Russia's interests. Critics believe that this is far from the truth: Putin's government is authoritarian, has restricted the freedom of the press, and cosied up to extreme right-wing leaders.

Michael McFaul and Jonathan Steele look at the issue further.

THE ERA OF LIBERALISM VERSUS COMMUNISM IN RUSSIA IS OVER
Michael McFaul

Michael McFaul is an associate professor of political science at Stanford University and a nonresident associate at the Carnegie Endowment for International Peace.

YES

✓ The results of the parliamentary vote last Sunday suggest that Russia has entered new political era. For the first decade of post-communist politics in Russia, the central cleavage was between left and right, communist and anti-communist, or "reformers" and non-reformers. The central issue was the economy and policies to reform it. The vote tally from Sunday's election suggests that a third parameter—nationalism—has overtaken these earlier divides and debates. The long term consequences could be terrifying.

Of the major Russian political parties, three are rising, and three are falling. United Russia, The Liberal Democratic Party of Russia, and Motherland (Rodina) all won more votes in the election than in the last election in 1999. The Communist Party of the Russian Federation (CPRF), Yabloko, and the Union of Right Forces all won fewer votes in 2003 than in 1999. The last two—Russia's liberal, democratic, pro-Western parties—did so poorly that they will not even be represented in the new Duma.

The State Duma is the lower house of the Russian Federation's parliament; it was created by the 1993 Constitution. The new Duma had its first plenary session on December 29, 2003.

Winners and losers

Several factors unite these winners and losers and distinguish them from each other. First, the winners—United Russia, LDPR, and Motherland—are all parties created initially by the state, the LDPR over a decade ago, United Russia (called Unity before) in 1999, and Motherland during this electoral cycle. In contrast, societal actors founded the Communist Party, Yabloko, and the Union of Right Forces. Parties beholden to the state are gaining popular support. Parties beholden to societal forces are losing strength.

What might be the negative effects of political parties owing their creation to the state?

Second, the three winners in last Sunday's voters are all loyal to the president. Unified Russia ran in this election as the party of Putin and is fully subservient to the Kremlin. Neo-nationalist Vladimir Zhirinovsky, the LDPR leader, and the leaders of Motherland are more colorful personalities than the gray suits leading Unified Russia, but these two parties will also serve the interests on the president on

Vladimir Putin speaking in Rome, Italy, on November 5, 2003.

Are nationalism and racism the same thing? Go to http://www.russia journal.com/misc/ opinion.shtml? id=64 to find out more about the situation in Russia.

Russian lawyer Vladimir Zhirinovsky (1946–) entered politics in 1988. His party— the Liberal Democratic Party of Russia (LDPR)— took one-quarter of the vote in the 1993 election. The LDPR won 11.5 percent of the parliamentary vote in the December 2003 elections, but Zhirinovsky withdrew from the presidential campaign. Vladimir Putin won the March 2004 election with over 71 percent of the vote; Oleg Malyshkin, the LDPR candidate, took just over 2 percent of the vote.

important issues. In contrast, the three losers are all parties are all opposition parties that have never fully succumbed to the president's will.

Third, and most importantly, all three winners in Sunday's vote are nationalist parties. Running on the coattails of President Vladimir Putin, Unified Russia leaders and campaign materials called for a "strong" state and "orderly" country. Motherland leader Dmitry Rogozin even more stridently echoed nationalist themes in his campaign appearances, compelling some of his opponents in other parties to publicly use the word "fascist" to describe his ideology. And the LDPR's head, Vladimir Zhirinovsky, is a long time populist demagogue who has relied on outrageous xenophobic and racist one-liners to keep his party in the parliament since it splashed on to the Russian political scene in the 1993 parliamentary vote by capturing a quarter of the popular vote. In this year's election, Zhirinovsky's main campaign slogan was "I am for Russians, I am for the poor," an echo of the nationalist–socialist cocktail that proved so explosive a half century ago.

The spectre of fascism

After the 1993 election, many (including me) worried about the specter of fascism in Russia. After his strong showing in 1993, however, Zhirinovsky and his ideas seemed to fade from the center of Russian politics. In 1999, his party barely made it in to the Duma, winning a mere six percent of the vote. At the end of the decade, it seemed as if one of Russia's greatest successes was that nationalism did not take hold as a major force in Russian politics—a sharp contrast to the deadly destructive role that nationalism played in Serbia, the only other empire to collapse after the fall of communism. Today, Zhirinovsky is back. So are his clones.

In ideological terms, the losers in this election can be mapped on traditional left–right scale. The Communist Party is the left of center party and the Union of Right Forces and Yabloko are right of center (with Yabloko closer to the center). For most of the 1990s, those on the right battled keep out of power those on the left. As in Western party systems, economic debates defined the battle lines between left and right in Russia. Now, this battle is over; serious debates about economic issues are no longer a central theme of Russian politics.

To be sure, the Communist Party has tried to capture the nationalist, patriotic vote before, but never with any success. And Union of Right Forces leader Anatoly Chubais recently has floated the idea of Russia as a "liberal empire," but the concept did not steal votes away from the three winning nationalist parties. Instead, these parties won votes in the past without inflaming nationalist sentiments within the Russian electorate. As of yesterday, their non-nationalist themes seem less important to Russian voters.

It is premature to predict Russia's long-term political trajectory after a single vote. We made that mistake back in 1993. This said, the trend line after Sunday does not look promising. During his presidency, Putin has sought to eliminate or emasculate alternative sources of political power. Since becoming president in 2000, Putin has chased away or arrested oligarchs with political ambitions, seized control of all national television networks, emasculated the power of the Federal Council (Russia's equivalent of the U.S. Senate), and tamed regional barons who once served as a powerful balance to Yeltsin's presidential rule. The individual rights of Russian citizens, including especially those living in Chechnya, are abused now more than anytime since the collapse of the Soviet Union. Putin believes that he is on a mission to clean up the mess left behind during the Yeltsin era and create a new and powerful Russia state. "Managed democracy" is the euphemism for this agenda of democratic erosion.

To this less democratic regime, the Kremlin has now added nationalism as the principle ideological theme, and helped to empower nationalists as the political leaders on the rise. Under the control of the more moderate, Western-oriented Putin, the increasingly centralized, less pluralistic political regime in Russia today has not been deployed to carry out massive repression against the Russian people or threaten countries on Russia's borders. But who takes power after Putin? The electoral results from yesterday suggest that the liberals have no chance, while the nationalists of a more virulent sort than Putin are up and coming. In their hands, the regime that Putin has built could become really threatening to the people of Russia, to Russia's neighbors, and eventually to the West.

On February 24, 2004, less than four weeks before the presidential election, President Putin sacked his own government. Some international commentators argued that the real target of this action was Prime Minister Mikhail Kasyanov, who was the most critical independent voice in Putin's administration. Would the U.S. political process allow a president to behave in the same way?

The author again suggests that nationalism is a bad thing. Do you think that U.S. nationalism is negative or positive?

THE AWFUL TRUTH
Jonathan Steele

Jonathan Steele is a
journalist for the
British newspaper
The Guardian.

Many international
observers—
including the
Organization for
Security and
Cooperation in
Europe (OSCE), an
international
monitoring group,
of which Russia is a
member—accused
the state-controlled
media of showing
bias toward
propresidential
parties.

Alexander Lebed
(1950–2002) was a
Russian army
general and
politician. A war
hero and successful
politician, he was
dismissed by
President Boris
Yeltsin, but became
governor of the
Krasnoyarsk region
of Siberia. He
refused to run in
the 2000
presidential
elections. He was
killed in a
helicopter crash in
2002, leading to
claims that he had
been assassinated.

NO

X The results of Russia's parliamentary elections ought to come as no shock. In spite of the huge accretion of power which they have handed to President Putin, they also contain more good news than bad. Stark though these judgments may sound, especially in the face of the hand-wringing tone of most official western reactions to Sunday's vote, they rest on the basis of historical evidence.

First, the no-shock issue. Low turnouts, a lack of debate, unfair use of the state-controlled media, heavy intervention by oligarchs in the funding process, and "virtual" parties which have no members or branches and offer voters empty slogans rather than detailed programmes—these have been characteristic of Russian politics for almost a decade.

In every Duma election since the collapse of the one-party state, the Kremlin has used "administrative resources" to promote its favourites (and in some cases to destroy them later, as with the one-time Afghan war hero General Alexander Lebed). The power of incumbency has been used ruthlessly to raise obstacles for potential challengers. TV and radio stations have manipulated public debate by saturating the airwaves with commentators who blatantly support the central government.

It has been a miserable process, especially after the hopes that accompanied the arrival of open political competition towards the end of the Gorbachev era. In 1993 when Boris Yeltsin broke the constitution by suspending parliament and writing a new constitution which reduced MPs' powers, a handful of Moscow-based reporters and western commentators denounced it as the start of a slippery slope. They have now been vindicated. We argued then that this was a kind of "market Bolshevism", designed to push through neo-liberal economic policies in the face of opposition not only in parliament but in the Russian public at large, at a time when gradual reform rather than wild revolution in both politics and the economy was necessary and possible.

The disputes between president and parliament in the first post-Soviet years were not a recipe for paralysis, as was claimed. They were the inevitable discomforts inherent in developing democratic compromises and a system of checks and balances that Russia had never had in its history. But leading western governments supported the strong-hand concept, falling for and in some cases promoting the false argument that there was an imminent danger of a return to power of Soviet-style communism if Yeltsin did not strike first.

A clear and present danger?

The much more real danger, which subsequently became reality, was that a return to excessive power in the Kremlin and hardline economic reforms would impoverish huge numbers of Russians and discredit the process of democratic change. One reason for the collapse of the Union of Right Forces in last Sunday's poll was the fierce unpopularity of Anatoly Chubais, the party's grey cardinal, who drove the neo-liberal privatisation of the early 1990s.

Anatoly Chubais (1955–) is the chairman of Russia's electricity monopoly UES (Unified Energy System of Russia). Labeled the "most hated man in Russia," Chubais was Boris Yeltsin's privatization minister and oversaw the much criticized sale of natural resources to a select group of Russian businessmen—the "oligarchs."

The Russian Communist party may be a linear descendant of the party of Lenin, but by 1993 it had become an amalgam of authoritarian nationalists and statists, with a few social democrats hidden in its midst. It retained a strong local organisation and had a certain nostalgic appeal for many Russians, but offered few ideas for change.

Since its high point in 1996—when its presidential candidate, Gennady Zyuganov, took 40 percent of the vote—the party has been in decline. Yeltsin began to steal some of its clothes with his use of nationalist symbols, but Putin has gone further in combining the Communist party's post-1991 nostalgia for order and discipline with its pre-Gorbachevian tradition of bureaucratic authoritarianism.

Gennady Zyuganov (1944–) is the leader of the Russian Communist Party and the communist faction in the State Duma—the lower parliamentary house.

In this election he stole some of its leftist populism by making a carefully calculated attack on a few selected oligarchs. This clearly took votes away from the communists, even though Putin himself is not only a friend of the oligarchs but their creature. It was the alliance of Yeltsin and the oligarchs, including the Chelsea Football Club owner Roman Abramovich, who chose Putin as Yeltsin's successor.

By stating that Putin is the "creature" of the oligarchs, is the author suggesting that he is their puppet? Is that a fair comment?

In advance of this election, the communists adopted the Kremlin's own cynicism. It literally sold places on its national and regional lists to millionaire oligarchs who, if elected, gain immunity from arrest and prosecution. Eleven of the top 18 people on the lists were not even party members, and five were linked to the oil giant Yukos, whose founder Mikhail Khodorkovsky is still in prison pending trial. This, too, alienated traditional communist voters and perfectly reflected the party's ideological bankruptcy.

Russian soldiers vote at an open-air polling station in Tajikistan on December 5, 2003. Russian border guards and people in remote regions vote before everyone else for technical reasons.

If western observers such as the Organisation for Security and Co-operation in Europe now denounce the election as a step backwards in Russia's eventual transition to democracy, the pity is that they did not do it when the European Institute for the Media was saying the same thing several years ago. In 1996 the west turned a blind eye to Yeltsin's electoral manipulations because they liked the result. The hope is that this time they are not criticising the election for similar reasons of expediency—the defeat of the Union of Right Forces and Grigory Yavlinsky's Yabloko party.

Optimism

The good news in the election is that it may lead to a realignment of Russian parties in the long term. The Communist party has split, not before time, with the creation of the new party—Rodina, or Motherland—which opposes neo-liberal economics. Although the party's formation owes much to the Kremlin, which wanted to break the communists apart, Rodina contains forces within it which could develop a genuinely independent and social democratic identity. Sergei Glaziev, its leader, is one of the brightest progressive economists in Russia. His alliance with the ultra-nationalist Dmitri Rogozin and an authoritarian former general helped him to get votes, but it ought not to last long. The communists may split further now that they see Rodina's success. Yabloko's defeat should provoke a rethink in its ranks.

The idea of a merger between Yabloko and the Union of Right Forces which is being pushed by some commentators is nonsense. Both parties may be pro-western and liberal in political terms, but their economic approaches are different. The rightists support the oligarchs and want to take the process of oil privatisation still further. With Russia's oilfields already in private hands, they want to sell off (or buy up) the pipelines which remain in the hands of a state-owned monopoly. Yavlinsky, by contrast, is more of a social democrat.

This week's election gives a chance for a complete reshuffling of the pack of political cards. The process will be long and hard, and it may lead nowhere. So many Russians have been turned off politics by the events of the past decade. So many are struggling to survive in conditions of economic hardship.

Russia may have several thousands of "new rich" but it also has millions of "new poor". Cynicism and apathy prevail, as people see the privileges and perks that go with being an MP and the interpenetration of government and parliament by narrow-minded business interests.

A realignment of Russia's political scene is long overdue. It will not happen overnight, but after this week's poll the chances that it could develop over the next few wilderness years are marginally better than at any time since the Yeltsin coup of 1993.

Go to www.cnn.com and find out how many Russians voted in the March 2004 presidential election. How does the figure compare to votes in the November 2004 U.S. presidential election?

Is the merging of the interests of government and business just a reality of 21st-century politics?

Summary

Is democracy under threat in Russia? The presidential elections of 2004 focused international attention on the subject and resulted in much heated debate. The preceding two articles examine some of the main issues.

Michael McFaul, the author of the first article, argues that Russian democracy is under threat from nationalism or fascism. He observes that the three main winning parties in the December 2003 election were all created by the Russian state, were loyal to the president, and had nationalist views. During his presidency Putin has sought to restrain alternative sources of political power and also supported nationalist political leaders. McFaul worries about Putin's successor. He argues that a nationalist president could potentially be threatening not only to the Russian people but also to the rest of the world.

However, Jonathan Steele, the author of the second article, is more optimistic about the future impact of the elections. Although he acknowledges that the Russian state unfairly promotes its favorites, Steele also gives some reasons why the losing parties were unpopular—for example, their association with the sale of national industries in the 1990s, and allowing rich oligarchs to buy places on election lists. Steele hopes that these failures may lead to a long overdue realignment of Russian political parties, which will eventually be good for Russian democracy.

FURTHER INFORMATION:

Books:

Service, Robert, *Russia: Experiment with the People*. London: Macmillan, 2002.

Useful websites:

http://edition.cnn.com/SPECIALS
CNN special edition site, featuring reports on the Russian elections.
http://news.bbc.co.uk/1/hi/world/europe/country_profiles/1102275
BBC country profiles site. Features key information on Russia's political economy since 1991. Also provides links to other relevant news agencies.
http://www.rferl.org/specials/russianelection/
Radio Free Europe and Radio Liberty site. Has features on the 2003 Duma elections.
http://www.washtimes.com/op-ed/20031217-091229-3042r.htm
Article by journalist Dan Perrin that examines controlled media and politics in Russia.

The following debates in the Pro/Con series may also be of interest:

In this volume:
Topic 1 Is liberal democracy the only viable political system?

In *Government*:
Topic 3 Are democracy and capitalism at odds with each other?

In *Economics*:
The rise and fall of communism, pages 34–35

IS DEMOCRACY UNDER THREAT IN RUSSIA?

YES: Russian oligarchs are damaging the economy and undermining stability and democracy. Since Putin is trying to prevent this, the oligarchs sponsor opposition political parties.

YES: The next president could be an extreme nationalist and install a more dictatorial regime. There has been a marked increase in nationalism in Russia since the mid 1990s.

CORRUPTION
Are Russia's oligarchs undermining democracy?

NATIONALISM
Is nationalism a threat to democracy?

NO: Many Russian oligarchs have financial and political ties with western Europe and support a more liberal and democratic Russia

NO: Extreme nationalist parties still comprise a minority of the vote. Russia is too aware of the dangers of nationalism, as its support of antiterrorist measures has shown.

IS DEMOCRACY UNDER THREAT IN RUSSIA?

KEY POINTS

YES: International observers have accused the state-controlled media of promoting propresidential parties

YES: The government has taken control of the formerly independent state television station and uses it to broadcast propaganda in support of the state

ELECTIONS
Are Russian elections undemocratic?

FREE SPEECH
Is free speech under threat in Russia?

NO: Independent observers have said the elections were well organized, with no evidence of vote rigging

NO: Profitable media outlets in Russia, such as radio stations, many newspapers, and magazines, operate as free press

FACT CHECKING

*"There is no such source of error as the
pursuit of absolute truth."*

—SAMUEL BUTLER (1835–1902), ENGLISH AUTHOR

*Most of the information we get is taken from the Internet, newspapers,
the television, and other media sources. While we usually accept that
what we are reading or hearing is true and based in fact, how do we
really know? The Internet, for example, provides a wealth of information
at the touch of a button, but how much of it has been checked?
It is very important to make sure that any information you use,
whether in an essay or in a formal debate situation, is true. Fact checking
is a way of doing this. By ensuring that the information you use is correct,
you will make your argument more convincing—and save yourself the
embarrassment of having an opponent or peer challenge you.*

Why fact check?

There are two key reasons why fact checking is important:
* It makes sure that everything in an article or speech is as accurate as possible.
* It ensures that there is nothing in the speech that can harm the writer or speaker. Facts that are incorrect can cause insult and in extreme situations can result in a lawsuit against the writer/speaker.

Fact checking vs. research skills

Fact checking uses many of the same resources and skills as research (see Volume 2, *Government*, *Research skills*, pages 58–59), but there are factors that set fact checking and research apart.

1. Written content: A fact checker verifies prewritten content and must be able to identify any information that may be questionable. Critical thinking (see Volume 5, *Science*, pages 60-61) is a useful technique for fact checking.

2. Proven sources: A fact checker uses credible sources, such as a dictionary, almanac, or encyclopedia, to check for validity. But it is not enough to rely on a single published source. A good fact checker will use several sources and attempt to resolve any contradictions.

3. Legitimacy: A fact checker does not find new information but checks the legitimacy, authenticity, and validity of the presented information. This can be a time-consuming process that requires patience.

4. Agility: A fact checker must be able to balance the need for thoroughness with the ability to sift through information and absorb the knowledge sources quickly and easily.

Fact-checking methodology

There is no cut-and-dried method of fact checking, but the following points may help make the process easier:

- Collect all the information relating to the text. Use the references or bibliography from the text as a guide if in doubt.
- Read through the article a few times to make sure you understand everything.
- Highlight anything that is questionable, including spellings, dates, names, and acronyms.
- Start researching. Use a respected dictionary like *Webster's* or an almanac or encyclopedia. Access to a school, college, or copyright library is also helpful.
- Check any statistics, dates, and spellings of names and places.
- Create a list of questions for the writer or source (if available) in order to check the veracity of a story or particular fact.
- List any research material that you have used. Note details such as the author, book or article title, page number, publisher, date of publication, or the URL.

FACT CHECKING AND THE INTERNET

Many people use the Internet as their major research source. It is, however, very important to remember that a lot of the information has been rekeyed, and that names and birth and death dates, for example, may be incorrect and need to be checked thoroughly. The following are useful sites:

American National Biography Online
www.anb.org
Lists information on over 18,000 people.

Distinguished Women of Past
and Present
www.distinguishedwomen.com
Includes information on women who
have achieved great things in the past.

Internet Movie Database
www.imdb.com
Features movie information, including
credits for current and past movies.

People Spot
www.peoplespot.com
Includes censuses, biographies, and
population figures.

POTUS
www.ipl.org/div/potus
Features information on U.S.
presidents and links to other
biographical resources.

U.S. Census Bureau
www.census.gov
Gives past and current population
information based on the Census.

U.S. Department of State
www.state.gov
Provides information on foreign affairs
and diplomacy.

The White House
www.whitehouse.gov
Features the latest presidential news.

PART 2
INTERNATIONAL CONFLICT AND SECURITY

In the last decade of the 20th century the abandonment of communism, the end of the Cold War, and the dismantling of totalitarian regimes—particularly in the former Soviet Union and eastern Europe—brought changes in how international conflict and security issues were perceived. Studies in these areas broadened beyond a traditional focus on military force and the superpower arms race to include contemporary challenges to international security, particularly regional and ethnic conflicts and international terrorism. Increasingly violent and shocking acts of terrorism, such as those taken against New York and Washington, D.C., on September 11, 2001, have focused international attention on both the power of international terrorist organizations in the 21st century and also the need for governments to work together to remove obstacles to world peace and to protect international security.

The post-Cold War world

In a well-known and provocative essay, "Why We Will Soon Miss the Cold War," written in 1990, in the midst of the euphoria following the fall of the Berlin Wall, political scientist John Mearsheimer wrote that "We may ... wake up one day lamenting the loss of the order that the Cold War gave to the anarchy of international relations." His warning about the likely outbreak of smaller regional conflicts in places like eastern Europe looks particularly prescient today, especially when viewed in light of the bloody dissolution of the former Yugoslavia in the 1990s and the ethnic conflict that tore the region apart for many years. Such examples of animosities between neighbors, otherwise termed regional conflicts, are not a new phenomena in human history. They were in fact a prominent feature of the Cold War. But some experts believe that the difference lies in the fact that even though regional conflicts have decreased in number in the post-Cold War world, those that remain are far more volatile and are more of a threat to international peace.

Many observers believe, however, that governments have got better at dealing with security issues—as shown by the decrease in the actual number of armed conflicts both between nations and within them, the overall decline in people being killed in armed conflict, and even though it may not seem like it at times, a decrease in the number of international terrorist incidents.

The end of the Cold War also gave supraorganizations such as the United Nations new freedom to have an active role in international security. This also opened such organizations up to intensive criticism. Some critics question whether they serve any purpose at all in the 21st-century political framework, and if such organizations actually help or hinder international security and conflict resolution (see Part 3).

Problem areas

Some experts argue that there are three main areas of risk to international security. The first is the growth in

overthrow the Taliban regime, which had provided a safe haven for Al Qaeda, a manhunt for its leader Osama Bin Laden, and most controversially, the invasion and conquest of Iraq. The latter conflict was justified in part by alleged acquisition of weapons of mass destruction by the Iraqi dictator Saddam Hussein.

Bush's administration has also promoted liberal democracy as the only political system, although some

---

"You have to take chances for peace, just as you must take chances in war."

—JOHN FOSTER DULLES, SECRETARY OF STATE (1953–1959)

---

international terrorist organizations, the second is the declining effectiveness of treaty regimes trying to achieve the nonproliferation of weapons of mass destruction, and the third is the existence and emergence of fragile, failing, or failed nation-states that pose problems not only to their own security but to the international community as well. At the heart of any study of international security and conflict is how these issues are dealt with.

Violence, terrorism, and war

Terrorist action, taken by groups such as Al Qaeda, has brought into sharp focus one of the greatest threats to international security—an organized global movement that has adopted terror and the use of weapons of mass destruction to achieve its political goals. The War on Terrorism launched by George W. Bush's administration (2001–) has involved a military campaign against Afghanistan to

people counter that this is not the case at all (see Topic 1).

Among the criticisms directed at a war against terror is that its primary achievements have been yet more war and even more terror. Topic 5 in this section discusses whether violence is an effective means of achieving political change, while Topic 6 focuses on the effect the War on Terrorism has had on U.S. global leadership.

Another issue that has caused huge debate is the U.S. relationship with Israel. This received much attention particularly after the 2004 killings of Sheikh Ahmed Yassin (1934–2004), the spiritual leader of the militant Islamic organization Hamas following an Israeli missile attack, and his successor Abdel Aziz al-Rantissi (1947–2004) just weeks later. Topic 7 examines whether Israel and Palestine will ever reach a peace settlement and its relevance to international security.

Topic 5

CAN VIOLENCE BRING ABOUT EFFECTIVE POLITICAL CHANGE?

YES

FROM "I AM PREPARED TO DIE"
RIVONIA TRIAL, PRETORIA, SOUTH AFRICA, APRIL 20, 1964
NELSON MANDELA

NO

"THE THEATRE OF GOOD AND EVIL"
LA JORNADA, SEPTEMBER 21, 2001
EDUARDO GALEANO, TRANSLATED BY JUSTIN PODUR

INTRODUCTION

People or groups have used violence to try to bring about political change for thousands of years. A violent act, such as killing a politician or bombing a famous landmark, is used for maximum impact: It immediately gains attention and creates fear among citizens. Often referred to as "terrorism," such violence is, many commentators believe, ineffective in challenging the accepted political or social order, whether it be legitimate or otherwise. Some, however, argue that violence is an extreme action and is usually only undertaken as a last resort.

Throughout history governments have been the target of violent action by groups that hold particular grievances. The violent protest made by these groups often falls into one of two categories: sabotage—usually carried out against property, including public utilities and government buildings—and violence against people. Although the first kind may sometimes involve the

second, some people, including former South African president Nelson Mandela, have claimed that there is distinction between them. A deliberate attack on individuals or groups is more likely to alienate potential allies. It also perpetuates violence even after the protesters have achieved their aims. But sabotage is intended to make it as difficult as possible for a regime to function, and it is, advocates argue, much more likely to attract sympathetic international attention to a cause.

But people do have a choice, critics argue, and nonviolent action, such as peaceful demonstrations, sit-ins, or strikes, has a proven record in helping achieve change. The Indian civil rights leader Mahatma Gandhi (1869-1948) challenged the unfair treatment of Indians in both South Africa and India by using nonviolent action. Similarly, Dr. Martin Luther King, Jr. (1929-1968) led the peaceful struggle to gain equal rights for U.S. blacks in the 1960s, and the freedom fighter Daw Aung San Suu Kyi (1945–) has advocated peaceful protest in the struggle to achieve democracy in Myanmar (Burma).

Some commentators counter that there are several examples of violence being a viable method for political change. Many cite the sabotage campaign conducted by the militant wing of the African National Congress (ANC) in South Africa, which they believe highlighted for the international community the injustices perpetrated by the white-minority government under the system of apartheid. Trade sanctions and political pressure from abroad helped end apartheid. Critics believe that the regime was ousted from power in 1990 only after changes in the world order made it socially and economically unsustainable.

"In an imperfect world, terrorism, like war, is a necessary evil."

—CURTIS F. JONES, "TERRORISM: ITS CAUSE AND CURE" (2001)

But is violence counterproductive since it either begets retaliatory violence or leads to extreme violations by governments of citizens' rights? In Northern Ireland violent action by the Irish Republican Army (IRA) and other extremist groups resulted in the British government's suspension, from 1969, of the civil rights normally guaranteed in United Kingdom. Internment (detention without charge) and criminal trials heard by judges, without juries, were among the measures introduced.

Similarly, many nations introduced laws curbing certain civil rights after the September 11, 2001 (9/11), terrorist action against the United States. The USA PATRIOT act, for example, was signed into law in October 2001 by George W. Bush's administration. This gave U.S. law-enforcement agencies significantly greater surveillance and investigative powers, but also infringed on the rights of citizens. Officials argued that the suspension of certain constitutional rights was necessary to prevent further terrorism. The War on Terrorism, which led to military action against Afghanistan and Iraq, was the United States' other response. Although the war could be seen as proof that violence begets violence, both nations may be experiencing democratization—and this could also arguably support the contention that violence does work.

But has the global response to terrorism changed since 9/11? The surprise change of power in the 2004 Spanish election indicates to many that it has. On March 11, 2004, 200 people were killed and more than 1,200 injured in the terrorist bombing of several trains in Madrid. The People's Party (PP) government was quick to blame ETA, the Basque terrorist group. Others believed that Al Qaeda had committed the crime in retaliation for the PP's support of U.S. military action against Iraq. Either way the action was strategically timed. Socialist leader José Luis Rodríguez Zapatero, whose party had opposed the war, promised to withdraw Spanish troops from Iraq: He won the March 14 election. Commentators claim the electorate blamed the bombings on the PP's hard-line response to terrorism.

The following articles examine issues in the debate further.

I AM PREPARED TO DIE
Nelson Mandela

Nelson Mandela (1918–) was heavily involved in the struggle for equal rights in South Africa. In 1950 he became part of the National Executive board of the anti-apartheid organization, the African National Congress. In 1962 Mandela was imprisoned for five years for leaving South Africa without a passport. In 1963 he was tried, along with Walter Sisulu, Ahmed Kathrada, Govan Mbeki (father of President Thabo Mbeki), Dennis Goldberg, Raymond Mhlaba, Elias Motsoaledi, and Andrew Mlangeni, for alleged sabotage designed to provoke revolution. Mandela made this speech in April 1964 during the Rivonia Trial. However, the men were sentenced to life imprisonment on Robben Island in June 1964. The UN Security Council condemned the trial, but Mandela remained in prison until February 11, 1990. He was elected president of South Africa in 1994, in the first democratic multiracial elections.

YES

…I admit immediately that I was one of the persons who helped to form Umkhonto we Sizwe, and that I played a prominent role in its affairs until I was arrested in August 1962.… I, and the others who started the organization, did so for two reasons. Firstly, we believed that as a result of Government policy, violence by the African people had become inevitable, and that unless responsible leadership was given to canalize and control the feelings of our people, there would be outbreaks of terrorism which would produce an intensity of bitterness and hostility between the various races of this country which is not produced even by war. Secondly, we felt that without violence there would be no way open to the African people to succeed in their struggle against the principle of white supremacy. All lawful modes of expressing opposition to this principle had been closed by legislation, and we were placed in a position in which we had either to accept a permanent state of inferiority, or to defy the Government. We chose to defy the law. We first broke the law in a way which avoided any recourse to violence; when this form was legislated against, and then the Government resorted to a show of force to crush opposition to its policies, only then did we decide to answer violence with violence. …

Never terrorism

[T]he violence which we chose to adopt was not terrorism. We who formed Umkhonto were all members of the African National Congress, and had behind us the ANC tradition of nonviolence and negotiation as a means of solving political disputes. We believe that South Africa belongs to all the people who live in it, and not to one group, be it black or white. We did not want an interracial war, and tried to avoid it to the last minute.…

The African National Congress was formed in 1912 to defend the rights of the African people which had been seriously curtailed by the South Africa Act, and which were then being threatened by the Native Land Act. For thirty-seven years—that is until 1949—it adhered strictly to a constitutional struggle.…

Even after 1949, the ANC remained determined to avoid violence. At this time, however, there was a change from the strictly constitutional means of protest which had been employed in the past. The change was embodied in a decision which was taken to protest against apartheid legislation by peaceful, but unlawful, demonstrations against certain laws. Pursuant to this policy the ANC launched the Defiance Campaign, in which I was placed in charge of volunteers. This campaign was based on the principles of passive resistance....

The idea of "passive resistance" can be found in Buddhism, Hinduism, and Jainism, among other religions. See Volume 15, Human Rights, page 108, for further information.

Harsher penalties

During the Defiance Campaign, the Public Safety Act and the Criminal Law Amendment Act were passed. These statutes provided harsher penalties for offences committed by way of protests against laws. Despite this, the protests continued and the ANC adhered to its policy of nonviolence....

In 1960 there was the shooting at Sharpeville, which resulted in the proclamation of a state of emergency and the declaration of the ANC as an unlawful organization. My colleagues and I, after careful consideration, decided that we would not obey this decree. The African people were not part of the Government and did not make the laws by which they were governed.... In 1960 the Government held a referendum which led to the establishment of the Republic. Africans, who constituted approximately 70 per cent of the population of South Africa, were not entitled to vote, and were not even consulted about the proposed constitutional change. All of us were apprehensive of our future under the proposed White Republic, and a resolution was taken to hold an All-In African Conference to call for a National Convention, and to organize mass demonstrations on the eve of the unwanted Republic, if the Government failed to call the Convention. The conference was attended by Africans of various political persuasions. I was the Secretary of the conference and undertook to be responsible for organizing the national stay-at-home which was subsequently called to coincide with the declaration of the Republic. As all strikes by Africans are illegal, the person organizing such a strike must avoid arrest.... The stay-at-home, in accordance with ANC policy, was to be a peaceful demonstration.... The Government's answer was to introduce new and harsher laws … designed to intimidate the people.

Under the circumstances do you think violent action was the only option for black South Africans? In a regime in which the majority of the population are denied political rights is there any other way to affect change?

[T]he hard facts were that 50 years of nonviolence had brought the African people nothing but more and more repressive legislation, and fewer and fewer rights. It may not be easy for this Court to understand, but it is a fact that for a long time the people had been talking of violence … and we, the leaders of the ANC, had nevertheless always prevailed upon them to avoid violence and to pursue peaceful methods. When some of us discussed this in May and June of 1961, it could not be denied that our policy to achieve a nonracial state by nonviolence had achieved nothing, and that our followers were beginning to lose confidence in this policy and were developing disturbing ideas of terrorism.…

Mandela implies that "organized violence" is more preferable than the "spontaneous" kind. Why might that be? Do you agree?

Already small groups had arisen in the urban areas and were spontaneously making plans for violent forms of political struggle. There now arose a danger that these groups would adopt terrorism against Africans, as well as Whites, if not properly directed.… It was increasingly taking the form, not of struggle against the Government—though this is what prompted it—but of civil strife amongst themselves, conducted in such a way that it could not hope to achieve anything other than a loss of life and bitterness.

Mandela lists clearly and systematically the many ways in which the ANC tried to challenge the accepted status quo nonviolently. He contrasts them with the white government's more aggressive response. Rationality and clarity are key to any well-structured argument.

At the beginning of June 1961, after a long and anxious assessment of the South African situation, I, and some colleagues, came to the conclusion that as violence in this country was inevitable, it would be unrealistic and wrong for African leaders to continue preaching peace and nonviolence at a time when the Government met our peaceful demands with force. This conclusion was not easily arrived at. It was only when all else had failed, when all channels of peaceful protest had been barred to us, that the decision was made to embark on violent forms of political struggle, and to form Umkhonto we Sizwe … in November 1961. The avoidance of civil war had dominated our thinking for many years, but when we decided to adopt violence as part of our policy, we realized that we might one day have to face the prospect of such a war. This had to be taken into account in formulating our plans.…

"Umkhonto we Sizwe" means "Spear of the Nation." Go to http://www.anc.org.za/ancdocs/history/mk/ to read its manifesto.

Four forms of violence were possible. There is sabotage, there is guerrilla warfare, there is terrorism, and there is open revolution. We chose to adopt the first method.… Sabotage did not involve loss of life, and it offered the best hope for future race relations.…

Hit where it hurts the most

We believed that South Africa depended to a large extent on foreign capital and foreign trade. We felt that planned destruction of power plants, and interference with rail and telephone communications, would tend to scare away capital from the country, make it more difficult for goods from the industrial areas to reach the seaports on schedule, and would in the longrun be a heavy drain on the economic life of the country, thus compelling the voters of the country to reconsider their position. Attacks on the economic life lines of the country were to be linked with sabotage on government buildings and other symbols of apartheid. These attacks would serve as a source of inspiration to our people.... Umkhonto had its first operation on 16 December 1961, when government buildings in Johannesburg, Port Elizabeth and Durban were attacked. The selection of targets is proof of the policy to which I have referred. Had we intended to attack life we would have selected targets where people congregated and not empty buildings and power stations....

The response ... among the white population was characteristically violent.... In contrast, the response of the Africans was one of encouragement. Suddenly there was hope again.... But we in Umkhonto weighed up the white response with anxiety.... The white newspapers carried reports that sabotage would be punished by death. If this was so, how could we continue to keep Africans away from terrorism?... If war were inevitable, we wanted the fight to be conducted on terms most favourable to our people. The fight which held out prospects best for us and the least risk of life to both sides was guerrilla warfare. We decided ... to make provision for the possibility of guerrilla warfare....

[I]it was decided that I should attend the Conference of the Pan-African Freedom Movement for Central, East, and Southern Africa, which was to be held early in 1962 in Addis Ababa, and ... it was also decided that, after the conference, I would undertake a tour of the African States with a view to obtaining facilities for the training of soldiers, and that I would also solicit scholarships for the higher education of matriculated Africans.... Wherever I went I met sympathy for our cause and promises of help. All Africa was united against the stand of White South Africa....

A democratic and free society

During my lifetime I have dedicated myself to this struggle of the African people. I have fought against white domination, and I have fought against black domination. I have cherished the ideal of a democratic and free society in which all persons live together in harmony and with equal opportunities. It is an ideal which I hope to live for and to achieve. But if needs be, it is an ideal for which I am prepared to die.

Was the ANC being naive in thinking that sabotage would bring about a change of heart in the white voting public?

How do you think the United States would respond to a similar attack against a government building or military installation? Do you think officials would differentiate between sabotage and terrorism?

The conference was held in Addis Ababa, Ethiopia, from February 2 to 10, 1962. It aimed to do everything possible to speed up the total emancipation of Africa, and to establish the necessary framework for a union between east and central African countries.

A powerful and memorable statement—like the one used in Mandela's closing sentence—is a good way to end an argument.

THE THEATRE OF GOOD AND EVIL
Eduardo Galeano

Uruguayan author Eduardo Galeano (1940–) is regarded as one of Latin America's most outspoken voices on issues of social conscience.

Is the author implying that evildoers sometimes serve a purpose for supposedly "good" powers? Can you think of a recent example of this?

The author adopts a slightly whimsical tone to show how evil and good are a matter of perception—even supposedly evil empires have to have a focus of evil.

NO

In the struggle of Good against Evil, it's always the people who get killed.

The terrorists killed workers of 50 countries in NYC and [Washington,] D.C., in the name of Good against Evil. And in the name of Good against Evil President Bush has promised vengeance: "We will eliminate Evil from the world", he announced.

Eliminate Evil? What would Good be without Evil? It's not just religious fanatics who need enemies to justify their insanity. The arms industry and the gigantic war machine of the U.S. also needs enemies to justify its existence. Good and evil, evil and good: the actors change masks, the heroes become monsters and the monsters heroes, in accord with the demands of the theatre's playwrights.

This is nothing new. The German scientist Werner von Braun was evil when he invented the V2 bombers that Hitler used against London, but became good when he used his talents in the service of the U.S. Stalin was good during World War Two and evil afterwards, when he became the leader of the Evil Empire. In the cold war years John Steinbeck wrote: "Maybe the whole world needs Russians. I suppose that even in Russia they need Russians. Maybe Russia's Russians are called Americans." Even the Russians became good afterwards. Today, Putin can add his voice to say: "Evil must be punished."

Enemies of humanity

Saddam Hussein was good, and so were the chemical weapons he used against the Iranians and the Kurds. Afterwards, he became evil. They were calling him Satan Hussein when the U.S. finished up their invasion of Panama to invade Iraq because Iraq invaded Kuwait. Father Bush [brought] that particular war against Evil upon himself. With the humanitarian and compassionate spirit that characterizes his family, he killed more than 100,000 Iraqis, the vast majority of them civilians.

Satan Hussein stayed where he was, but this number one enemy of humanity had to step aside and accept becoming number two enemy of humanity. The bane of the world is

German scientist Werner von Braun (1912–1977) holds a model of the V2 rocket developed for the Nazis during World War II. Von Braun later went to work for the United States.

In 1985, 40th President Ronald Reagan (1981–1989) led a group of Mujahideen (Islamic freedom fighters opposed to the Russian invasion of Afghanistan) onto the lawn outside the White House and made this comment in a television broadcast. In 1996 Mujahideen leaders formed the Taliban administration in Afghanistan. Reagan's comments have been quoted to show how U.S. attitudes toward Afghanistan—and the Middle East— have changed since the end of the Cold War.

now called Osama Bin Laden. The CIA taught him everything he knows about terrorism: Bin Laden, loved and armed by the U.S. government, was one of the principal "freedom fighters" against Communism in Afghanistan. Father Bush occupied the Vice Presidency when President Reagan called these heroes "the moral equivalents of the Founding Fathers." Hollywood agreed. They filmed Rambo 3: Afghani Muslims were the good guys. Now, 13 years later, in the time of Son Bush, they are the worst of the bad guys.

Henry Kissinger was one of the first to react to the recent tragedy. "Those who provide support, financing, and inspiration to terrorists are as guilty as the terrorists themselves," he intoned, words that Son Bush would repeat hours later.

If that's how it is, the urgent need right now is to bomb Kissinger. He is guilty of many more crimes than Bin Laden or any terrorist in the world. And in many more countries. He provided "support, financing, and inspiration" to state terror in Indonesia, Cambodia, Iran, South Africa, Bangladesh, and all the South American countries that suffered the dirty war of Plan Condor.

The United States disapproved of the democratically held 1970 presidential election results that brought Marxist Salvador Allende to power in Chile. Declassified documents show that Henry Kissinger and the CIA helped bring about the 1973 military coup that resulted in Allende's death.

On September 11 1973, exactly 28 years before the fires of last week, the Presidential Palace in Chile was stormed. Kissinger had written the epitaph of Allende and Chilean democracy long before when he commented on the results of the elections: "I don't see why we have to stand by and watch a country go communist because of the irresponsibility of its own people."

A contempt for the people is one of many things shared by state and private terror. For example, the ETA, an organization that kills people in the name of independence in Basque Country, says through one of its spokespeople: "Rights have nothing to do with majorities or minorities."

Is it fair to compare the terrorist action of "fanatics," such as Bin Laden, with the political actions of legitimate governments?

Low- and high-tech terrorism

There is much common ground between low- and high-tech terrorism, between the terrorism of religious fanatics and that of market fanatics, that of the hopeless and that of the powerful, that of the psychopath on the loose and that of cold-blooded uniformed professional. They all share the disrespect for human life: the killers of the 5,500 citizens under the Twin Towers that fell like castles of dry sand—and the killers of 200,000 Guatemalans, the majority of whom were indigenous, exterminated without television or the newspapers of the world paying any attention. Those Guatemalans were not sacrificed by any Muslim fanatic, but by terrorist squads who received "support, financing, and inspiration" from successive U.S. governments.

All these worshippers of death are in agreement as well on the need to reduce social, cultural, and national differences to military terms. In the name of Good against Evil, in the name of the One Truth, they resolve everything by killing first and asking questions later. And by this method, they strengthen the enemy they fight. It was the atrocities of the Sendero Luminoso that gave President Fujimori the popular support he sought to unleash a regime of terror and sell Peru for the price of a banana. It was the atrocities of the U.S. in the Middle East that prepared the ground for the holy war of terrorism of Allah.

Although the leader of the Civilized World is pushing a new Crusade, Allah is innocent of the crimes committed in his name. At the end of the day, God did not order the Holocaust against the followers of Jehovah, nor did Jehovah order the massacres of Sabrah and Shatila or the expulsion of Palestinians from their land. Aren't Allah, God and Jehovah are, after all, three names for the same divinity?

A tragedy of errors: nobody knows any more who is who. The smoke of the explosions forms part of the much larger curtain of smoke that prevents all of us from seeing clearly. From revenge to revenge, terrorism obliges us to walk to our graves. I saw a photo, recently published, of graffiti on a wall in NYC: "An eye for an eye makes the whole world blind."

The spiral of violence creates violence and also confusion: pain, fear, intolerance, hatred, insanity. In Porto Alegre, at the beginning of this year, Ahmed Ben Bella warned: "This system, that has already made mad cows, is making mad people too." And these mad people, mad from hate, act as the power that created them.

A three year old child, named Luca, told me: "The world doesn't know where its house is." He was looking at a map. He could have been looking at a reporter.

Is preemptive action ever right? See Volume 22, International Law, Topic 3 Is it legal for one nation to attack another preemptively?

The author refers to George W. Bush as the "leader of the Civilized World" and to the War on Terrorism as a "Crusade." Some commentators believe that George W. Bush's foreign policy has been directed more by Christian ethics than by human rights issues or a desire to eradicate weapons of mass destruction.

The author uses imagery to help prove his point. Do you think it detracts from or enhances his argument?

Summary

Violent action for political gain has increased greatly during the last hundred years or so. This has resulted in many commentators questioning whether it is a viable method of effecting political change. The two preceding extracts look at the issue from very different points of view. The first is an extract from the famous speech Nelson Mandela made in his defense at the Rivonia Trial in 1964. In it Mandela makes a distinction between the violence finally adopted by the militant wing of the ANC—sabotage—and terrorism. He states that the decision to adopt a more aggressive stance was only taken after 50 years of passive resistance had failed, and violent action became inevitable. He states that it was the only viable method by which South African blacks could challenge apartheid, and that the ANC's organized violence might prevent civil war from occurring in the country.

The second article, by Uruguayan author Eduardo Galeano, makes the point that "good" and "evil" have no objective meaning since people always think that they have God on their side. Among the many examples he gives is Osama Bin Laden, whom the United States once regarded as a freedom fighter and aided while he was fighting communist insurgents in Afghanistan, but who was denounced as a terrorist when he opposed U.S. operations in the same country. Galeano also criticizes Henry Kissinger, former secretary of state (1973-1977), for condemning sponsors of terrorism when he supported armed insurgency in many countries—including the 1973 overthrow of the democratically elected government of Chile. Murder is murder, no matter whether the killer is a terrorist or a government agent, Galeano says.

FURTHER INFORMATION:

Books:

Chomsky, Noam, *The Culture of Terrorism*. London: Pluto Press, 1988.

Mandela, Nelson, *No Easy Walk to Freedom*. New York: Penguin, 2002.

Useful websites:

http://www.fas.org/irp/threat/terror.htm
Intelligence Resource Program site with lots of links to reports and articles on terrorism.

http://www.terrorism.com/
The Terrorism Research Center site.

http://usinfo.state.gov/topical/pol/terror/
State Department site on the U.S. response to global terrorism.

http://www.us-israel.org/jsource/Terrorism/usterrtoc.html
State Department list of terrorist incidents and key events.

The following debates in the Pro/Con series may also be of interest:

In this volume:
  Topic 6 Has the War on Terrorism reinforced U.S. global leadership?

In *Individual and Society*:
  Topic 10 Is violent protest ever justified?

In *U.S. Foreign Policy*:
  September 11, 2001, pages 176–177

CAN VIOLENCE BRING ABOUT EFFECTIVE POLITICAL CHANGE?

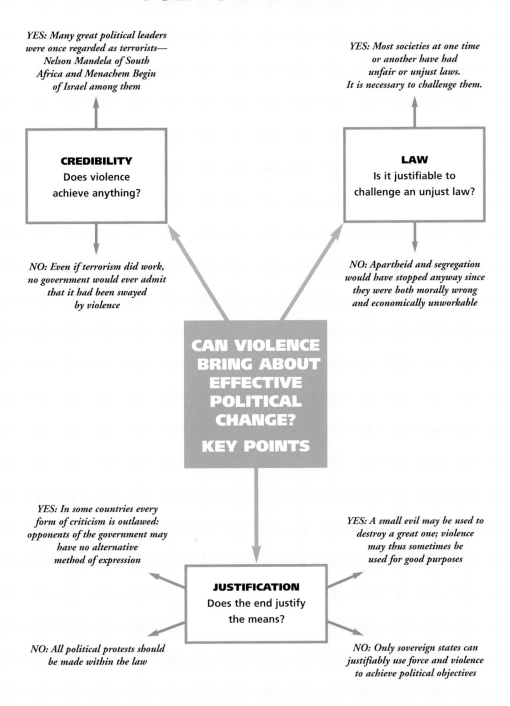

YES: Many great political leaders were once regarded as terrorists— Nelson Mandela of South Africa and Menachem Begin of Israel among them

YES: Most societies at one time or another have had unfair or unjust laws. It is necessary to challenge them.

CREDIBILITY
Does violence achieve anything?

LAW
Is it justifiable to challenge an unjust law?

NO: Even if terrorism did work, no government would ever admit that it had been swayed by violence

NO: Apartheid and segregation would have stopped anyway since they were both morally wrong and economically unworkable

CAN VIOLENCE BRING ABOUT EFFECTIVE POLITICAL CHANGE?

KEY POINTS

YES: In some countries every form of criticism is outlawed: opponents of the government may have no alternative method of expression

YES: A small evil may be used to destroy a great one; violence may thus sometimes be used for good purposes

JUSTIFICATION
Does the end justify the means?

NO: All political protests should be made within the law

NO: Only sovereign states can justifiably use force and violence to achieve political objectives

Topic 6

HAS THE WAR ON TERRORISM REINFORCED U.S. GLOBAL LEADERSHIP?

YES

"LAWMAKER PRAISES INTERNATIONAL COOPERATION IN WAR ON TERRORISM"
PRESS RELEASE, DECEMBER 12, 2001
U.S. STATE DEPARTMENT

NO

FROM "THIS WAR ON TERRORISM IS BOGUS"
THE GUARDIAN, SEPTEMBER 6, 2003
MICHAEL MEACHER

INTRODUCTION

On September 20, 2001, days after the terrorist attacks on Manhattan and Washington, D.C., President George W. Bush announced a "war on terror," a multifaceted approach to battling global terrorism. He vowed to bring those responsible for the attacks on the United States to justice, to apply pressure on countries that sponsor terrorism, and to shut down terrorists' financial networks. Several years on and two military campaigns in Afghanistan and Iraq later, the War on Terrorism remains, in the words of Secretary of State Colin Powell, "the United States' number one foreign policy priority." For some critics, however, it is a policy that is costing the United States its reputation as leader of the free world.

At the end of World War II (1939-1945) the United States' financial and military power enabled it to play a decisive part in shaping the postwar world. America had a key role in developing new intergovernmental economic and security organizations. They included the International Monetary Fund (IMF) for promoting global economic growth, the United Nations for finding peaceful resolutions to international conflicts, and the North Atlantic Treaty Organization (NATO) for protecting the West through the containment of communism. Throughout the Cold War—the ideological conflict with the Soviet Union—the United States took the lead in resisting communism, becoming involved in military conflicts in Korea (1950-1953) and Vietnam (1964-1973), among other places. Since the collapse of the Soviet Union in 1991 some commentators describe the position of the United States as "consensual hegemony"—that is, an acknowledged leadership in which the United States is the custodian of world order.

In his September 20, 2001, speech, President Bush called on "every nation to join us" in the fight against terror.

Secretary of State Powell has reiterated that victory in the War on Terrorism depends on "constructive ties among the world's major powers." Proponents of this view claim that the administration's "strategy of partnerships" is working. They offer proof in NATO's formal invocation for the first time in history of its mutual defense clause—that an attack against one or more members is considered an attack against all members of the alliance—after the United States provided evidence that Al Qaeda was behind the September 11, 2001, attacks. The decision was a green light for the U.S.-led invasion of Afghanistan, which had the backing of the most of the international community.

> *"You're either with us or against us in the fight against terror."*
> —GEORGE W. BUSH,
> 43RD PRESIDENT (2001–)

However, the Bush administration was criticized for its emphasis on unilateral and preemptive military responses to the terrorist threat, which critics argued undermined a tradition of global leadership based on alliances and partnerships. Critics accused the administration of conducting foreign policy on the basis of two dangerous assumptions. The first was that since Americans cannot count on others to protect them, the best way to ensure national security is therefore to remove the constraints imposed by friends, allies, and international institutions.

The second was that an America unbound by international constraints should use its power to change the global status quo. This aggressive unilateralism, critics argue, was evident in the administration's arguments regarding the use of force. In the 2002 "National Security Strategy," for example, the government stated that "We will not hesitate to act alone, if necessary, to exercise our right of self-defense by acting preemptively against such terrorists." In the view of critics this amounts to a wholesale rejection of the kind of U.S. global leadership that had previously characterized the world order. A *New York Times* editorial of January 3, 2004, accused the Bush administration of disregarding the United Nations' "founding principle of collective security" with its decision to invade Iraq in March 2003. "Since the day the administration took office," the editorial said, "it has been chipping away at the multinational diplomatic system that America did so much to build in the past two generations." According to President Bush's harshest critics, the Iraq invasion signaled a new phase in the War on Terrorism that equates to empire building. Some insist that the United States did not go to war because Iraqi dictator Saddam Hussein allegedly possessed weapons of mass destruction but because it wanted to control oil reserves in the Middle East and Central Asia. They claim that the War on Terrorism is a pretext for removing any enemy who stands in the way of turning U.S. world leadership into actual hegemony.

Congressman Ike Skelton and British politician Michael Meacher offer opposing opinions about U.S. global leadership in the post-September 11 world in the following extracts.

LAWMAKER PRAISES INTERNATIONAL COOPERATION IN WAR ON TERRORISM
U.S. State Department

The House Armed Services Committee has jurisdiction over the activities of the Department of Defense. Go to http://www.house.gov/hascl to find out more. Missouri Congressman Ike Skelton, the senior Democratic member of the committee, made this speech two months after the terrorist attacks of September 11, 2001, on the Pentagon and the World Trade Center.

YES

The ranking minority member of the House Armed Services Committee took to the floor of the House of Representatives December 12 to praise the help provided by foreign nations in the war on terrorism.

"The State and Defense Departments provided me with a list of 29 countries plus the European Union who have contributed to our current counter terrorist efforts," Representative Ike Skelton told fellow lawmakers.

"While each country is helping in specific ways, they all are making a difference in our ability to thwart the global threat posed by terrorist groups like Al Qaeda," Skelton said.

A "multifaceted" war

The Missouri Democrat cited President Bush's warning that the war on terrorism "will be a long and multifaceted one."

To succeed, Skelton said, the United States will need the "continued strength and commitment of the American people," as well as "the ongoing support of our friends around the world."

Skelton, one of the foremost defense experts in the Congress, said it was in everyone's interest to end terrorist activity, "and it will take global efforts to achieve this goal."

Skelton gave special thanks to Great Britain, "who has stood with us diplomatically and fought alongside us in Afghanistan. The depth of this special friendship is one for which we should be profoundly grateful."

See http://www.bjreview.com.cn/2001/200125/Global Observer-200125(A).htm for a brief history of U.S.–Indian relations from the Cold War to 2001.

Beyond Europe, Skelton continued, "our allies in Asia—Korea, Japan, Australia and New Zealand—have all provided combat or support forces for this fight."

Skelton also said U.S. relations with Russia and India "have improved greatly because of our common struggle against terrorism and their continued efforts to support us."

Skelton also noted "the remarkable actions of Muslim countries in this global struggle."

Following is the text of Representative Skelton's December 12 remarks from the Congressional Record:

Secretary of State Colin Powell has argued that some people overstate the role of preemption in the War on Terrorism. U.S. foreign policy is, he says, a "strategy of partnerships."

In May 2003 Francis X. Taylor, assistant secretary for diplomatic security, reported that the United States and over 160 other countries had frozen $124 million in terrorist assets from over 600 bank accounts around the world. See http://www.state. gov/s/ct/terfin/ for the latest news from the Counterterrorism Finance and Designation Unit, part of the Counterterrorism Office within the State Department.

See Topic 9 Is NATO still needed in the post-Cold War world?

See http://news. bbc.co.uk/1/hi/ uk_politics/ 3264169.stm for "US and UK: a transatlantic love story?" a history of U.S.–UK relations from the BBC.

International contributions to the War on Terrorism

House of Representatives December 12, 2001

Mr. Skelton: Mr. Speaker, in the aftermath of the devastating attacks on New York and Washington on September 11, the United States has taken a range of swift and decisive actions to bring the terrorists responsible to justice and to ensure that sponsors of terrorism are uprooted. Our military has helped drive the Taliban from power in most of Afghanistan and has tightened the noose on Osama bin Laden and his compatriots. We have seized terrorist assets around the world, putting those who would help terrorists on notice that we will dry up those sources of support.

A global fight

In our military, diplomatic and financial efforts, the United States has received unprecedented support from the international community. Many countries around the world have converted their sympathy into real acts of solidarity. Our battle against terrorism is a global fight. Success requires sustaining a broad coalition of diplomatic and military partners over the long term.

Recently, the State and Defense Departments provided me with a list of 29 countries plus the European Union who have contributed to our current counter terrorist efforts. While each country is helping in specific ways, they all are making a difference in our ability to thwart the global threat posed by terrorist groups like Al Qaeda.

Our allies in Europe are among our most committed partners. NATO took the unprecedented step of invoking article 5 of its charter, considering the attacks on the United States as attacks on the alliance as a whole. The European Union has offered broad diplomatic support and nations throughout Europe, from France and Germany to Poland, have offered military and domestic counter terrorism units. Unique among these loyal European partners is Great Britain who has stood with us diplomatically and fought alongside us in Afghanistan. The depth of this special friendship is one for which we should be profoundly grateful.

Beyond our European partners, our allies in Asia—Korea, Japan, Australia and New Zealand—have all provided combat or support forces for this fight. Our relationships with Russia and with India have improved greatly because of our common struggle against terrorism and their continued efforts to support us.

Finally, I would like to note the remarkable actions of Muslim countries in this global struggle. So many are our friends and recognize that the war against terrorism is not a war against Islam. Pakistan has been crucial to our efforts in Afghanistan and has demonstrated great courage in helping lead the struggle against radical terrorism. Our NATO partner, Turkey, has provided special operations troops and has helped bridge the gap between the West and other Muslim nations. States in the Gulf and throughout Central Asia have also chosen to stand with the global community, seizing terrorist assets, providing public support for our military efforts and granting critical overflight and basing rights.

As President Bush has said many times, this war will be a long and multifaceted one. To succeed, we will need the continued strength and commitment of the American people, but we will also need the ongoing support of our friends around the world. It is in the global interest to end terrorist activity and it will take global efforts to achieve this goal.

Relations between Turkey and the United States cooled during 2003 when Turkey refused to allow U.S. forces to use Turkish bases for the invasion of Iraq. The Turkish government later gave the United States the right to use Turkish airspace to establish a northern front in the conflict. It also allowed some supplies to pass through Turkey to reach U.S. forces in Iraq and permitted U.S. aircraft to land at Turkish bases if they were in distress.

THIS WAR ON TERRORISM IS BOGUS
Michael Meacher

British Member of Parliament Michael Meacher was a minister in Tony Blair's Labour government from 1997 until 2003, but later became a critic of Blair's "presidential" style of leadership.

NO

Massive attention has now been given—and rightly so—to the reasons why Britain went to war against Iraq. But far too little attention has focused on why the US went to war, and that throws light on British motives too. The conventional explanation is that after the Twin Towers were hit, retaliation against Al Qaeda bases in Afghanistan was a natural first step in launching a global war against terrorism. Then, because Saddam Hussein was alleged by the US and UK governments to retain weapons of mass destruction, the war could be extended to Iraq as well. However this theory does not fit all the facts. The truth may be a great deal murkier.

A global Pax Americana

We now know that a blueprint for the creation of a global Pax Americana was drawn up for Dick Cheney (now vice-president), Donald Rumsfeld (defence secretary), Paul Wolfowitz (Rumsfeld's deputy), Jeb Bush (George Bush's younger brother) and Lewis Libby (Cheney's chief of staff). The document, entitled "Rebuilding America's Defenses", was written in September 2000 by the neoconservative think tank, Project for the New American Century (PNAC).

The PNAC's "fundamental propositions" are "that American leadership is good both for America and for the world; that such leadership requires military strength, diplomatic energy and commitment to moral principle; and that too few political leaders today are making the case for global leadership." Do you agree that the United State should take a leading role in world affairs?

The plan shows Bush's cabinet intended to take military control of the Gulf region whether or not Saddam Hussein was in power. It says "while the unresolved conflict with Iraq provides the immediate justification, the need for a substantial American force presence in the Gulf transcends the issue of the regime of Saddam Hussein."

The PNAC blueprint supports an earlier document attributed to Wolfowitz and Libby which said the US must "discourage advanced industrial nations from challenging our leadership or even aspiring to a larger regional or global role".… It describes peacekeeping missions as "demanding American political leadership rather than that of the UN". It says "even should Saddam pass from the scene", US bases in Saudi Arabia and Kuwait will remain permanently … as "Iran may well prove as large a threat to US interests as Iraq has". It spotlights China for "regime change", saying "it is time to increase the presence of American forces in SE Asia".…

Finally—written a year before 9/11—it pinpoints North Korea, Syria and Iran as dangerous regimes, and says their existence justifies the creation of a "worldwide command and control system". This is a blueprint for US world domination. But before it is dismissed as an agenda for rightwing fantasists, it is clear it provides a much better explanation of what actually happened before, during and after 9/11 than the global war on terrorism thesis. This can be seen in several ways.

Without such a system, however, how can the United States protect itself?

The United States did nothing to prevent 9/11

First, it is clear the US authorities did little or nothing to preempt the events of 9/11. It is known that at least 11 countries provided advance warning to the US of the 9/11 attacks. Two senior Mossad experts were sent to Washington in August 2001 to alert the CIA and FBI to a cell of 200 terrorists said to be preparing a big operation. The list they provided included the names of four of the 9/11 hijackers, none of whom was arrested.

Mossad is the most important Israeli intelligence organization.

It had been known as early as 1996 that there were plans to hit Washington targets with aeroplanes. Then in 1999 a US national intelligence council report noted that "Al Qaeda suicide bombers could crash-land an aircraft packed with high explosives into the Pentagon, the headquarters of the CIA, or the White House".

Fifteen of the 9/11 hijackers obtained their visas in Saudi Arabia. Michael Springman, the former head of the American visa bureau in Jeddah, has stated that since 1987 the CIA had been illicitly issuing visas to unqualified applicants from the Middle East and bringing them to the US for training in terrorism for the Afghan war in collaboration with Bin Laden. It seems this operation continued after the Afghan war for other purposes. It is also reported that five of the hijackers received training at secure US military installations in the 1990s.

From 1979 until 1989 Afghanistan was occupied by the Soviet Union. Soviet troops joined communist government forces fighting Muslim rebels. The CIA covertly armed and trained Muslim guerrillas to fight the Soviet Union.

Instructive leads prior to 9/11 were not followed up. French Moroccan flight student Zacarias Moussaoui (now thought to be the 20th hijacker) was arrested in August 2001 after an instructor reported he showed a suspicious interest in learning how to steer large airliners. When US agents learned from French intelligence he had radical Islamist ties, they sought a warrant to search his computer, which contained clues to the September 11 mission. But they were turned down by the FBI. One agent wrote, a month before 9/11, that Moussaoui might be planning to crash into the Twin Towers.

All of this makes it all the more astonishing—in the war on terrorism perspective—that there was such slow reaction on September 11 itself…. Not a single fighter plane was scrambled to investigate from the US Andrews airforce base, just 10 miles from Washington, D.C., until after the third plane had hit the Pentagon at 9.38 am. Why not? There were standard FAA intercept procedures for hijacked aircraft before 9/11…. It is a US legal requirement that once an aircraft has moved significantly off its flight plan, fighter planes are sent up to investigate.

"FAA" stands for "Federal Aviation Administration." The FAA is responsible for the safety of civil aviation.

Was this inaction simply the result of key people disregarding, or being ignorant of, the evidence? Or could US air security operations have been deliberately stood down on September 11? If so, why, and on whose authority?…

Do you think that Meacher's case supports his implication that 9/11 involved a U.S. conspiracy?

Just a pretext?

The catalogue of evidence does, however, fall into place when set against the PNAC blueprint. From this it seems that the so-called "war on terrorism" is being used largely as bogus cover for achieving wider US strategic geopolitical objectives….

In fact, 9/11 offered an extremely convenient pretext to put the PNAC plan into action. The evidence again is quite clear that plans for military action against Afghanistan and Iraq were in hand well before 9/11. A report prepared for the US government from the Baker Institute of Public Policy stated in April 2001 that "the US remains a prisoner of its energy dilemma. Iraq remains a destabilising influence to … the flow of oil to international markets from the Middle East"….

Similar evidence exists in regard to Afghanistan. The BBC reported that Niaz Niak, a former Pakistan foreign secretary, was told by senior American officials at a meeting in Berlin in mid-July 2001 that "military action against Afghanistan would go ahead by the middle of October". Until July 2001 the US government saw the Taliban regime as a source of stability in Central Asia that would enable the construction of hydrocarbon pipelines from the oil and gas fields in Turkmenistan, Uzbekistan, Kazakhstan, through Afghanistan and Pakistan, to the Indian Ocean. But, confronted with the Taliban's refusal to accept US conditions, the US representatives told them "either you accept our offer of a carpet of gold, or we bury you under a carpet of bombs"….

In 1996 extremist Islamic Taliban forces captured the Afghan capital, Kabul. By the end of 1998 the Taliban controlled about 90 percent of the country. The regime banned television and music, and their human rights violations prompted worldwide criticism.

[I]t is not surprising that some have seen the US failure to avert the 9/11 attacks as creating an invaluable pretext for attacking Afghanistan in a war that had clearly already been well planned in advance. There is a possible precedent for this. The US national archives reveal that President Roosevelt used exactly this approach in relation to Pearl Harbor on December 7 1941. Some advance warning of the attacks was received, but the information never reached the US fleet. The ensuing national outrage persuaded a reluctant US public to join the second world war....

It's all about energy

The overriding motivation for this political smokescreen is that the US and the UK are beginning to run out of secure hydrocarbon energy supplies. By 2010 the Muslim world will control as much as 60% of the world's oil production and, even more importantly, 95% of remaining global oil export capacity. As demand is increasing, so supply is decreasing, continually since the 1960s.

This is leading to increasing dependence on foreign oil supplies for both the US and the UK. The US, which in 1990 produced domestically 57% of its total energy demand, is predicted to produce only 39% of its needs by 2010.... The UK government has confirmed that 70% of our electricity will come from gas by 2020, and 90% of that will be imported. In that context it should be noted that Iraq has 110 trillion cubic feet of gas reserves in addition to its oil.

A report from the commission on America's national interests in July 2000 noted that the most promising new source of world supplies was the Caspian region, and this would relieve US dependence on Saudi Arabia. To diversify supply routes from the Caspian, one pipeline would run westward via Azerbaijan and Georgia to the Turkish port of Ceyhan. Another would extend eastwards through Afghanistan and Pakistan and terminate near the Indian border. This would rescue Enron's beleaguered power plant at Dabhol on India's west coast, in which Enron had sunk $3bn investment and whose economic survival was dependent on access to cheap gas....

The conclusion of all this analysis must surely be that the "global war on terrorism" has the hallmarks of a political myth propagated to pave the way for a wholly different agenda—the US goal of world hegemony, built around securing by force command over the oil supplies required to drive the whole project. Is collusion in this myth and junior participation in this project really a proper aspiration for British foreign policy? If there was ever need to justify a more objective British stance, driven by our own independent goals, this whole depressing saga surely provides all the evidence needed for a radical change of course.

> On December 7, 1941, Japanese planes attacked the U.S. Navy's Pacific Fleet at Pearl Harbor in Hawaii. Then President Franklin D. Roosevelt (1882– 1945) has sometimes been accused of ignoring warnings of the attack so that it would provide a pretext for the United States to enter World War II (1939–1945). See Volume 13, U.S. History, Topic 9 Did Franklin D. Roosevelt provoke Pearl Harbor?

> "Hegemony" means the domination or authority of one nation over others.

Summary

These two articles paint starkly different pictures of U.S. global leadership in the post-September 11, 2001, world. In the first article Ike Skelton praises the swift action taken by the United States in trying to bring the terrorists to justice and uncover their sponsors. He highlights the "unprecedented support" the United States received from the international community and stresses that the War on Terrorism is a "global fight" that will need to rely on "a broad coalition of diplomatic and military partners over the long term." Skelton singles out the efforts made by individual states in combating terrorism and urges them to maintain this level of assistance in the future.

In the second article the British MP Michael Meacher claims to reveal the real thinking behind the Bush administration's War on Terrorism. He cites a document called "Rebuilding America's Defenses," which was written in 2000 by the Project for the New American Century (PNAC). Meacher insists that the document proves the administration planned to take control of the Gulf states regardless of whether Saddam Hussein was still in power in Iraq or not. He claims that the document is a "blueprint for US world domination" and says that this can be substantiated by the events before, during, and after the September 11 attacks. According to Meacher, the PNAC document is proof that the War on Terrorism is being used by the United States as a cover for wider geopolitical goals, namely, securing energy supplies in Central Asia.

FURTHER INFORMATION:

Books:

Frum, David, and Richard Perle, *An End to Evil: How to Win the War on Terror.* New York: Random House, 2003.

Sammon, Bill, *Fighting Back: The War on Terrorism from Inside the Bush White House.* Washington, D.C.: Regnery Publishing, 2002.

Useful websites:

http://www.foreignaffairs.org/20040101faessay83104/colin-l-powell/a-strategy-of-partnerships.html
"A Strategy of Partnerships" by Colin L. Powell.
http://www.theatlantic.com/issues/2003/12/soros.htm
"The Bubble of American Supremacy" by George Soros.
http://usinfo.state.gov/topical/pol/terror/
State Department site on responses to terrorism.
http://www.whitehouse.gov/news/releases/2001/09/20010920-8.html
George W. Bush's address to a joint session of Congress and the American people, September 20, 2001.

The following debates in the Pro/Con series may also be of interest:

In this volume:
Part 4: The United States and the World

In *U.S. Foreign Policy*:
Topic 15 Should the United States use military force against nations that harbor terrorists?

In *International Law*:
Topic 3 Is it legal for a state to attack another nation preemptively?

HAS THE WAR ON TERRORISM REINFORCED U.S. GLOBAL LEADERSHIP?

YES: George W. Bush announced the War on Terrorism shortly after the attacks and called for international cooperation

YES: The war is motivated by the desire of the international community to defend freedom, law, and order

RESPONSE TO 9/11
Is the War on Terrorism a response to the attacks of 9/11?

MOTIVES
Is the War on Terrorism motivated by more than U.S. economic considerations?

NO: The U.S. government wanted to invade Iraq before 9/11. The War on Terrorism is a cover for the United States' wider geopolitical goals.

NO: The ultimate goal of the war is to secure oil supplies for the United States in Central Asia

HAS THE WAR ON TERRORISM REINFORCED U.S. GLOBAL LEADERSHIP?
KEY POINTS

YES: The United States is the most powerful country in the world. Its diplomatic relations with other countries, extensive intelligence resources, and law-enforcement capabilities will help defeat global terror networks.

YES: The United States is militarily strong enough to defend itself without having to make alliances or justify its actions

AN UNWINNABLE WAR?
Can the War on Terrorism be won?

ACTING ALONE
Was the United States justified in ignoring international opinion concerning the war on Iraq?

NO: The military approach to fighting terrorism does not offer a solution to its causes; it has undermined U.S. credibility in global affairs

NO: The decision to go to war in Iraq in 2003 fundamentally damaged the United Nations and international relations

85

Topic 7

CAN ISRAEL AND PALESTINE EVER REACH A PEACE SETTLEMENT?

YES

FROM "GENEVA ACCORD: OPEN FORUM"
AMERICANS FOR PEACE NOW, THE FOUNDATION FOR MIDDLE EAST PEACE, AND THE
AMERICAN TASK FORCE ON PALESTINE, WASHINGTON, D.C., DECEMBER 3, 2003
WITH YOSSI BEILIN, DANIEL LEVY, SHAUL ARIELI, YASSER ABD RABBO, SAMIH AL-ABED,
AND NABIL KASSIS

NO

"STRIKING ACCORD"
THE ECONOMIST ONLINE, GLOBAL AGENDA, DECEMBER 4, 2003
THE ECONOMIST ONLINE

INTRODUCTION

On March 22, 2004, Sheikh Ahmed Yassin (1934–2004), the spiritual leader of the militant Islamist organization Hamas, was killed when an Israeli helicopter fired rocket missiles at a group of Palestinians. Several weeks later Yassin's successor, Abdel Aziz al-Rantissi (1947–2004), was killed in another rocket attack. Both attacks were authorized by Israeli Prime Minister Ariel Sharon (1928–).

The international community condemned Israel's actions; the UN stated that Israel had acted unlawfully. Images of Arabs swearing vengeance were broadcast around the world, but polls suggested that the majority of Israelis supported the actions. Many people, however, viewed the killings as the final nail in the coffin of the Israeli–Palestinian peace process.

Historically relations between Arabs and Jews have been troubled. Since 1948, however, when the state of Israel was created by the partition of Palestine (located between Egypt and southwest Asia) into three separate areas—an Israeli state, a Palestinian state, and an international zone encompassing Jerusalem—relations have become increasingly more violent. The region has suffered several bloody Arab–Israeli wars. The 1967 Six-Day War, for example, resulted in Israeli occupation of territories not in the original UN mandate suggesting partition, including the Golan Heights and the West Bank. Intifadas (uprisings) and terrorist action, including an increasing incidence of Palestinian suicide bombings, have resulted in a great loss of life on both sides.

Much of the conflict stems from disputed territorial rights, and the issue of repatriation—the "right to return"—for the Palestinian Arabs displaced by partition. Both Muslims and Jews have religious ties to the area. Muslims believe that the Prophet Muhammad was conveyed from the Kabah (Mecca) to Jerusalem's Temple Mount. Jewish claims date back to biblical times, when the region was the site of the kingdoms of Israel and Judah.

Palestinian opposition has manifested itself in the Palestinian Liberation Organization (PLO), which as part of its manifesto vowed to destroy the state of Israel and reclaim Palestinian lands. Under the leadership of Yasser Arafat (1929–), and the rise to prominence of the militant Fatah organization in the PLO, Palestinian protest became more violent. Israel also continued to create new settlements in the West Bank. In 1987 the Palestinians launched their first intifada against Israel.

> *"The forces of extremism and terror are attempting to kill progress and peace by killing the innocent."*
> —GEORGE W. BUSH (2002)

Despite several UN resolutions, the first serious internationally brokered attempt to settle the problem once and for all came with the Norwegian-negotiated Oslo Accords in 1993. Although around 400 million people watched the broadcast of Israeli Prime Minister Yitzhak Rabin (1922–1995) and PLO leader Yasser Arafat shaking hands outside the White House, Israel and Palestine remained deadlocked over several issues. Israeli right-wing groups also perceived Rabin as weak

for his "surrender" of Israeli lands to Palestine under the accords. When Rabin was assassinated on November 4, 1995, violence escalated, and the peace plans faltered. Despite negotiations with successive Israeli governments, the five-year interim period defined by the Oslo agreement in which a final resolution had to be made passed on May 4, 1999.

Ehud Barak's 1999 election as prime minister brought new hope. With help from the United States Barak (1942–) pressured Arafat into discussing peace at Camp David, the U.S. presidential retreat, in 2000. They were, however, unable to agree on issues such as the "right to return" and Jerusalem. Barak resigned in December 2000 following the outbreak of violence. An intifada (Sepember 2000) broke out in response to Ariel Sharon, the leader of the right-wing Likud party, touring the Arab Al Aqsa/Temple Mount complex in Jerusalem. But Sharon later swept to power in the February 2001 election.

Some commentators believe that Sharon's hard-line response to the conflict, his rejection of the 2003 Geneva Accord—an unofficial peace agreement negotiated by Palestinian and Israeli politicians—and his 2002 sanction of the construction of a "security fence" between Israel and Palestine make peace unlikely. Others claim that he has always acted in Israel's best interests. He has supported the U.S.-backed "road map to peace" (a two-state solution to the conflict) and has agreed to pull Jewish settlers out of the Gaza Strip. But this resulted in Hamas declaring a military victory over Israel, which, some argue, may have contributed to Yassin's and Rantissi's assassinations.

The following extracts focus on the Geneva Accord peace negotiations.

GENEVA ACCORD: OPEN FORUM
Yossi Beilin, Samih Al-Abed, et al.

YES

 Q: What is the position of the Geneva Accord on the right of return?

Yossi Beilin: The issue of the refugees is one of the most difficult. We tried to tackle it in a way that would answer the needs of both parties, not as a zero-sum game, but a win-win game.... The agreed solution to the refugee issue is fair to both sides and balanced. It includes compensation for everyone who meets the definition of a refugee, compensation for assets that are in Israel and belong to the refugees, and it give the refugees five options for a permanent place of residence. The first is the new Palestinian state. Once it is sovereign, all refugees will be invited. The second is to resettle in territories that were under Israeli sovereignty but will be annexed to the Palestinian state as a result of the exchange of land. The third option for resettlement is the countries where refugees live today, if those countries agree. Jordan accepts this, but Lebanon is a problem. For those countries that agree, there will be a process of rehabilitation and then they will live there permanently. The fourth option is third countries, like the U.S., Canada, Germany Australia, Spain, and other countries, which are willing to absorb refugees. The fifth option is Israel itself. Of course, this is the most delicate issue. Israel will make a sovereign decision on how many refugees it is willing to take. In deciding, it will have to take into consideration as a basis for its decision, the average quotas that third countries are accepting. It is not surprising that the major criticism in Israel of our solution is that the Palestinians did not give up, in writing, the right of return, and the main criticism on the Palestinian side is that the Palestinians gave up on the right of return. For us, the question was not who is right and who is wrong? The question for us was how do we solve the problem....

Q: How are you going to sell this plan to your respective communities…?

Samih al-Abed: This is the first time that Israelis and Palestinians have started to talk about specific issues in more detail. In contrast to the Oslo Declaration of Principles, which failed, we did not talk about principles or a framework for the solution.… [W]e sought detailed agreements on specific issues that we had been unable to obtain … in earlier talks. We also presented our draft to the population, both in Palestine and in Israel, to consider it before any official agreement is made.… We want the public to feel like they own this document and the solution, and that they can solve the problem themselves without having solutions imposed on them.…

Daniel Levy: We Israelis who have participated in this agreement have been arguing that the narrative that says there is no one to talk to and nothing to talk about was unacceptable to us. There is a whole new public debate now that we have produced this document. Formerly, we argued that there was, indeed, a partner for peace. But now we have a document that proves we have a partner and a plan. Now we are both in a position to give a very different message to our publics. We are already shifting the debate in Israel. The polls are relatively encouraging. The latest poll in Ha'aretz, on the day of the launching event on Monday, showed 31 percent of Israelis supporting Geneva, 37 percent against, and 20 percent undecided. This is very encouraging. We have to thank the government of Ariel Sharon for coming out in such a hysterical fashion against the agreement, which really pumped it up in the media. The way in which they did this was very revealing. They attacked the document as illegitimate, claiming we went behind the backs of the government, and that this was not democratic. They chose not to attack the substance of the document because they understood that it is acceptable to the silent majority in Israel and Palestine. Our challenge is to mobilize and re-empower that silent majority. It has been very difficult to do, and we hope that this will give a tool to those in our camp who had lost faith, and to those beyond our camp who were not convinced that we could change our situation.…

Q: How are you going to sell this to the White House, Capitol Hill and Colin Powell? …

Yasser Abed Rabbo: …Throughout our history, the world was trying to persuade us to solve our problem. Now for the first time, we have come up with a solution ourselves.… The most difficult thing for us in the past two-and-a-half years has been trying to find a line of balance that cuts all through the

Yitzhak Rabin, the prime minister of Israel, and Yasser Arafat signed the Oslo Declaration of Principles on August 20, 1993. They agreed, among other things, to the withdrawal of Israeli forces from the Gaza Strip and the West Bank. In 2000, however, the Oslo negotiations came to a standstill.

Daniel Levy is Beilin's adviser. He is in charge of foreign affairs for the accord. He is also the son of British Middle East envoy Lord Michael Levy, a close friend of British Prime Minister Tony Blair.

Israeli Prime Minister Ariel Sharon condemned the accord. He said that the road map to peace was a more viable option.

Yasser Abed Rabbo (1945–) has been a leading Palestinian negotiator in the peace talks for many years. He was minister of culture and information (1994–2001).

issues in this package, so that both Israelis and Palestinians will conclude that their basic aspirations and needs are met and do not contradict each other.… We are offering a very concrete solution, based on previous experience. Second, our solution proves to the two nations, Palestinian and Israeli, to the other nations in the region and to the Americans, that there is a possible way for solving your problems through reconciliation, through historical compromise, and through negotiations that take into account the basic interests and needs of both sides and find a balance between them. Our work shows that there is an alternative to the extremists and fundamentalists who oppose reconciliation, compromise, and dialogue.… If it fails, the forces of extremism will grow even stronger. That's why the White House should support our way of solving things, in order to protect not only our interests, but American interests as well.…

Why should the United States involve itself in the peace process? Go to Volume 8, U.S. Foreign Policy, Topic 16 Should the United States take more responsibility for promoting peace in the Middle East?

Q: After the breakdown of peace at Camp David, Barak and Clinton blamed the Palestinians and the American people were led to believe that Israel has no partner for peace. Have any former Clinton administration officials … endorsed endorse the Geneva proposal?

In 2000 Israeli Prime Minister Ehud Barak and Yasser Arafat met at Camp David to discuss a peace settlement. The negotiations broke down, and Arafat was blamed.

Yossi Beilin: President Clinton sent an endorsement letter to us in Geneva, and we have received warm support from Madeleine Albright and Sandy Berger. Generally speaking, the people who were around Clinton, and Clinton himself, are supporting this initiative.

Yasser Abed Rabbo: Whom do we represent? On the Palestinian side, we represent the mainstream. We have our extremists, but we have always had them. What we have lacked in the last three years is a platform that will unite all the moderates, and that will reunite the Palestinian mainstream. Our plan provides this. On the Israeli side, besides Yossi Beilin, you have Avram Burg, Amram Mitzna, retired generals from the army, retired officials from Israeli Security, and people from left, center and right. The plan is winning over 30 percent of the Israeli support, in spite of what I call the brainwashing that has been directed through the years, to both the Palestinians and the Israeli public, saying there is no partner and no possible solution and that we have no choice but to go on destroying and killing each other. It is unbelievable that we have won support from 30 percent of the Israelis in the first days after releasing the plan, notwithstanding all the negative propaganda that has

Go to http://www.americantaskforce.org/geneva.htm to read the text of the Geneva Accord. Is it feasible?

demonized the other side and argued that it is impossible to achieve anything....

Q: ...I understand Arafat hasn't come out in support of the Accord.... How can you prove that if there were an Israeli government that would support it, then the PLO would also support it? ...

Yasser Abed Rabbo: In some circles, all the evils of the world are attributed to Arafat, yet when Arafat says something positive publicly and openly, it is ignored. Arafat sent an official message in his name, and it was read in Geneva, in front of the hundreds of participants, including of course, world dignitaries, presidents and ex-presidents, including former President Carter. Chairman Arafat's message supported this initiative and called upon the entire world to support it, because it gives a real basis for hope for both sides. Before that, two statements were made by the Palestinian leadership headed by Arafat. I'm a member of the Palestinian leadership, I report to the Palestinian leadership, I'm not an amateur, and I've been working as a politician for over 35 years. Nor is Arafat an amateur. He supports and endorses this, and he believes that this is a way that we all should take in order to return back to the normal forms of solving our problems. At every turning point over the years, Arafat was the key figure who influenced Palestinian public opinion for the better. This is not propaganda; this is history, recent history, today's history. Without his support, I tell you, our road will be very difficult.... Ahmed Qureia, the prime minister, supports what we are doing. Abu Mazen, the ex-prime minister, supports what we are doing. They know where we are heading. And without this, of course, it would be very difficult for us. We had 200 Palestinians with us at Geneva. Among them were ex-prisoners, mostly Fatah people, and among them were young generation militants, who are still leading a struggle in the streets. There were also intellectuals, peasants, businessmen, and wealthy Palestinians who came from the United States, Europe, and elsewhere abroad. It was a very strange and unique scene.... These people represent the majority of Palestinian society.

Remember that we are still in the first month after we started the campaign.... But 31 percent have already expressed support. That's a very good beginning in the first month. ... We are overcoming decades of hatred and suspicion.... The situation is urgent, and we have a large responsibility. So does the American administration....

Do you think Yasser Arafat has been treated fairly by the media? Go to www.google.com and search for articles about him.

Ahmed Qureia (1937–), better known as Abu Ala, became the Palestinian Authority's prime minister in September 2003. He has been a chief negotiator in the Palestinian–Israeli peace talks and is believed to have persuaded Arafat to meet with Yitzhak Rabin in the secret talks that led to the Oslo Accords.

Go to http://news.bbc.co.uk/1/hi/in_depth/middle_east/2000/mideast_peace_process/340237.stm to look at a history of Israel–Arab peace agreements.

STRIKING ACCORD
The Economist Online

On June 5, 1967, Israel began a preemptive war with Egypt, Jordan, and Syria, believing that a massive Arab attack was imminent. Egypt had ordered the withdrawl of UN Emergency Forces stationed on the Egypt–Israel border and had blocked Israeli trade through the Straits of Tiran; Syria mobilized its forces and attacked the border along the Golan Heights. The war, which lasted six days, left Israel in control of the Sinai Peninsula, eastern Jerusalem, the Golan Heights, Judea Samaria, and the Gaza Strip.

In 2003 the United States, the UN, the EU, and Russia, with Israeli and Palestinian consultation, drew up the "road map to peace." It was a two-state solution to the Israeli–Palestinian conflict by which an independent Palestinian state would be set up in the West Bank and Gaza Strip, the occupied territories bordering Israel.

NO

Ten years after the Oslo peace process was launched with similar fanfare in Washington, on Monday December 1st Palestinian and Israeli negotiators met in Switzerland to seal a comprehensive peace agreement between their warring nations, known as the Geneva accord. Under it, Israel would withdraw from most of the Palestinian territories it occupied in the 1967 war. The Palestinians would accept shared sovereignty in occupied East Jerusalem and effectively give up their refugees' right of return to their homes in what was once Palestine but is now Israel. Dignitaries and politicians from America, Europe and the Arab world applauded the historic compromise in a star-studded ceremony. The accord's two main authors—Yossi Beilin, a former Israeli justice minister, and Yasser Abed Rabbo, a former Palestinian information minister—are expected to meet Colin Powell on Friday. The American secretary of state has welcomed the "peace".

Not a real peace

It isn't a real peace, of course, and not simply because the hope raised by Oslo has long been washed away by the despair of the Palestinians' armed struggle, or intifada. Neither the dozens of Palestinians nor the 200 Israelis at Geneva were there as representatives of their governments. Yasser Arafat, the president of the Palestinian Authority (PA), has blessed the enterprise without endorsing the outcome. Ariel Sharon, the Israeli prime minister, denounced the accord before once again nailing his colours to the "road map"—a peace plan sponsored by the so-called Quartet (America, the European Union, Russia and the United Nations)—which collapsed in the summer. On Tuesday Mr Sharon's deputy, Ehud Olmert, went so far as to say that it would be a mistake for Mr Powell to meet the Geneva negotiators. Mr Powell rejected the advice, asking: "Why should we not listen to others who have ideas?"

A wakeup call?

The Geneva peace agreement has a long way to go before it replaces the road map or topples the Palestinian or Israeli

Colin Powell meets Yasser Arafat during peace talks in 2002.

Yasser Arafat established Fatah (The Movement for the National Liberation of Palestine) in the early 1960s. It carried out civilian terrorist raids on Israeli targets from 1965. When Arafat became chairman of the PLO, Fatah became the PLO's most popular faction.

governments. But it has shaken all three. Four of the Palestinian signatories nearly bailed out from the Geneva ceremony, alarmed by the rising tide of protest the concessions on Jerusalem and refugees have caused among the Palestinian factions, including Mr Arafat's Fatah movement. The fall-out among Israelis has been similarly pronounced. Since the Geneva Accord was first drawn up, they have been swamped with a plethora of other "peace plans": the settlers have proposed Jewish and Arab cantons in "Judea, Samaria and Gaza" (as they call the occupied territories); the opposition Labour Party has promoted an agreement that mirrors Geneva in outline while differing with it on detail; and Mr Sharon has been forced to face down all of these proposals with an ill-defined "initiative" of his own, which he has said he would pursue if the road map goes nowhere.

First, says Mr Sharon, he will seek to revive the road map by talking to the PA's new prime minister, Ahmed Qureia. To increase the chances of such talks bearing fruit, the Israeli leader has quietly dropped his precondition that the PA's security forces engage in "a real war" against militant groups like Hamas and Islamic Jihad. Mr Sharon has also hinted that he may evacuate a few Jewish settlements. However, if these efforts fail, he will replace a negotiated solution with an imposed one. The Palestinians assume this means the establishment of new borders that would leave a future Palestinian state with less than half the West Bank and perhaps not all of Gaza.

Timeframe

This is unlikely to happen anytime soon, if only because of a revived American interest in the road map. For the first time in months, America's envoy to the peace process, William Burns, has been in the region. In meetings over the weekend he told Mr Qureia there could be no substitute for rooting out the "terrorist infrastructure" of Hamas and Islamic Jihad. He also told Mr Sharon that Israel would have to dismantle settlement outposts and freeze settlement construction in the occupied territories, as it is bound to do under the road map. Mr Sharon has said he is prepared to remove some—but not all—of the 60 outposts established during his tenure as prime minister. He has said and done nothing about a construction freeze.

As for Mr Qureia, he is awaiting the outcome of talks between the various Palestinian factions meeting in Cairo this week. He wants them to agree a ceasefire so that he has

From December 3 to 7, 2003, Qureia met with 10 Palestinian groups in Egypt to discuss a full ceasefire. The groups could not reach an agreement on terms, however.

something in his hand when he finally sits down with Mr Sharon. In return for a truce he will demand that Israel stop military incursions like the one that ended with three Palestinians dead and 30 arrested in Ramallah on Monday. He will also insist Israel end construction of the barrier in and around the West Bank. Mr Sharon says the barrier is vital for Israel's security. The Palestinians say it is charting the borders of their future "provisional" and utterly unviable state.

Pie-in-the-sky

Mr Qureia is unlikely to get very far. His Israeli counterpart has made it clear he regards the Palestinian terms for a return to the road map as every bit as pie-in-the-sky as the accord signed in Geneva.

"No [Palestinian] conditions will be accepted, whether they concern ceasing construction of the separation fence or dismantling it or any other demands," Mr Sharon told his cabinet on Sunday.

In May 2002, following the increase in suicide bombings, the Israeli government began building a security fence along the Israeli–Palestinian border. It claimed that it was to help deter terrorist action. It has been a very controversial project. Go to www.cnn.com and www.bbc.co.uk and look at articles on the subject.

Summary

The first of the two articles features Yossi Beilin and Daniel Levy from Israel, and Yasser Abed Rabbo and Samih al-Abed from Palestine—four of the six Geneva Accord negotiators involved in the Open Forum held to discuss the viability of the accord. They claim that the accord is different from other peace proposals since it is the first time that "Israelis and Palestinians have started to talk about specific issues in more detail." Yasser Abed Rabbo claims that it is groundbreaking since Palestinians and Israelis have tried to resolve the conflict themselves. He says, "our solution proves to … Palestinian and Israeli, to the other nations in the region, and to the Americans, that there is a possible way for solving your problems through reconciliation, through historical compromise, and through negotiations that take into account the basic interests and needs of both sides and find a balance between them." They are all very positive about the possibility of peace.

The article from *The Economist,* however, compares the Geneva Accord to the Oslo peace process of 1993, in which all hope was "washed away by the despair of the Palestinian's intifada." The key point made is that the Israeli and Palestinian negotiators of the accord do not represent their governments. While Yasser Arafat might be giving the process some behind-the-scenes support, the Israeli government is completely against it. Indeed, the article does not hold out much hope for the deadlock being broken at all. Sharon sees Palestinian terms for both the Geneva Accord and a return to the road map as equally "pie in the sky." The final word is his: "No [Palestinian] conditions will be accepted, whether they concern ceasing construction of the separation fence or dismantling it or any other demands."

FURTHER INFORMATION:

Books:

Tessler, Mark A., *A History of the Israeli–Palestinian Conflict* (Indiana Series in Arab and Islamic Studies). Bloomington, IN: Indiana University Press, 1994.

Useful websites:

www.bbc.co.uk

Site of the BBC. Country-by-country profiles. It also features a timeline on the Arab–Israeli conflict.

www.guardian.co.uk

Features various articles on this subject. Also has useful links to newspapers and sites focusing on the conflict.

www.mideastweb.org/history.htm

Useful for history and conflicts of Middle Eastern countries.

The following debates in the Pro/Con series may also be of interest:

In this volume:
Arab–Israeli relations after 1948, pages 98–99

In *U.S. Foreign Policy*:
Topic 16 Should the United States take more responsibility for promoting peace in the Middle East?

CAN ISRAEL AND PALESTINE EVER REACH A PEACE SETTLEMENT?

YES: Sometimes minority groups think their only option lies in violence—wars have illustrated this in the past

YES: The United States could put financial pressure on Israel to stop all settlement in Palestinian territory

VIOLENCE
Is violence a justifiable way to resolve the conflict?

UNITED STATES
Could the United States do more to bring about a settlement?

NO: Violence has caused such hatred and resentment that peace will never be possible

NO: The United States has taken the lead in the road map to peace proposal, but it cannot force either side to comply

CAN ISRAEL AND PALESTINE EVER REACH A PEACE SETTLEMENT?

KEY POINTS

YES: The accord was sent to every home in Israel and was printed in Palestinian newspapers. A poll, held shortly afterward, implied that over 55 percent of Palestinians and 53 percent of Israelis would back it in principle.

YES: A two-state solution is practicable if both sides are prepared to compromise

GENEVA ACCORD
Is the Geneva Accord viable?

PROBLEMATIC
Is the problem solvable?

NO: Neither the Israeli nor Palestinian legislative councils have backed the agreement

NO: The conflict that exists between the two nations is complicated. Both sides want the same land, and neither will accept the presence of the other.

ARAB–ISRAELI RELATIONS AFTER 1948

At midnight on May 14, 1948, the state of Israel—a homeland for the Jewish people—officially came into being. It was created by UN Resolution 181, which divided the ancient land of Palestine into three separate areas—one for the Jews, one for the Arabs, and an international zone around Jerusalem. Palestine held religious significance for both Jews and Arabs—Jewish claims date back to biblical times when it was the site of the kingdoms of Israel and Judah, and Arabs believe that Jerusalem is the third holy Muslim city. The creation of Israel was met with great hostility by the Arab community. On May 15 Arab states invaded Israel, beginning the first of many Arab–Israeli wars. Since then the area has been the site of bitter conflict and violence, suicide bombings, and terrorism, resulting in massive casualties and many deaths on both sides. This timeline examines key dates in Arab–Israeli relations since 1948.

1948 May 14: The state of Israel is created. **May 15:** The First Arab–Israeli War begins when Arab states invade Israel.

1949 A series of ceasefires leaves Israel with 77 percent of former Palestine; Egypt controls the Gaza Strip; Jordan occupies the West Bank and East Jerusalem.

1956–1957 October 29: The Second Arab–Israeli War begins when Israel—backed by Britain and France—attacks the Gaza Strip and occupies most of the Sinai Peninsula. Israel withdraws in spring 1957.

1964 The Palestinian Liberation Organization (PLO) is established. Yasser Arafat also forms the Fatah, an anti-Israeli armed unit.

1967 June 5–10: The Six-Day War/Third Arab–Israeli War. Israel launches preemptive strikes on Arab armies amassed on its borders. It captures Sinai and the Gaza Strip from Egypt, the West Bank and East Jerusalem from Jordan, and the Golan Heights from Syria. **November 22:** UN Security Council Resolution 242 calls for Israel's withdrawal from occupied lands.

1969 Arafat becomes chairman of the PLO. It becomes more militant. In the early 1970s its headquarters move from Jordan to Lebanon.

1973 October 6: Egypt and Syria attack Israel on the Jewish holy day Yom Kippur (the Fourth Arab–Israeli War, or Yom Kippur War). Israel retaliates, gaining land in the Sinai and the Golan Heights. **22:** UN Security Resolution 338 calls for a ceasefire. Saudi Arabia places an oil embargo on nations that have helped Israel (until 1974). There are oil shortages and a drastic rise in world oil prices.

1974 Yasser Arafat asks for a peaceful resolution to the conflict at a meeting at the UN. In 1975 the United States acknowledges that Palestinian interests should be taken into account in peace negotiations.

1977 Menachem Begin wins the Israeli elections, He intensifies settlement in the West Bank and Gaza. In November Egyptian

President Anwar Sadat addresses the Israeli parliament in the first tacit recognition of Israel's sovereignty by an Arab leader.

1978–1979 September: Egypt and Israel sign the Camp David Accords, which provide for the introduction of limited Palestinian autonomy. **April:** The countries sign a mutual recognition pact, which states, among other things, that Israel will withdrawal from Sinai. Other Arab states boycott Egypt. **October 6:** Sadat is assassinated.

1982 June 6: Israel invades Lebanon to destroy PLO bases. The PLO relocates to Tunisia. **September 16–18:** The Phalangists, allies of Israel, kill hundreds of Palestinians in the Sabra and Shatila refugee camps while Israeli troops surround them. Three years later Israel withdraws from most of Lebanon, but maintains a security zone there.

1987 Palestinians in Gaza and the West Bank begin an intifada (uprising) against Israeli occupation in December.

1988 In November the Palestinian National Council proclaims an independent Palestinian state.

1991 January–March: Following the expulsion of its forces from Kuwait during the Persian Gulf War, Iraq launches missiles against Israeli targets, but the United States persuades it not to respond. **October:** Talks between Israel and the Arab states take place in Spain and America.

1993–1994 September 13: The Declaration of Principles (Oslo Accords) provides mutual recognition of Israel and the PLO, and for the gradual Israeli withdrawal from the occupied territories. **May 4:** Israel and the PLO sign an agreement specifying Israel's withdrawal from most of the Gaza Strip and Jericho (West Bank). It establishes a

Palestinian National Authority (PNA). **October 26:** Jordan and Israel sign a peace treaty.

1995 September 28: The Oslo II Agreement divides the West Bank into three zones under Palestinian, Israeli, or joint control. **November 4:** Yitzhak Rabin, Israel's prime minister, is assassinated.

1996–1997 January: Arafat is elected president of the PNA. **May:** Binyamin Netanyahu, who opposes the Oslo Accords, becomes prime minister of Israel. **January 17:** 80 percent of the West Bank city of Hebron is placed under Palestinian control.

1999 January: Netanyahu's government collapses. **May:** The Oslo Accords' five-year timeframe for a final settlement expires.

2000 September 28: Ariel Sharon, leader of the Israeli Likud party, sparks a second intifada when he visits the Al Aqsa mosque; he claims it will remain under Jewish control.

2001–2002 February 6: Sharon is elected prime minister of Israel. **September:** Following the 9/11 terrorist attacks against America, Israel increases strikes against Palestinian territories. **March:** Israel reoccupies Palestinian areas. **June:** Israel constructs security fences—compared to the Berlin Wall—around the West Bank.

2003 April 30: The UN, the United States, Russia, and the EU release a "road map" for peace. Mahmoud Abbas becomes the Palestinian prime minister. **September:** Abbas resigns; he is replaced by Ahmed Qureia in November. **October:** The Geneva Accord (see pages 88–95) is released.

2004 March: Sharon authorizes the killing of the head of Hamas, Sheikh Ahmed Yassin. **April:** Yassin's successor, Abdel Aziz al-Rantissi, is assassinated.

PART 3
INTERNATIONAL ORGANIZATIONS

INTRODUCTION

Throughout modern history the principal actors in world politics have been sovereign nation-states. The realist theory of international relations holds that nation-states seek to maximize their power in an inherently anarchic environment. Realism, therefore, tends to emphasize noncooperative behavior between states and downplays evidence of international cooperation. Critics, however, point out that a great deal of mutually beneficial cooperation takes place in the practice of states. It has largely been fostered by international organizations—institutions that operate across national borders. Although such institutions have not removed conflict between states, they have arguably enhanced international security.

IGOs and NGOs

There are two principal types of international organizations: intergovernmental organizations (IGOs), to which states belong and are bound by a formal agreement, and nongovernmental organizations (NGOs), to which private individuals and groups belong. Although nations have formed alliances to further their common interests throughout history, the rise of the modern international organization is associated with the growth in transnational commerce and communications that accompanied

industrialization in the 19th century. The number of such organizations increased dramatically during the 20th century. By one common count there were 37 IGOs in 1909 and 293 in 1990. Some IGOs are global in scope and general in purpose; others are regional or have specific functions. The League of Nations, established after World War I (1914–1918), was the first quasi-universal, multipurpose IGO. In the post-World War II era the most prominent global organization has been the United Nations (UN). The UN is involved in collective security, human rights, world health, economic development, and environmental protection, among many other areas.

NGOs—of which there are many thousands—tend to be more specialized than IGOs. Many have economic or business-related functions. For example, the International Air Transport Association coordinates the work of airlines. Other NGOs have political purposes and seek to influence government policies. For instance, Amnesty International campaigns for human rights. Others, such as the International Committee of the Red Cross, have humanitarian concerns. Religious organizations are among the largest NGOs; their memberships often span many countries. Although IGOs have a more direct effect on

100

international relations because their members are states, NGOs are gaining increasing importance on the world political stage.

International organizations now connect people in all countries, seeming to reflect a rising level of interdependence. Yet they also mirror degrees of conflict and cooperation that characterize world politics

adversarial environment. For example, membership in IGOs gives small states a voice that they otherwise would not have in setting global political agendas.

Existing tensions

Advocates maintain that the high level of participation in IGOs by the world's most powerful states is proof of their importance in international relations.

> *"[O]nly justice, fairness, consideration, and cooperation can finally lead men to the dawn of eternal peace."*
> —DWIGHT D. EISENHOWER, 34TH PRESIDENT (1953–1961)

generally. In fact, some scholars have called their effectiveness into question: In his 1994 essay "The False Promise of International Institutions" political scientist John Mearsheimer argues that "institutions have minimal influence on state behavior." As a consequence, he says in his 1995 article "A Realist Reply," institutions cannot prevent states behaving as "short-term power maximizers." If this were true, critics ask, why would self-interested states take part in international organizations?

A competing theoretical approach to international relations is liberal institutionalism, which holds that states generally refrain from taking maximum short-term advantage of each other. In fact, they often work together by following rules they develop to govern their interactions. Over time the rules become established, and institutions grow up around them. States gradually get used to working through those institutions. They do so out of self-interest: States can realize greater gains through cooperation than in an

However, critics question whether institutions that were established during the Cold War have evolved to meet the challenges of a new era. Topics 8 and 9 respectively consider the contemporary relevance of the UN and the military alliance NATO.

Observers point out that even in the European Union, the most advanced example of integration between states, there remains unresolved tension between the principles of sovereignty and supranational authority. Topic 10 looks at whether a fully integrated United States of Europe is possible. Institutions that promote free trade, such as the World Trade Organization (WTO), the subject of Topic 11, reveal similar tensions. The removal of trade barriers can benefit all nations in terms of global wealth creation, but the costs to individual states, such as the effect on domestic industries, can be high. The final topic examines the controversial issue of the role that the regional IGO the Arab League could play in achieving Middle East peace.

Topic 8
SHOULD THE UNITED NATIONS BE DISBANDED?

YES

FROM "THE TIME IS NOW: THE UNITED NATIONS—IRRELEVANT AND DANGEROUS"
AMERICAN POLICY CENTER, MARCH 28, 2003
TOM DEWEESE

NO

"PRESIDENT BUSH MEETS WITH UN
SECRETARY-GENERAL KOFI ANNAN"
THE OVAL OFFICE, FEBRUARY 3, 2004
OFFICE OF THE PRESS SECRETARY

INTRODUCTION

In a 2003 speech on the importance of the United Nations (UN) to the future of the world, UN Secretary-General Kofi Annan insisted that the organization remains "indispensable to the security and progress of all nations." But some critics argue that the UN is ill equipped to face modern challenges, and they question its continued existence. At the end of 2003—a year that saw the UN divided over the U.S. decision to go to war in Iraq—Annan acknowledged that the organization had "come to a fork in the road," and he appointed a panel to examine its reform.

According to its charter, the main purposes of the UN are to maintain international peace and security, to advance friendly relations between countries, and to cooperate in resolving international problems and promoting human rights. The UN was established as a successor to the League of Nations in 1945. The league, which was set up in 1920, proved unable to resolve a number of disputes in the 1930s or prevent a second world war. Its failure was largely blamed on the lack of great-power support: The United States never joined the league. In contrast, it led the way in the creation of the UN.

Each of the UN 192 member states has a vote in the General Assembly, where issues such as security and budgetary matters are debated. The UN body tasked with maintaining global peace is the Security Council. It has 5 permanent members (Britain, France, China, Russia, and the United States) and 10 members who are elected by the General Assembly for two-year terms. Each member casts one vote in decisions on council resolutions. The council has the power to authorize the use of force in conflicts and to send peacekeepers to troublespots. In 2003 there were peacekeeping missions in 13 countries. Commentators mostly agree that the UN has been successful in about half of the missions it has undertaken. It became increasingly involved in conflicts after the end of the Cold War in the early 1990s. The UN was criticized during this period after peacekeepers failed to help prevent both the ethnic cleansing of Muslims by Serbs in Bosnia and also the Hutu genocide of 800,000 Tutsis in Rwanda. However, operations during this time also brought peace to El Salvador, Cambodia, Mozambique, and East Timor. Supporters also point out that since 1945 the UN has arranged over 170 peace settlements.

"The United Nations is not perfect, but it is precious."

—KOFI ANNAN, UN SECRETARY-GENERAL (2003)

The run-up to the U.S.-led invasion of Iraq in 2003 was a crucial test of the UN's authority. The United States and Britain argued that Security Council Resolution 1441 of 2002, which called for Iraq to disarm and cooperate with UN weapons inspectors, allowed for military action. France proposed to veto a second resolution authorizing action, and the United States decided to go to war without UN approval. Critics say that this response highlighted the UN's increasing irrelevance. They argue that the UN needs to adapt to survive. They insist that, apart from the United States, the other permanent members of the Security Council must accept they no longer have the same influence they

had in 1945, and they should give up their seats. Critics also argue that the UN, with more than 50,000 staff and an annual budget of around $2.6 billion, is too bureaucratic and needs to improve accountability. The UN is funded by member states, with each country assessed on its ability to pay. Some critics suggest that smaller nations should contribute more money to give them a greater stake in UN operations.

Other critics go further and say that the UN should be disbanded. They argue that the lack of strong support from the United States has made it as ineffectual as the League of Nations. Not only did the United States invade Iraq without UN backing, but it has also refused to ratify key agreements such as the treaty establishing the International Criminal Court (ICC). Critics also point out that the UN's reputation has been undermined by allowing representatives of repressive regimes such as Sudan to sit on the UN Commission on Human Rights. There have also been damaging allegations that peacekeepers in West Africa committed human rights abuses and that some UN staff were involved in corruption in Iraq.

Supporters of the UN counter that it has achieved great successes through its wider agenda of reducing poverty, fighting disease, promoting education, and upholding human rights. Advocates claim that the ability of the UN to tackle these problems will be the true test of its value in the 21st century. They point out that UN efforts have halved the rate of child mortality and eradicated smallpox in developing countries, and that the UN remains one of the world's largest sources of aid to the poor, children, and refugees.

The following two articles look at the importance of the UN.

THE TIME IS NOW: THE UNITED NATIONS...
Tom DeWeese

Tom DeWeese is president of the American Policy Center, which advocates "individual liberty, free enterprise, property rights, and back-to-basics education." This article dates from March 28, 2003. On March 20 the United States led an invasion of Iraq to remove Saddam Hussein (1937–) from power and to search for weapons of mass destruction, which the U.S. government claimed Iraq was hiding in violation of the peace treaty that ended the 1991 Persian Gulf War.

YES

✓ The world is in chaos and, quite frankly, it's the United Nations' fault. It gives validity to zealots and petty bigots. It helps to keep tyrannical dictators in power. It provides money and aid to international terrorists. And it sets itself up as the international economic and environmental standard to which all nations are to mirror. The truth is, the United Nations is the root of international trouble, not the answer.

Saddam Hussein is in power, able to threaten world peace today, because the United States allowed the United Nations to dictate the terms for the finish to the Gulf War after an American-organized coalition all but annihilated Iraq.

In the intervening ten years, Iraq has time and again broken the terms of that treaty. The UN's response has been to pass 17 resolutions to demand that Iraq behave itself. Those resolutions are toothless and irrelevant because other nations that have economic dealings with Iraq refuse to take action for fear of losing money.

A simple question

When President Bush went before the UN to make his case against Iraq, he simply was asking the Security Council if it agreed with the U.S. assessment that Iraq "has been and remains in material breach," of the terms of the Gulf War disarmament provisions.

True to form, the UN was unable to act on so clear of a position. Instead, France, Russia and China, all nations who have Iraqi economic ties to lose in a war, and all members of the Security Council, used their power to delay and deny U.S. action.

As a result, the UN resolution #17 does not allow for U.S. action if a breach is found. Instead it demands that the UN basically issue resolution #18.

Delay. Negotiate. Recommend. Study. Reconsider. Do nothing. This is the same game the UN has played in nearly every international crisis. It is the reason North Korea remains a threat and its violent dictator remains in power

On November 8, 2002, the UN Security Council passed resolution 1441—its 17th resolution on Iraq since the end of the Gulf War. It threatened serious consequences if Iraq did not heed this "final opportunity to comply with its disarmament obligations."

after 50 years. It's the reason why Zimbabwe's murderous dictator, Robert Mugabe, is able to steal his election and then steal the land of white property owners and still have a voice at the UN's Sustainable Development Conference a few months ago in South Africa. It's the reason why the Communist Chinese are able to ignore any UN rules not to their liking while growing as an international military and economic threat. It's the reason why a terrorist nation like Syria can be given a seat on the UN's Human Rights Council while the United States is removed.

The United Nations' main purpose is to provide voice and power to irrelevant or vicious nations to counter the United States. The UN will never approve U.S. military action against Iraq or any tin horn dictators who threaten the peace, because they are the very dictators who now control UN decisions.

In May 2001 the United States was voted off the UN Human Rights Commission for the first time since it was established in 1947. The commission investigates human rights abuses. Some commentators suggested that the vote was a reaction to U.S. foreign policy. The United States was voted back onto the commission in April 2002.

It's our fault

It is, however, the United States that is to blame for this situation, because we allow this circus on the East River to exist. The only credibility the UN possesses comes from recognition by the United States. The only financial security the UN enjoys comes from funds provided by U.S. taxpayers. The only military punch controlled by the UN comes from American military might.

The UN headquarters building stands on the East River in Manhattan.

The United States is dutifully providing an elegant clubhouse in which pouting and jealous bureaucrats and self-inflated international diplomats can pretend to matter. As long as the United States allows them to exist and as long as this nation goes along with their demands, they do matter. The United Nations is nothing more than a house of cards, but it's a very dangerous house of cards.

The UN is dangerous because its most vocal membership stands in opposition of the American values of controlled representative government, justice, free enterprise, privacy of individuals and private property rights. Most of the UN's membership comes from nations controlled either by communist regimes, kingdoms or mad dictators where American values are either unknown or viewed as a threat.

Do you agree that these are "American values"?

Those same UN members are busy working to implement plans for UN global governance. Already, the UN's International Criminal Court is in place. The UN has held an international meeting to discuss the possibilities and methods of implementing global taxes. More plans are under consideration to establish a UN global army or police force. Most member states participating in these planning sessions

See Volume 22, International Law, Topic 1 Does the International Criminal Court undermine national sovereignty?

are from brutal dictatorships like China and Cuba and a number of brutal fundamental Islamic states like Syria and Iran. Can any clear thinking American honestly believe that the ideas coming out of this group would have a possibility of favoring ideals readily accepted as rights in the United States?

Many Americans simply do not believe that the United States would voluntarily give up its sovereignty to the United Nations. They say our people would never stand for it. Those who think this way somehow seem to believe the issue will come up for a national vote to determine if the United States will agree to dismantle its federal government in acceptance of UN global governance. If it were that simple, even UN opponents wouldn't worry about the UN threat. Such a thing will never happen.

It's already happening

See Volume 8, U.S. Foreign Policy, Topic 6 Does NAFTA work?

It happens in increments of well meaning, innocent-sounding policies and treaties. The North American Free Trade Agreement (NAFTA) was sold as simply a way for American producers to broaden their markets to the international level. Instead, many have found that details of the treaty dictate rules and regulations, particularly of the environmental kind, that tilt the playing field to other nations. As a result, American markets are flooded with foreign goods as American businesses and jobs head out of the country....

On January 1, 2002, 12 member states of the European Union changed their national currencies to a single currency called the euro. Sweden rejected membership in the euro in a referendum in 2003.

The European Union was originally sold as another NAFTA through which nations could join together to compete with the United States on the international market. Now, once-proud nations have given up their national sovereignty, ancient currencies like the Italian Lira and the French Franc have disappeared in place of the Euro. Would the citizens of France, Italy or Greece ever have agreed to such a move had the whole plan been put on a ballot?

Now there is discussion of an African Union, a South American Union and a North American Union in which the United States would meld its borders with Canada and Mexico. The move will be easy since NAFTA has already set the precedent.

How long will it be after the establishment of all of these geographical unions before the world moves towards one international union? It will be easy to complete after all of these nations have been through the process of letting go of their national identity. And the United Nations is already putting the pieces together with its World Court, global tax schemes and military planning.

Imagine a world run by the justice of China, with the economics of Cuba and the military might of the United States. Such is the world of the future under the United Nations. The United States holds all of the cards, but it has only one vote in this cesspool of Socialism.

The United Nations exists simply because there is an established mindset that says it's supposed to. It is the established mindset of too many Americans who simply view the United Nations through the televised images of the UN's Security Council, as the President of the United States, hat in hand, asks that body to allow the United States to defend itself against murderers. It is the mindset that they somehow have a legitimacy to grant or deny that request. It is the mindset that Resolution #17 means anything. It is the established mindset of NAFTA, the European Union and the International Criminal Court that are already part of our lives. It is the mindset that accepts the movement toward a North American Union and UN global governance as simply the next natural step. These are the reasons why the United Nations is so dangerous.

The United States can end it all now if it wishes. The mindset must be changed. President Bush has proven that we don't need the United Nations to grant us permission to protect our national interests. The United States can and will fight its own war on terrorism. It can and will organize its own coalition of allies, use its own money, its own weapons and its own troops to defeat an enemy who threatens us.

We're propping up this circus

The United Nations is irrelevant as a body to deliver world peace. But it is United States' participation in propping up the circus that makes the UN dangerous.…

As the new 108th Congress opens in January, Congressman Ron Paul will once again introduce H.R. 1146, the American Sovereignty Restoration Act. His bill calls for the United States to withdraw from the United Nations. It also calls for the United Nations to remove its headquarters from our shores. H.R. 1146 would relieve the United States from participating in UNESCO and UN environmental policies that endanger our economy and property rights. It would end U.S. participation in UN peace keeping missions, meaning we would no longer be helping to prop up criminal governments and enemies who seek our demise.

As the UN's irrelevance becomes clearer to the nation … the time has never been better to change the national mindset to say, "Get us out of the UN." The time is now.

Do you think that DeWeese's argument justifies his choice of words here? Does such language help or weaken his argument?

Many experts believe that Iraq had nothing to do with the terrorist attacks of 9/11. Who do you think are the "murderers" that Americans are defending themselves against?

Go to http://www.theorator.com/bills 108/hr1146.html to read the American Sovereignty Restoration Act of 2003. Do you think the United Nations could survive without the United States?

PRESIDENT BUSH MEETS WITH UN SECRETARY-GENERAL KOFI ANNAN...
The Office of the Press Secretary

On February 3, 2004, George W. Bush and Secretary-General Kofi Annan met in the Oval Office in the White House to discuss a range of issues. The meeting was viewed by observers as significant. Only a month before—at the World Economic Forum meeting in Switzerland—Annan had warned that the U.S. War on Terrorism could sharpen global tensions and endanger human rights and civil liberties.

Kofi Annan (1938–), from Ghana, has been secretary-general of the United Nations since 1997. In 2001 he and the UN jointly received the Nobel Peace Prize for "bringing new life" to the organization.

NO

THE PRESIDENT:

It's my honor to welcome the Secretary-General here to the Oval Office. We've just had a really constructive dialogue about a lot of issues. And the world is changing for the better and the United Nations is playing a vital role in that change. And we talked about Iraq and Afghanistan, Pakistan, India, the Middle East, the continent of Africa. And I'll let the Secretary-General speak for himself, but I'm upbeat and optimistic about the future of the world.

We've got a lot of work to do in certain areas and, obviously, a lot of focus right now on Iraq. And I have always said that the United Nations needs to play a vital role and it's an important role. And we have discussed ways to make sure that by working together the Iraqi people can be free, and their country stable and prosperous, and an example of democracy in the Middle East. And the United Nations does have a vital role there, and I look forward to working with the Secretary-General to achieve that.

THE SECRETARY-GENERAL:

Thank you very much, Mr. President. As you heard the President, we've had a very good and lengthy meeting on a whole host of issues. We realize that last year we were all taken up with war, the question of war and peace in Iraq. But we have many other issues to work on together, the President and I have agreed, other areas which are important that we will be working on.

Iraq

On Iraq, I believe that the stability of Iraq is in everyone's interest. The UN does have a role to play, and that's why following the meeting of 19 January, I have decided to send in a team, a team that will go in to try and work with the Iraqis in finding the way forward. Everyone agrees that sovereignty should be handed over to Iraq as soon as possible. The date of 30 June has been suggested, but there is some disagreement as to the mechanism for establishing

President George W. Bush and UN Secretary-General Kofi Annan shake hands at the 58th session of the UN General Assembly, New York, September 23, 2003.

An Iraqi man passes by a UN sign next to a banner of Saddam Hussein, former president of Iraq (Umm Qasr demilitarized zone on the Iraqi–Kuwait border).

the provisional government. And I hope this team I'm sending in will be able to play a role getting the Iraqis to understand that if they could come to some consensus and some agreement on how to establish that government, they're halfway there.

Building a future

We are going to go there to help the Iraqis, to help them establish a government that is Iraqi, a government that will work with them to assure their future, in terms of political and economic destiny. And the team will talk to as many Iraqis as possible and help them steer things in the right direction. The CPA—that is the Coalition led by Mr. Bremer, and the Iraqi Governing Council, when they met me in New York, indicated that they would accept the conclusions of the UN team. So we do have a chance to help break the impasse which exists at the moment and move forward.

On other issues, as the President indicated, we are going to work very closely together. We've had some successes and there are very positive developments around the world, which we are also going to try and build on and consolidate.

So thank you very much, Mr. President.

THE PRESIDENT:

Thank you.

Do you think UN involvement in the future of Iraq is crucial to the establishment of a democratic and free government? Go to www.cnn.com and www.bbc.co.uk to search for articles on this subject.

The Coalition Provisional Authority (CPA) was the temporary governing body of Iraq. It was designated by the UN as the lawful government of Iraq until the country became politically and socially stable enough to assume its own sovereignty. The CPA, administered by Ambassador L. Paul Bremer, III, was in power from the overthrow of Saddam Hussein's dictatorship in April 2003 until the restoration of self-rule in June 2004. Sheikh Ghazi al-Yawar (1958–) is president, and Dr. Ayad Allawi (1945–) is prime minister of the interim government.

Summary

In the first article Tom DeWeese lays the blame for the state of the world squarely at the feet of the United Nations. He argues that the organization consistently reacts to international crises with strategies of negotiation and dialogue that ultimately lead to inaction. He is critical of the UN for allowing nondemocratic countries to become member states. These same members, he contends, are seeking to impose global governance on sovereign states through their plans for, for example, the International Criminal Court (ICC). DeWeese claims that the United States is responsible for this situation because it allows the UN to exist through its financial support. He believes that the organization is irrelevant to world peace and insists that it would be in the interests of the United States to leave the international body.

The second extract, taken from comments made by President George W. Bush and UN Secretary-General Kofi Annan at the White House in February 2004, shows the valid role that the UN has to play in the War on Terrorism. Bush states, "the world is changing for the better and the United Nations is playing a vital role in that change." He claims that there is much still to be done in regions such as Africa and the Middle East, and that the UN has an important part in achieving peace in these areas. Annan validates this by stating that the United States and the UN will work closely together to achieve peace and bring order to regions that are in conflict. He says that although Iraq has taken up a great deal of time, there are other problems that also need to be addressed.

FURTHER INFORMATION:

Books:

Fasulo, Linda, *An Insider's Guide to the UN*. New Haven, CT: Yale University Press, 2004.

Meisler, Stanley, *United Nations: The First Fifty Years*. New York: Atlantic Monthly Press, 1995.

Schlesinger, Stephen, *Act of Creation: The Founding of the United Nations*. Boulder, CO: Westview Press, 2003.

Articles:

Pauken, Heidi, "UNderappreciated." *The American Prospect*, vol. 14, no. 7, July 3, 2003.

Useful websites:

http://www.lawac.org/speech/annan%202003.htm
Kofi Annan 2003 speech on the importance of the UN.

www.un.org
Official United Nations site.

The following debates in the Pro/Con series may also be of interest:

In this volume:
  Topic 6 Has the War on Terrorism reinforced U.S. global leadership?

In *Human Rights*:
  Topic 5 Has the Universal Declaration of Human Rights achieved anything significant?

  Topic 12 Is the UN an effective advocate for children's rights?

SHOULD THE UNITED NATIONS
BE DISBANDED?

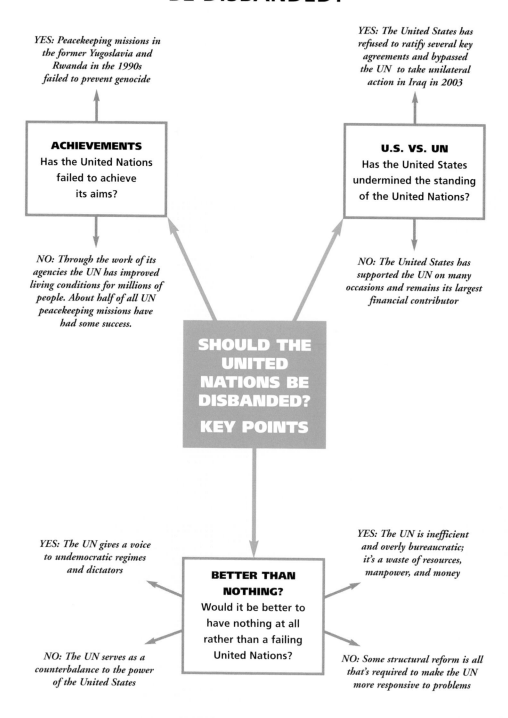

YES: Peacekeeping missions in the former Yugoslavia and Rwanda in the 1990s failed to prevent genocide

YES: The United States has refused to ratify several key agreements and bypassed the UN to take unilateral action in Iraq in 2003

ACHIEVEMENTS
Has the United Nations failed to achieve its aims?

U.S. VS. UN
Has the United States undermined the standing of the United Nations?

NO: Through the work of its agencies the UN has improved living conditions for millions of people. About half of all UN peacekeeping missions have had some success.

NO: The United States has supported the UN on many occasions and remains its largest financial contributor

SHOULD THE UNITED NATIONS BE DISBANDED?

KEY POINTS

YES: The UN gives a voice to undemocratic regimes and dictators

YES: The UN is inefficient and overly bureaucratic; it's a waste of resources, manpower, and money

BETTER THAN NOTHING?
Would it be better to have nothing at all rather than a failing United Nations?

NO: The UN serves as a counterbalance to the power of the United States

NO: Some structural reform is all that's required to make the UN more responsive to problems

Topic 9

IS NATO STILL NEEDED IN THE POST-COLD WAR WORLD?

YES

FROM "WINSTON CHURCHILL LECTURE"
WWW.NATO.INT, LONDON, NOVEMBER 24, 2003
LORD ROBERTSON

NO

"ADVICE FOR BUSH ON NATO: END IT, DON'T EXTEND IT"
WWW.LP.ORG, NOVEMBER 21, 2002
LIBERTARIAN PARTY ONLINE

INTRODUCTION

On April 4, 1949, the United States, Belgium, Canada, Denmark, France, Great Britain, Iceland, Italy, the Netherlands, Norway, and Portugal signed the North Atlantic Treaty in Washington, D.C., creating a military alliance of European and North American nations. The North Atlantic Treaty Organization (NATO) was created to provide mutual assistance should any one member of the alliance be attacked. It was formed after World War II (1939–1945) to combat and contain the perceived threat of Soviet communism. But since 1989, the end of the Cold War, and the dismantlement of the Soviet Union people have questioned what relevance NATO has to modern international security.

Critics believe that the development of new political alliances, the ongoing War on Terrorism, U.S. military superiority, and political and security developments in the European Union, among other things, mean that NATO

has no place in international affairs. Supporters, however, counter that NATO has played a vital part in late 20th- and early 21st-century conflict resolution. They argue that its expanding membership—it grew to 26 nations when seven former communist nations joined in 2004—shows how much it is valued.

The fundamental role of NATO is to safeguard the freedom and security of its member countries by political and military means. Member nations that participate in the military aspect of the alliance contribute forces and equipment that make up NATO's integrated military structure. Resources remain under national control until NATO requires them for a specific purpose, such as peacekeeping.

Since the 1990s NATO has played an increasingly important role in crisis management and peacekeeping. An example of this was its role in conflict resolution in the Balkans. In the early to mid-1990s, civil war and ethnic conflict made the region Europe's first post-Cold War challenge to peace. Solving the crisis in the Balkans required new forms of political and military cooperation. From 1995 NATO and Russian joint peacekeeping efforts were a key part of this process. Some believe that the establishment of the NATO–Russia Council in May 2002 shows how far their relationship has progressed since 1949.

> *"The ability to get to the verge without getting into … war is the necessary art."*
> —JOHN FOSTER DULLES, SECRETARY OF STATE (1953–1959)

NATO's involvement in European conflicts, however, has led opponents to claim that the organization is largely irrelevant to the United States and, thus, is a waste of taxpayers' money. They assert that the United States is militarily very strong, and that it can pursue any necessary action unilaterally or form alliances as and when they are needed. Critics also believe that U.S. military technology is so vastly superior to that of its European NATO allies that the United States has ended up defining how some conflicts have been resolved—again making the organization redundant. NATO's supporters, however, believe that the organization still fulfills an essential role: It provides an international forum in which European and North American countries can find a united way of dealing with security issues.

NATO's support of the United States following Al Qaeda's terrorist action on September 11, 2001, is, supporters claim, a good example of how this works. Less than 24 hours after the attack, and for the first time in its history, NATO invoked Article 5 of the North Atlantic Treaty, which states that an armed attack against one member nation is an attack against all.

Since then, supporters argue, NATO has provided essential support in the War on Terrorism by, among other things, sending Airborne Warning and Control Systems aircraft to help protect the United States and using NATO forces in the Balkans to act against terrorist groups with links to Al Qaeda. In 2003 NATO also took over command of the UN-mandated International Security Assistance Force established to provide security in Kabul Afghanistan, after U.S. military intervention in the country—NATO's first operation outside of Atlantic–European borders.

Some commentators believe that NATO is trying to adapt to the demands of the post-Cold War world. In 1999 NATO accepted the former Warsaw Pact members of Poland, the Czech Republic, and Hungary, and, in 2004, Estonia, Romania, Bulgaria, Latvia, Lithuania, Slovakia, and Slovenia as new members. It also has a good relationship with Russia. But NATO's existence has also been challenged by European countries: Both Germany and France want to establish a military alliance within the European Union, which some people believe is meant to undermine NATO.

Lord Robertson and the Libertarian Party discuss NATO's relevance further.

WINSTON CHURCHILL LECTURE
Lord Robertson

Former British Member of Parliament George Allen McNeil Robertson (1946–) was the 10th secretary-general of NATO (1999–2003). This extract is from the Winston Churchill Lecture that he gave in London on November 24, 2003.

At the Prague Summit, held in November 2002, NATO heads of state and governments invited Bulgaria, Estonia, Latvia, Lithuania, Romania, Slovakia, and Slovenia to begin discussions to join NATO. They became members in the May 2004 NATO session. If NATO is irrelevant to 21st-century international affairs, why might new countries be eager to become member states?

YES

✓ … My predecessor in NATO, Lord Carrington, used to say that NATO's strength was that the members sang in harmony, not in unison. He was right. It is not my job alone to argue the case for a strong Europe. My main focus will therefore be on the NATO Alliance, the embodiment of the transatlantic relationship.

The fact is, however, that a vibrant transatlantic relationship can only be sustained if Europe is healthy and strong. As we saw earlier this year over Iraq, dissension among Europeans damages NATO, the European Union and the UN just as surely as dissension across the Atlantic…. But this audience will know only too well that there always have been differences, among Europeans, and between Europeans and Americans. Suez, Vietnam, Star Wars, cruise missiles, Bosnia, Kosovo, the list is a long one. What you may be less aware of is the level of agreement that exists today among all 19 NATO members, plus the seven countries soon to join the Alliance and the EU members who are not part of NATO. Agreement on the challenges faced by all of us in this post 9/11 world, and agreement on how these challenges should be met.

It is often said that the strength of the Cold War alliance stemmed from a common understanding of the Soviet threat. The threat has changed beyond recognition. But the same common understanding has endured….

21st-century overspill

[The] five characteristics of the 21st century—instability, overspill, terrorism, failed or rogue states, and the proliferation of weapons of mass destruction—add up to a guaranteed supply chain of disorder. They add up to a security environment in which threats can strike at any time, without warning, from anywhere. Threats that could vary from a terrorist with a box-cutter on an airliner to a chemical weapon mounted on a ballistic missile. Threats that nobody can confidently predict. The good news is not only that there is agreement within Europe and across the Atlantic about this analysis, but that we also agree on how to respond. There is no chasm between unilateralists and multilateralists. Nor is there an unbridgeable gap between Atlanticists and

Europhiles.… The bottom line, recognised on both sides of the Atlantic, is that to face the post September 11 spectrum of transnational threats, the only credible response is multinational. And the most effective multinational co-operation in security and defence takes place where it has done for the past 50 years—in NATO.…

NATO can adapt

NATO had long since ceased to be a Cold War warrior. During the 1990s the Alliance intervened to bring peace and security to stricken Bosnia after the bloodiest civil war in recent European history. It acted to end Milosevic's brutal ethnic cleansing in Kosovo. In 2001 it prevented a civil war in Macedonia. It reached out to new democracies across Europe and into the former Soviet Union to build understanding and promote co-operation throughout a Euro-Atlantic partnership area stretching from Vancouver to Vladivostock. It began the process of engagement with Russia, tentative steps but a welcome contrast to the hostility of the Cold War. September 11 changed the rules completely. But NATO proved equal to the task.

Our declaration of Article 5 of NATO's Washington Treaty on 12 September 2001, which made the attack on the United States an attack on all nineteen NATO countries, turned Churchill's famous dictum on its head. The old world came to the aid of the new. A commitment to common defence, designed to enable the United States to save Europe, was invoked for the first time ever to allow Europeans to help protect the United States. Article 5 was an immense political symbol. But it was much more than that. It made NATO an active participant in the war against terrorism.…

Four themes underpin NATO's transformation. Four themes which bind Europe and America together in a common cause to protect our people from the dangers of today, just as NATO did from the dangers of the Cold War and its aftermath. The first derives directly from September 11. NATO has formally taken on a range of vital new missions. We continue to fight terrorism on the ground and at sea in Europe and North America. But we have also abandoned the geographical constraints on NATO operations which hamstrung the Alliance throughout the 1990s.

Then we were told by critics that NATO had to go out of area or out of business. In 2002, the 19 NATO members agreed that the Alliance must meet threats from wherever they may come. In 2003, NATO is in Afghanistan doing just that. In parallel, we have turned NATO into the motor for

Some people believe that the terrorist action of September 11, 2001, taken against the United States by Al Qaeda, changed how international security and defense issues were dealt with. If this is the case, is NATO really the best organization through which "effective multinational" cooperation can take place? Go to www.nato.int (the official website) and www.cnn.com to look at recent analysis of the issue.

The North Atlantic Treaty came into being on April 4, 1949. Article 5 (see http://www.nato.int/docu/basictxt/treaty.htm#Art05) states that an armed attack against one member nation is an armed attack against all member nations.

Weapons of mass destruction (WMD) can be used to annihilate large numbers of people. They can be nuclear, chemical biological, or radiological weapons. The War on Terrorism has been directed partly by the desire to eliminate the threat of WMDs by taking action against nations that may use them.

Following a request from Turkey, NATO sent surveillance aircraft and defense forces in February 2003 to protect the Turkish people in the event of an Iraqi attack resulting from the invasion of Iraq. The operation was conducted under the overall command of the Supreme Allied Commander Europe (SACEUR) and was run by NATO's regional headquarters southern Europe (AFSOUTH). It ended on April 16, 2003.

developing military plans and concepts to guide the contribution of armed forces in the war against terrorism and in defending ourselves against weapons of mass destruction....

[N]ew partnerships was the second transformation theme at Prague. No single organisation can defeat today's threats alone. We are stronger and more effective when we work closely together.... Most striking of all these new partnerships is that between NATO and Russia. No longer is our relationship clouded by Cold War stereotypes and suspicions. September 11 put us firmly on the same side in a new war against disorder and extremism.... We do not agree on everything. But we have at last booted the Cold War firmly into the history books where it belongs....

Nato in crisis vs. action

[L]et me give you two vignettes, one of NATO in crisis and one of the new NATO in action. Both are unashamedly intended to show that the transatlantic Alliance remains a real working partnership. The first example is what many said was NATO's most difficult hour, the row over Iraq and in particular the so-called crisis over Turkey's request for help to deter an attack by Saddam in the run up to the war last spring. This was indeed a real crisis for the Alliance, with deeply and honestly held views on both sides. Turkey felt vulnerable. Most Allies, whether or not they were involved in the anti-Saddam Coalition, believed that it was right for NATO to help. But four countries believed that to do so would deepen the crisis. They argued that NATO support was premature. For eleven days we met, talked and failed to reach agreement. The press became frenzied. There was talk of the end of the Alliance. Yet during those eleven days, the four countries separately came to the view either that circumstances had changed and the time was right for NATO to act, or that the case for joining consensus now outweighed that for staying aloof. NATO's decision-making machinery was also sufficiently flexible to allow consensus to be reached without loss of face on any side. Eleven days may sound a long time. For those of us directly involved, it seemed like a lifetime. It was, in fact, a shorter time than NATO took to agree a similar deployment to Turkey before the first Gulf War. More importantly, NATO reached an agreement on action. No other international organisation was able to do so....

Commitments were met. Collective security worked. Sceptics worried, however, that NATO had been broken in the process. Consensus would be impossible in future. In fact, NATO healed quickly. It always does....

My second vignette follows on from the decision on Afghanistan. Since last August, NATO has been supporting the efforts of President Karzai, a good and able leader, to bring security to the capital, Kabul. ... Afghanistan matters, really matters, to everyone in Europe. As I said earlier, if we do not go to Afghanistan and deal with its problems, Afghanistan and those problems will come again to us.

It was therefore an uplifting experience to visit the International Security Assistance Force in Kabul for the first time a matter of weeks ago.... Everyone was working with a sense of common purpose which flowed from fifty years of mutual trust and cooperation in NATO. I pay tribute to all of those whose work and dedication during those years is now paying dividends in such unexpected circumstances, a continent and a half away from the Cold War theatres where NATO first came into being....

In December 2001 Hamid Karzai (1957–) was appointed the U.S.-sponsored interim president of Afghanistan. The first post-Taliban elections were scheduled for June 2004. They were later postponed to September 2004 in order that the parliamentary and presidential elections could be held at the same time.

Confidence

One of the reasons that I am so confident about this is that the two institutional manifestations of Atlanticism and of Europe, NATO and the European Union, are locked together not in competition but in cooperation....

[T]o those of you who are following the twists and turns of the EU's Intergovernmental Conference Negotiations, which some observers see as another blow by Europeans against NATO, I say: remember that this is not a zero sum game. A stronger Europe does not automatically mean a weaker NATO. Look instead at what a stronger Europe actually delivers in practice.

A "zero sum game" is one in which the gain for one player entails a loss for the other.

If the result is a Europe able to put more, better equipped soldiers into the field, whether in NATO or, where more appropriate, under EU, UN or coalition command, I will welcome it. Because that will reinforce not weaken NATO....

Today's transformed NATO, of which I have been proud to be Secretary General for these past four extraordinary years, is I believe the right vehicle for much of this action to be successfully pursued.

NATO bridges the Atlantic. It binds in partners from Ireland through Russia to Central Asia. It allows friends to disagree without falling out. It is the platform for all successful military operations. And it has a record of unparalleled success.

Most of all, it makes hard choices unnecessary.

Go to www.NATO.int and look at the archived articles. Has NATO been as successful as the author claims? Would a wider international military force be more effective?

ADVICE FOR BUSH ON NATO: END IT, DON'T EXTEND IT
Libertarian Party Online

NO

Instead of welcoming several new countries into NATO at the summit that begins today in Prague, President Bush should pull the United States out of the unnecessary alliance and save taxpayers billions of dollars in "military welfare" costs, Libertarians say.

The Libertarian Party view

"NATO might as well stand for Never-ending American Taxpayer Obligation," said Geoff Neale, the national chair of the Libertarian Party. "There's no reason that the United States should keep paying to defend rich European nations like France, England and Germany against a Soviet threat that no longer exists."

Bush intends to use the two-day NATO summit as a forum to consult with European leaders over his possible war plans on Iraq. The president also plans to welcome into NATO several new members—including Estonia, Latvia and Lithuania—which he says will "bring new life to the trans-Atlantic alliance."

But the last thing NATO needs is new members, Libertarians say, especially since U.S. taxpayers will be paying part of their membership dues.

Nothing so permanent

"NATO is living proof that there's nothing quite so permanent as a temporary government program," Neale said. "This alliance was created after World War II to protect Western Europe from a belligerent communist dictatorship in the USSR. Yet instead of letting NATO quietly expire when the Soviet Union collapsed, politicians have put it on life support by constantly finding new missions."

For example, NATO currently has thousands of troops on peacekeeping and humanitarian missions in Bosnia, Macedonia, and Albania—deployments that cost Americans an estimated $13 billion per year, Neale noted.

Humanitarian missions should be performed by humanitarian organizations, such as the Red Cross, not done

Although the Cold War has ended, international security is under threat from a number of sources, and NATO has helped in peace resolution in the last 15 years or so. Since NATO's original mandate no longer exists, should it automatically be disbanded?

George W. Bush (front) with the American delegation at the opening meeting of Nato Council, Czech Republic, November 21, 2002. The delegation from left to right behind Bush includes Nato Ambassador Nicholas Burn, Security Adviser Condoleezza Rice, and Defense Secretary Donald Rumsfield.

COMMENTARY: NATO in the 21st century

At the November 2002 Prague summit NATO heads of state gave the green light for a further seven countries to join the organization. Three former Warsaw Pact countries (Bulgaria, Romania, and Slovakia), three former Soviet republics (Estonia, Latvia, and Lithuania), and Slovenia, formerly part of Yugoslavia, became full member states of NATO in May 2004. They followed in the footsteps of Poland, Hungary, and the Czech Republic, which joined the organization in 1999.

NATO's admission of new member states has brought mixed reactions from the international community. Although their addition has brought NATO's membership up to 26 countries and has made it responsible for around 44 million more citizens, some commentators question what benefits these new nation states can bring to the organization at a time when many question NATO's relevance in international security at all.

NATO vs. the European Union

Some security analysts worry that NATO's enlargement will make it more difficult to reach a consensus on important decisions. Lord Robertson, the former secretary-general, however, believes that the opposite will be true. He argues that new members will help make Europe a united security space and will also reduce the risk of future European-based conflicts. In September 2003, however, the British newspaper *The Financial Times* published an internal document agreed at a weekend summit between British Prime Minister Tony Blair, French President Jacques Chirac, and German Chancellor Gerhard Schroeder, which stated, "The European Union should be endowed with a joint capacity to plan and conduct operations without recourse to NATO resources and capabilities." This, commentators believe, would considerably undermine the military importance of NATO.

A two-tier system

Some people have particularly questioned NATO's role since the terrorist action against the United States on September 11, 2001. They believe that the United States has sidelined NATO on many occasions in order to provide a quick military response. They assert that U.S. military technology is vastly superior to that of most European NATO member states, and that the latter would have to spend billions of dollars to upgrade their surveillance and precision-weapon capability, for example, to bring them up to U.S. standards. In the absence of increased European spending some commentators have suggested a two-tier system within NATO in which U.S. operations would involve high-intensity, technology-led conflict, and European countries would come in to clean up afterward. Critics, however, believe that this scenario is completely unrealistic, proving that NATO does not work anymore.

by NATO at taxpayer expense," Neale said. "If wealthy European nations want to spend billions of dollars on humanitarian missions, that's their business. But there's no reason to force Americans to pick up the tab for an international welfare program masquerading as a military alliance."

Does the United States, as a leading advocate of democracy and peace, have a duty to fund humanitarian missions?

Estimating the actual costs of NATO expansion is difficult, Neale explained. "Perhaps sensing that the U.S. public resents subsidizing Europe's defense, previous budget figures have been classified by NATO bureaucrats," he said. "But military analysts estimate that in 1997, when the alliance expanded to include Poland, Hungary, and the Czech Republic, the U.S. share came to more than $35 billion—a sum that could be equaled by Bush's proposed expansion. "That's a lot to spend defending Europe from an imaginary enemy."

Earlier this week, even Bush seemed to admit that NATO was unnecessary, Neale noted, when he told Radio Free Europe that, "The Warsaw Pact doesn't exist."

But apparently a sense of sympathy for the taxpayers who must fund NATO doesn't exist either, Libertarians say.

"Remaining in this obsolete military alliance may be a good deal for foreign politicians, but it's a raw deal for the American public," Neale said. "It's time to kick European governments off the welfare wagon, and pull the United States out of NATO."

The author refers to U.S. support of NATO as "welfare." Is this a fair comparison? Or is it clever use of an emotionally charged word?

Summary

The preceding two articles take opposing views on whether NATO has any relevance in the post-Cold War world.

Lord Robertson, the author of the first article, is strongly in favor of continuing and expanding NATO. His main point is that a militarily strong European Union would not damage NATO but would instead serve the interests of all concerned. Europe and North America share many common security concerns in the 21st century, and NATO is the perfect organization to collaborate on these issues. The bottom line is that post-September 11, 2001, the only credible response to transnational threats is multinational, and NATO is the most effective body for such action.

The Libertarian Party, on the other hand, believes that George W. Bush should withdraw the United States from NATO and save taxpayers billions of dollars. The LP argues that there is no reason for the United States to keep paying to support rich European nations, such as France, England, and Germany, against a Soviet threat that no longer exists. Since the end of the Cold War, it argues, politicians have kept NATO going by continually finding new missions that should be instead funded by the Europeans.

In short, NATO may be a good deal for foreign politicians, but it is a raw deal for the American public that must stop.

FURTHER INFORMATION:

Books:

Duigan, Peter, *NATO: Its Past, Present, and Future.* Stanford, CA: Hoover Institute Press, 2000.
Galen, Ted (ed.), *NATO Enters the 21st Century.* London: Frank Cass, 2001.

Useful websites:

http://www.cato.org/pubs/handbook/hb108/hb108-51.pdf
Cato Institute analysis of Congress's policy toward NATO.
http://www.cesd.org/natonotes/natorel.htm
Center for European Security and Disarmament article on NATO's relevance.
http://www.csis.org/europe/euroforum/v3n2.pdf
Center for Strategic Studies document on reassessing NATO's importance.
http://www.isn.ethz.ch/php/
Site of Parallel History Project (PHP), features many declassified documents relating to NATO.
www.nato.int
NATO's official site.

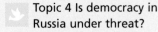

The following debates in the Pro/Con series may also be of interest:

In this volume:
Topic 4 Is democracy in Russia under threat?

Topic 8 Should the United Nations be disbanded?

In *U.S. Foreign Policy*:
Part 1: The United States' position in the world

September 11, 2001, pages 176–177

IS NATO STILL NEEDED IN THE POST-COLD WAR WORLD?

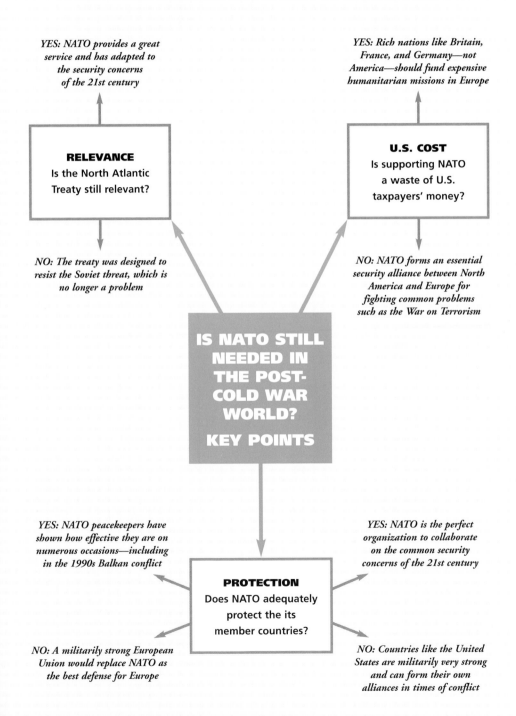

YES: NATO provides a great service and has adapted to the security concerns of the 21st century

YES: Rich nations like Britain, France, and Germany—not America—should fund expensive humanitarian missions in Europe

RELEVANCE
Is the North Atlantic Treaty still relevant?

U.S. COST
Is supporting NATO a waste of U.S. taxpayers' money?

NO: The treaty was designed to resist the Soviet threat, which is no longer a problem

NO: NATO forms an essential security alliance between North America and Europe for fighting common problems such as the War on Terrorism

IS NATO STILL NEEDED IN THE POST-COLD WAR WORLD?

KEY POINTS

YES: NATO peacekeepers have shown how effective they are on numerous occasions—including in the 1990s Balkan conflict

YES: NATO is the perfect organization to collaborate on the common security concerns of the 21st century

PROTECTION
Does NATO adequately protect the its member countries?

NO: A militarily strong European Union would replace NATO as the best defense for Europe

NO: Countries like the United States are militarily very strong and can form their own alliances in times of conflict

INTRODUCTION

The European Union (EU) is a treaty organization that manages economic and political cooperation between its members. In 2004 the EU grew from 15 to 25 states. Commentators predict that enlargement will have a great impact on the future of the EU. Member states debated a constitution outlining reform of the organization. While people agree that it is vital to streamline the EU, some fear that states risk delegating too much decision-making power. Others argue that the future of the EU lies with integration. They favor a more centralized, federal system that equates to a "United States of Europe."

The first leading politician to advocate a united Europe was Aristide Briand (1862–1932). In 1930, as French foreign minister, he proposed a federal union of European states within the structure of the League of Nations (the forerunner of the United Nations). His initiative did not find support, but the destruction caused by World War II

(1939–1945) gave Europe's leaders new impetus to find a way of rebuilding the continent and achieving lasting peace. Speaking in 1946, Winston Churchill (1874–1965), Britain's wartime prime minister, argued that only "a kind of United States of Europe" could prevent future conflict.

The EU has its roots in the 1951 treaty that founded the European Coal and Steel Community (ECSC). The ECSC pooled the coal and steel supplies of France, Belgium, Italy, Luxembourg, the Netherlands, and West Germany (the "Six") under a supranational authority. It was established in the belief that war between states would be impossible if they bound their economic interests and delegated part of their sovereignty to a higher power. In 1956 the Six set up the European Economic Community (EEC) with the aim of promoting a common market based on free trade. The ultimate goal, a single currency, was achieved in 2002 when 12 member states adopted the euro. After the 2004 enlargement, the EU—as it has been known since the Maastricht Treaty on European Union came into force in 1993—became the world's largest trading bloc, with 455 million citizens.

"There is no alternative to ever-closer integration among the European peoples."
—HELMUT KOHL, FORMER GERMAN CHANCELLOR (1998)

Some commentators insist that a United States of Europe represents a logical progression for the EU. Their opinion is that the EU must address political matters now that economic integration has been successful. They say that reform is vital to accommodate the new member states, and this should entail taking a larger view of the EU's direction. The Maastricht Treaty moved toward developing the EU's political dimension. It made provision for states to collaborate on a unified foreign and security policy and to cooperate more in judicial and domestic affairs. The EU constitution may bring full integration closer still. It proposes to make the EU Charter of Fundamental Rights, which sets out the civil, political, economic, and social rights of citizens, legally binding on member states. It also plans to institute a European defense force, an EU public prosecutor, an EU foreign minister, and a permanent president for the European Council. Some supporters of a United States of Europe say that the pace of political integration is still too slow, and that more power should be

given to a radically reformed European Parliament. They argue that an "inner core" of states should pursue faster, more advanced integration.

Critics of further integration say that a federation is unworkable because the continent has many peoples of different cultures, languages, and histories. These peoples, critics say, identify with their national institutions more than those of the EU, and they regard themselves as citizens of their own countries rather than Europeans. Some critics also maintain that the EU is financially inefficient. They cite the common agricultural policy (CAP), a system of subsidies for farmers, as an example of how close economic and political ties between member states can prove costly. They claim that EU laws place a bureaucratic burden on businesses and reduce their ability to compete. Critics insist that member states should be able to retain control over policies that serve their national interest. For example, Britain said that it would sign the EU constitution only if key areas such as foreign policy, criminal justice, taxation, and defense remain the prerogative of state governments. The constitution's critics say that far from simplifying the EU, it would give it the attributes of a state, such as its own legal system. They argue that the EU can work well as a model of close cooperation without imposing what Michael Howard, the leader of the British Conservative Party, has called a "straitjacket of uniformity" on member states. For example, Britain, Denmark, and Sweden chose not to join the single currency, but neither their national economies nor the euro were adversely affected by this decision.

BusinessWeek reporter John Rossant and British journalist Ian Black consider these issues in the following articles.

A UNITED STATES OF EUROPE?
John Rossant

John Rossant is European editor of BusinessWeek magazine. He reports on a speech given in May 2000 by German Foreign Minister Joschka Fischer. European Affairs journal described the speech as likely to be a key document on Europe's future.

YES

It's not every day that a high German official lobs a bomb into the European body politic. But that's what German Foreign Minister Joschka Fischer did in a May 12 speech at Berlin's venerable Humboldt University. With as many as 12 new members joining the European Union from Eastern and Southeastern Europe over the next decade, the loosely organized EU must become a more cohesive political federation, Fischer forcefully argued, or risk losing the benefits of a half-century of economic integration. "And that means nothing less than a European Parliament and European government which really do exercise legislative and executive power." There's another way to say this: Fischer is talking about a United States of Europe.

That's a fearsome thought to some Europeans, accustomed to the tradition of the nation-state. So it's no surprise that many commentators sought to devalue Fischer's remarks. Some figured Fischer wanted to revive the sagging fortunes of his Green Party with a splashy speech. Others saw more sinister motives: French Interior Minister Jean-Pierre Chevenement attacked Fischer's ideas as proof that Germany was not yet cured of Nazism.

Joschka Fischer (1948–) has been consistently rated as the most popular politician in Germany in recent years. He became the country's foreign minister and vice-chancellor in 1998. Fischer survived a scandal in 2001 when it was revealed that he attacked a policeman during a demonstration in 1973.

Think about the endgame

But Fischer's point is one all Europeans must face: It's time Europe began thinking seriously about the endgame of integration. For years, political leaders have discussed the future only by way of linguistic contortions and subterfuges—from "subsidiarity" to "variable geometry." In effect, Fischer's bomb explodes the notion that Europe can continue to muddle along as no more than an economic construct. As he asserted, economic integration—the industrial and financial consolidation that has followed the launch of the euro last year—must be accompanied by parallel innovations on the political side....

A "Gaullist" follows the philosophy of Charles de Gaulle (1890–1969), president of France from 1958 to 1969. In 2004 Alain Juppé was convicted of involvement in a political funding scam in the 1980s.

[E]ven prominent Gaullists such as Alain Juppé, Bordeaux's mayor and a former prime minister, are out in support of Fischer's vision. There are numerous signs that French leaders, happy to have others put the issue on the agenda, gave an advance nod to the speech.

German Foreign Minister Joschka Fischer (right) created controversy with his call for nation-states to have a much smaller role in a federal Europe.

COMMENTARY: Scandal hits the EU

The European Commission is the driving force of the EU. As its executive body, it proposes new legislation to the European Parliament and the Council of the European Union; it implements the policies of the EU and manages its budget; and it represents the EU on the international stage. A new commission is appointed every five years. It is composed of a president and a team of commissioners.

In March 1999 the EU faced one of the biggest crises in its history when an independent investigation into allegations of corruption—led to the resignation of all 20 commissioners. The president of the commission at the time was Jacques Santer (1937–), the former prime minister of Luxembourg. He had been appointed in 1995 as a compromise choice after the United Kingdom refused to allow the job to go to the Belgian Jean-Luc Dehaene, whom the British feared as having a European "superstate" agenda. Critics accused Santer of weak management at a crucial time for the EU, when it was beginning to discuss reform in preparation for enlargement and when the single currency, the euro, had just been officially launched as the centerpiece of economic and monetary union.

The report of the investigation, which had been instigated by the European Parliament, appeared to confirm the image that some skeptics have of the EU—that it is an overpaid, underworked bureaucracy. It found that the commission had lost control of its 19,000-strong staff in Brussels, Belgium, and it accused several commissioners of mismanagement and cronyism. Edith Cresson, a former French prime minister, was criticized for having lax control over a vocational-training program and for appointing a dentist friend of hers to head a research project. Two other commissioners were also singled out for putting friends and relatives on their payrolls. Santer faced less serious criticism for failing to deal with allegations of fraud within the commission's security services. While the report made it clear that no commissioner was "directly and personally" involved in fraud or had enriched him- or herself, its stinging conclusion—that "it is becoming difficult to find anyone who has even the slightest sense of responsibility"—was enough to oblige the commission to resign en masse the day after its publication.

Controversy continues for the commission

Santer's replacement was Romano Prodi (1939–), prime minister of Italy between 1996 and 1999. In the fall of 2003 scandal threatened the commission again with the publication of a series of reports on fraud allegations at the EU statistics agency, Eurostat. Prodi courted further controversy when he urged Italy's center-left political parties to join forces in the 2004 European elections. Critics accused him of acting irresponsibly and undermining the neutrality of his position within the EU.

Fischer and like-minded allies are already fielding ideas as to the organization of a federation. A new parliament could have two chambers: Member states might send two or more senators to the upper body, while the lower would consist of members who also sit in their national legislatures. Fischer calls it "a Europe of nation-states and a Europe of citizens."

It's years away, surely. Despite some reforms, the European Commission in Brussels remains an unelected and largely unaccountable bureaucracy: Important political decisions require the unanimous approval of all member states. It's a recipe for inaction. Remember Henry Kissinger's barbed quip? "When I need to get in touch with the Kremlin, I know who to call. When I need to get in touch with Europe, who do I call?" It's as true now as it was during Kissinger's days as U.S. Secretary of State.

Commentators argue that the fact the commission, which is the EU executive, is unelected is part of the reason why so many Europeans appear uninterested by EU politics. Do you think that this is a valid point?

Europe's political weakness

No European can be happy with the Continent's political weakness. For one thing, it's the dirty secret behind at least some of the euro's decline: Faced with a cacophony of national voices on this policy and that, no wonder investors have been dumping the common currency. For another, it's impossible to contemplate EU enlargement without doing some new political thinking. Utter paralysis is the alternative.

Fischer's speech may seem futuristic, but he has advanced a logical first step: Nations eager to move quickly on political reform should form a "core group" others can join. Fischer thus teams up with former EC President Jacques Delors, former German Chancellor Helmut Schmidt, and former French President Valéry Giscard d'Estaing. All three have recently called for an avant-garde that can form a constitutional convention to hammer out the terms of the federal experiment.

Do you think that it is realistic to draw a comparison between modern Europe and the creation of the United States?

Americans should find this familiar. The first 13 states spent years feeling their way toward what became the U.S.— which was a work in progress even after Washington was elected the first President in 1789. So it will be in Europe. Joschka Fischer has announced an era that promises to be as exhilarating as those formative years in U.S. history.

GISCARD UNVEILS DRAFT FOR "UNITED EUROPE"
Ian Black

NO

The former French president Valéry Giscard d'Estaing ran into immediate British opposition to some of his key ideas when he unveiled a carefully-balanced draft for a European Union constitution yesterday.

Senior government sources insisted that there was "not a cat in hell's chance" that the union could be renamed the United States of Europe or United Europe: two of the suggestions in the document.

Mr Giscard began the final phase of the convention on the EU's future by presenting his document after months of heated discussion about how to run an enlarged union of 25 or more members from 2004.

Tony Blair gave a guarded welcome to the blueprint in a Commons statement devoted to last week's Brussels summit spat with Jacques Chirac, the current French president, about the reform of the common agricultural policy.

Mr Giscard's draft proposals, the prime minister said, clearly emphasising the positive, made it clear that "Europe should cooperate as a union of European states, not a federal superstate".

What's in a name?

But government sources were adamant that there were "red lines" in the document that Britain found unacceptable, especially what the EU should be called in 2004.

Article one says it could be called the European Community, the European Union, United Europe (Mr Giscard's favourite) or the United States of Europe.

Britain's response was swift and blunt. "There is not a cat in hell's chance of it being called the United States of Europe," a senior official said. "If anything, it will be called the European Union."

The convention, which is preparing the most ambitious reorganisation the union has ever undergone, has 105 representatives of the 15 current member states, the 13 candidate countries [10 new entrants, plus Bulgaria, Romania, and Turkey] and the European and national parliaments.

The former French President Valéry Giscard d'Estaing headed the convention that drafted the EU constitution. The draft received criticism from euroskeptics and enthusiasts alike.

The full text of the draft constitution was completed in July 2003. It was debated at an intergovernmental conference in the fall, but at a summit in Brussels in December the EU heads of government reached deadlock on the final text. They disagreed on a new system of voting rights. Discussions resumed in 2004.

A "euroskeptic" is someone who opposes further European integration. This attitude is associated with some members of the British Conservative, or Tory, Party.

"MEP" stands for "member of the European Parliament." MEPs have been directly elected by the citizens of the EU member states since 1979. Elections are held every five years. The European Parliament shares the legislative power of the EU with the Council of the European Union.

Its brief is to make the union's unwieldy and outdated structures work better and to try to bridge the often yawning gap between disenchanted citizens and remote institutions, partly by explaining precisely the complex division of powers between the union and its members.

British officials gave a warm welcome to the proposed article eight, which makes clear the primacy of the nation state. "Any competence not conferred on the union by the constitution rests with the member states," it says.

Mr Giscard's text is a skeleton, suggesting only brief chapter headings for the constitutional treaty, but it nevertheless gives a clear sense of the direction he is likely to take when the final version is published next summer.

It contains something for almost everyone. Article one, for example, describes "a union of European states which, while retaining their national identities, closely coordinate their policies at the European level, and administer certain common competences on a federal basis".

Unsurprisingly, the draft attracted praise and condemnation from across the political spectrum. David Heathcoat-Amory, a Tory Euroskeptic and convention delegate, said the draft would endow the EU with "all the attributes of a state", and condemned what he called a "federal advance".

But Andrew Duff, the British chairman of the convention's Liberal Democrat caucus, was jubilant. "It allows for a radical refoundation of the EU along explicitly federalist lines," he said.

A moral dimension

Another key point is that that the constitution should include the EU's charter of fundamental rights, to give a moral dimension to the union and underline that the project is about more than just a single market and currency.

Britain has in the past fiercely opposed this, on the grounds that it might anchor new social rights in EU law, but government sources said it might now be acceptable.

The draft also suggests a way for countries to leave the EU, and the idea of a congress, including MEPs and members of national parliaments, to oversee its strategic direction.

The text refers to the term of office and appointment procedures for a president for the European council. This proposal is strongly backed by Britain, France and Spain, but opposed by smaller states which fear a loss of influence.

Mr Giscard said last week that there was a "very broad consensus" for having a European president and ending the current practice of a six-month rotating presidency.

SOME OF THE MAIN POINTS:

Values and objectives

The draft constitution sets out the foundation stones of
the EU: "human dignity, fundamental rights, democracy, the
rule of law, tolerance, etc." Its aims include promoting social
cohesion, strengthening economic and monetary union,
and high employment.

Name

The European Union, the European Community, United States
of Europe or United Europe. Membership would be open to
"all European states which share the same values".

Citizenship

It establishes and defines union citizenship, giving citizens of
member states dual citizenship.

Powers and competences

The constitution will define the powers of the EU's
main bodies: the supranational European commission,
the directly elected European parliament and the European
council. It lists areas of union competence and those
shared with the states.

Go to http://europa. eu.int/institutions/ index_en.htm to read an explanation of the main EU institutions.

Withdrawal

The document will establish the procedure for leaving the
club. Article 45 establishes the procedure for the suspension
of a member state which violates its principles and values.

Summary

In the first article John Rossant reports on a May 2000 speech given by Joschka Fischer, the German foreign minister. He agrees with Fischer that the EU must consider its long-term political future. Rossant states that other leading European politicians share Fischer's views on a federation of states; he outlines their ideas for a bicameral (two-house) European Parliament. But he maintains that the organization has a long way to go before this vision becomes a reality. Rossant is critical of the EU's political impotence, which he considers to be responsible for the relative weakness of the single currency, the euro. He argues that enlargement of the union is unthinkable without reform. Rossant backs Fischer's call for a core group of nations to take the first steps toward a federation, and he draws a parallel between the idea for a constitutional convention with the formation of the United States.

Ian Black, on the other hand, writes about the reception that an early draft of the new EU constitution got from the government of the United Kingdom. He reports that there was fundamental British opposition in particular to proposals for renaming the European Union "United Europe" or the "United States of Europe." Black also cites the views of other British politicians, both those who condemn what they see as an advance toward federalism and those who welcome it. He details other issues raised by the draft constitution, such as the inclusion of the EU Charter of Fundamental Rights and the appointment of a permanent European president. Black concludes by outlining some of the main points of the draft, such as the powers to be held by each of the EU institutions.

FURTHER INFORMATION:

 Books:

Bomberg, Elizabeth, and Alexander Stubb (eds.), *The European Union: How Does It Work?* New York: Oxford University Press, 2003.

Booker, Christopher, and Richard North, *The Great Deception: A Secret History of the European Union*. New York: Continuum, 2003.

McCormick, John, *Understanding the European Union: A Concise Introduction* (2nd edition). New York: Palgrave Macmillan, 2002.

 Useful websites:

http://europa.eu.int/index_en.htm
Europa, the official EU site.
http://eurunion.org/
European Union in the United States, a good guide to the basics of the EU.

http://www.jeanmonnetprogram.org/papers/00/joschka_fischer_en.rtf
Text of Joschka Fischer's speech on European integration in May 2000.

The following debates in the Pro/Con series may also be of interest:

In this volume:
 Topic 2 Is the nation-state consistent with the idea of globalization?

The European Union (EU), pages 138–139

IS A UNITED STATES OF EUROPE POSSIBLE?

YES: Economic integration has succeeded in establishing a single market and a common currency

SUCCESS STORY?
Is the European Union an effective organization?

NO: The EU is bureaucratic and inefficient; without political reform it will reach administrative gridlock after enlargement

YES: The unrestricted movement of people, goods, services, and capital in Europe has made state borders redundant

NATION-STATE
Is the idea of independent nation-states outdated?

NO: Europe is a continent of many different cultures, languages, and histories. Its peoples retain strong allegiances to individual nation-states and their institutions.

IS A UNITED STATES OF EUROPE POSSIBLE?

KEY POINTS

YES: Some of the reforms proposed in the constitution, such as an EU legal system, will give the organization the trappings of an actual state

EU CONSTITUTION
Will the EU constitution bring political integration closer?

NO: The basic purpose of the constitution is to simplify the day-to-day running of the EU; its proposed reforms are not greatly significant

YES: A USE would have a more coherent role in international affairs and would simplify foreign policy for the United States

USA AND USE
Would the United States of America prefer a United States of Europe?

NO: France and Germany would be likely to be core states within a USE; the United States has traditionally had a much closer relationship with Britain

THE EUROPEAN UNION (EU)

"Our task … is to shape a responsive European Union—in touch with the people, transparent and easier to understand, strengthened by its nations and regions, an EU whose vision of peace is matched by its vision of prosperity …"

—TONY BLAIR, BRITISH PRIME MINISTER, WARSAW (2000)

The European Union (EU) is an international organization composed of 25 member states. The EU is the latest stage in a process of economic and political integration that began with the establishment of the European Coal and Steel Community (ECSC) in 1951. The authority of the EU has gradually developed through a series of treaty agreements covering certain areas in which member states have agreed to pool their sovereignty—they include trade, transport, the environment, and employment. The three main institutions of the EU are the European Parliament, the Council of the European Union, and the European Commission.

May 9, 1950 French Foreign Minister Robert Schuman (1886–1963) proposes that France, West Germany, and any other European country that wishes to join them should pool their coal and steel resources.

April 18, 1951 France, West Germany, Belgium, Italy, Luxembourg, and the Netherlands ("the Six") sign the Treaty of Paris, which establishes the European Coal and Steel Community (ECSC). The production and use of coal and steel are planned by an independent supranational body called the High Authority.

May 27, 1952 The Six sign the European Defence Community (EDC) treaty in Paris. Its aim is to establish a common European army.

1954 August 30: The French parliament refuses to ratify the EDC treaty. **October 23:** In response to the failed EDC treaty the Western European Union comes into being. Its members—the Six plus Britain—agree to cooperate on defense and security.

June 1–2, 1955 The Six agree to aim for the complete integration of their economies.

March 25, 1957 The Six sign the Treaties of Rome, which establish the European Economic Community (EEC) and the European Atomic Energy Community (Euratom). The aim of the EEC is to create a common market with no trade barriers.

January 4, 1960 The agreement establishing the European Free Trade Association (EFTA) as an alternative to the ECC is signed by Austria, Denmark, Norway, Portugal, Sweden, Switzerland, and the United Kingdom.

July 30, 1962 The EEC launches a common agricultural policy (CAP). It pays subsidies to farmers in order to guarantee minimum levels of production.

July 1, 1967 The executive bodies of the ECSC, EEC, and Euratom merge to form a single Council and a single Commission of the European Communities (EC).

July 1, 1968 Customs duties on goods traded within the EC are abolished. The Common Customs Tariff is introduced to replace national customs duties in external trade.

January 1, 1973 First enlargement: Denmark, Ireland, and the United Kingdom join the EC.

December 9–10, 1974 The EC's heads of government agree to institutionalize summit meetings in the form of a European Council, to set up direct elections to the European Parliament, and to establish the European Regional Development Fund (ERDF).

February 28, 1975 The EC and 46 African, Caribbean, and Pacific (ACP) states sign the Lomé Convention, which gives the ACP states aid, investment, and free entry for their goods into the EC. Further conventions are signed in 1979, 1984, and 1989.

1979 March 13: The European Monetary System (EMS) is introduced. It aims to encourage stability by pegging exchange rates to a European Currency Unit (ECU). **June 7–10:** The first direct elections to the European Parliament are held.

January 1, 1981 Greece joins the EC.

1986 January 1: Spain and Portugal join the EC. **February:** The Single European Act, the first major revision of the Treaties of Rome, is signed in Luxembourg and The Hague. It lays down the framework for completing the single market by 1992. It also gives more power to the European Parliament.

1992 February 7: EC member states sign the Treaty on European Union (TEU) in Maastricht in the Netherlands. The treaty creates a common European citizenship, establishes a Common Foreign and Security Policy (CFSP), expands cooperation in judicial and home affairs, and sets up a timetable for Economic and Monetary Union (EMU) and a single currency. **May 2:** The EC and EFTA sign an agreement to form a European Economic Area (EEA).

1993 January 1: The Single European Market takes effect. It allows the unrestricted movement of people, goods, services, and capital between member states. **November 1:** The TEU enters into force; the EC becomes the EU.

January 1, 1995 Austria, Finland, and Sweden join the EU.

October 2, 1997 The Amsterdam Treaty is signed. It updates and clarifies the TEU and allows closer cooperation between countries wanting to forge ahead on certain issues.

1999 January 1: The single currency, the euro, is officially launched in 11 member states. **March:** The European Commission resigns after publication of a report detailing fraud, mismanagement, and nepotism.

2001 January 2: Greece becomes the 12th country to join the eurozone. **February 26:** The Treaty of Nice is signed. It overhauls the EU institutions in preparation for further enlargement.

January 1, 2002 Euro coins and notes enter into circulation to replace the national currencies of Austria, Belgium, Finland, France, Germany, Greece, Ireland, Italy, Luxembourg, the Netherlands, Portugal, and Spain.

July 18, 2003 The European Convention submits its draft EU Constitution to the European Council.

May 1, 2004 Cyprus, the Czech Republic, Estonia, Hungary, Latvia, Lithuania, Malta, Poland, Slovakia, and Slovenia join the EU.

Topic 11

IS THE WORLD TRADE ORGANIZATION ANTI-AMERICAN?

YES

"VISCLOSKY CALLS ON PRESIDENT TO REJECT WTO RULING ON STEEL SAFEGUARDS"
PRESS RELEASE, NOVEMBER 10, 2003
WWW.HOUSE.GOV

NO

"LONE SHARKS"
THE NEW REPUBLIC, JULY 17, 2003
ROBERT LANE GREENE

INTRODUCTION

The World Trade Organization (WTO) was established in 1995; it replaced the existing system of international trade negotiations and agreements enshrined in the 1947 General Agreement on Tariffs and Trade (GATT). The principal aims of the WTO—and GATT before it—are to liberate world trade through the reduction of tariffs (taxes on imported goods) and subsidies, and to help boost global economic growth.

Trade negotiations between WTO's member countries—of which there were 146 in 2004—cover areas such as trade and the environment, antidumping and subsidies, competition policy, intellectual property, and measures to help developing countries. The 2001 WTO negotiations held in Doha, Qatar, were aimed specifically at placing developing countries at the heart of international trade negotiations; this followed accusations that the WTO acted in the best interests of developed nations.

However, in trying to help trade flow "smoothly, predictably, and freely," as its website asserts, the WTO has come into conflict with nations over their trade practices. Both the United States and Europe, for example, heavily subsidize agriculture; the United States has also used tariffs to protect its domestic steel industry from foreign competition. Many people argue that these policies have been vital to the domestic economy and have helped save flagging industries from ruin. By criticizing them, they claim that the WTO has shown that it is biased and, therefore, anti-American.

The government-produced "Economic Report of the President: 2003" stated that the United States had demonstrated its willingness to "liberalize trade with countries from around the world, both developing and developed." It claimed that the United States wanted to work on trade negotiations through the WTO, and that it supported the organization's processes for resolving trade disputes, which helped ensure that all the members received the benefits to which they were entitled. Trade problems are settled by the dispute settlement panel, which uses experts to decide whether a country is in violation of an existing trade agreement. As of September 2003 the United States had filed 63 complaints against other countries, 39 of which had been resolved in panel discussions, including 3 that they had lost in litigation. In the same period the United States had been the respondent in 77 cases and had defended itself successfully in 4 out of the resulting 38 panel discussions.

> *"The U.S. is a country that doesn't like being told what to do."*
> —TIMOTHY WU, U.S. PROFESSOR OF LAW, ON THE WTO (2004)

Some WTO supporters contend that successive U.S. governments have paid mere lip service to free trade. They believe that the United States is happy to take its own disputes to the WTO—to press for the European Union to accept genetically modified U.S. food, for example—but that as soon as its own trade decisions are challenged by others, the United States criticizes the WTO and undermines its authority. Law professor Timothy Wu states that what the United States really wants is to live in "a world in which everyone else is bound to WTO decisions, and the U.S. is not."

Meanwhile, American critics have objected to U.S. adherence to WTO policy, which they believe leads to essential trade decisions being handed over to "unelected bureaucrats." They argue that the WTO does not act in the interests of U.S. citizens, some of whom have lost much-needed jobs and income through the demise of domestic industry. The U.S. steel and oil industries and its food-processing and agriculture sectors, in particular, have all suffered as a result of WTO rulings. A ruling on behalf of Venezuela and Brazil in 1996, for example, held that U.S. gasoline regulation discriminated against the two countries' product. Yet the gas had higher levels of pollutants than were allowed by the U.S. Clean Air Act at the time. President Clinton was forced to modify the act or face economic sanctions.

Economists support the WTO on the basis that free trade is at the very center of good economics—the theory of comparative advantage holds that only through specialization and trade can economies grow and nations prosper. Therefore, trade liberalization across the world will, in the long run, benefit all—consumers and producers alike. In fact, the "Economic Report of the President: 2003" asserted that the removal of tariffs and subsidies could raise world income by $355 billion by 2015. Thus, supporters argue, the WTO is not biased against the United States or any other nation, since its policies benefit everyone. The U.S. government has also given more money to the WTO—in 2003 it donated $1 million to a voluntary WTO trust fund to help developing countries—showing that it does not perceive it as anti-American.

The two pieces that follow look at some of the key issues in the debate.

VISCLOSKY CALLS ON PRESIDENT TO REJECT WTO RULING...
www.house.gov

YES

Congressman Pete Visclosky (D-Merrillville) today blasted the World Trade Organization (WTO) for rejecting a U.S. appeal of its anti-steel safeguard decision announced July 11, 2003. The WTO Appellate Body upheld the organization's original ruling that the tariffs imposed on March 5, 2002, against illegally traded foreign steel violated the WTO Safeguards Agreement.

Visclosky fights tariffs

Visclosky, who fought to have the tariffs imposed in order to preserve good-paying steelworker jobs in Northwest Indiana, insisted that the Bush Administration must not cave in to another predictable, anti-American decision by the WTO. President George W. Bush imposed the tariffs five days after Visclosky met with him at the White House, on February 28, 2002, to discuss the domestic steel crisis. Visclosky, vice-chairman of the Congressional Steel Caucus, called upon the President to keep safeguards in place despite today's ruling.

"Once again, the WTO has displayed a clear bias against the United States and its working families," Visclosky said. "Keeping these safeguards in place is absolutely necessary to keep hardworking men and women in Northwest Indiana on the job, and I call upon the President to reject the WTO's arbitrary and biased action against American workers."

Is the imposition of tariffs on competitive foreign goods a fair response if an industry—such as steel—is not competitive enough?

Bush's call

It is now up to President Bush to decide whether to keep the safeguards in place or modify them. He is under no legal obligation to modify the tariffs based on the WTO's biased ruling.

"When the President spoke with the American people about terrorism, he said the nations of the world must decide whether they were with us or against us," Visclosky said. "Now, the President must make a similar choice. He must decide whether he is with America's workers, or against them. The choice is clear, and the ball is in his court."

Visclosky refers to George W. Bush's speech about the international community being with America or against it in response to the War on Terrorism. He argues that the president must make a similar decision regarding U.S. workers and the WTO. Is this comparison appropriate?

A striker holds a U.S. flag while he demonstrates against the World Trade Organization.

COMMENTARY: Visclosky and U.S. steel

As a lifelong resident of northwest Indiana, Congressman Pete Visclosky believes that the steel industry is essential to the region. He has fought hard to save the domestic steel industry against foreign competition and to protect worker rights.

Visclosky's efforts to save U.S. steel

Visclosky has authored several acts protecting the steel industry. H.R. 4646, the Steel Industry Legacy Relief Act, was introduced on May 2, 2002. Visclosky was also responsible for H.R. 975, the Bipartisan Steel Recovery Act; this bill passed the full House on March 17, 1999, but failed to get passed by the Senate. On March 1, 2001, he authored and introduced H.R. 808, the Steel Revitalization Act, which called for quotas against foreign steelmakers in violation of U.S. trade law through dumping steel into the U.S. market. As a result of Visclosky's efforts, the ITC recommended that tariffs of up to 40 percent be enforced against countries dumping steel; President George W. Bush imposed 30 percent tariffs for three years in March 2002. Although the measure was heavily criticized by the international community and the WTO, tariffs remained in place until December 2003.

Steel and the War on Terrorism

Since the War on Terrorism began, Visclosky has emphasized the importance of the steel industry to national defense. He said, "As a nation it is not in our interests to be dependent on the good will of foreign nations to supply us for the steel we need for our ships, tanks, and weapons." He has, however, been criticized for this view, since it is not in line with the free-trade policies advocated by the WTO.

Letter to the president

Visclosky and 60 colleagues sent a letter to President Bush after the WTO's initial July 11, 2003, decision asking that the United States appeal the ruling, which it did.

Visclosky pushed for the imposition of steel safeguards as a response to the flood of illegally dumped steel that had saturated the American market and driven more than 30 domestic steel companies into bankruptcy, depriving thousands of steelworkers of good-paying jobs. He convinced the U.S. International Trade Commission (ITC) to come to Merrillville on October 5–6, 2001, to hear from steelworkers who had either lost or stood to lose their jobs. Within two weeks, the ITC ruled unanimously that foreign steel dumping had caused substantial injury to the domestic

The U.S. International Trade Commission (ITC) is an independent nonpartisan quasi-judicial agency that provides trade advice to government and monitors the effect of imports on U.S. industry.

steel industry, and recommended that President [George W.] Bush impose tariffs.

Testifying before the ITC

In July, Visclosky testified on four occasions before the ITC, as part of its legally mandated midterm review of the tariffs, to make the case that the tariffs are working and need to be kept in place. To turn back the clock now, just as tariffs are beginning to work, would have catastrophic results for steelworkers and the entire domestic steel industry.

"It is immoral and irresponsible for the WTO to rule that foreign steelmakers have the right to deprive hardworking American steelworkers, and their families, of their livelihoods," Visclosky said. "The WTO has a long history of slapping America and its workers in the face. It is wrong, it is unacceptable, and we must not allow it to stand."

The WTO was set up to establish fair trade between countries. It has, in the past, ruled against nations that have violated U.S. trade agreements. Is it fair to object when the WTO denounces U.S protectionist policy in return?

LONE SHARKS
Robert Lane Greene

Robert Lane Greene is countries editor at the economist.com. He wrote this piece for The New Republic in July 2003.

NO

If your interest in the subject of trade is a casual one, you might think George W. Bush is a true free-trader. To hear him talk, he sounds not only like he believes free trade is a good thing, but that it can save the world. Last week in Africa, he touted the virtues of free trade to that continent, saying in Senegal, "We will ensure that the nations of Africa are full partners in the trade and prosperity of the world." In May, he proposed a free-trade deal with Middle Eastern countries that are willing to adopt basic standards of good government, in the hope that it would lead them toward democracy. True, the president did slap big tariffs on foreign steel last year—but, his trade-loving supporters explain, that was only to build up capital in Congress for bigger, more comprehensive trade deals down the road. And, yes, the monstrous farm subsidies that the president approved in 2002 badly distort trade and hurt the world's poorest countries, but the president diverts attention from this by saying (correctly) that European farm policy is even worse.

In 2003 U.S. farmers received around $14 billion in subsidies. Critics, such as the Environmental News Network (ENN), argue that the subsidies make it impossible for farmers in developing countries to compete in the export market. In a time of budget deficits the United States can also no longer afford to fund such subsidies.

Protectionism

Still, as frustrating as it is that George W. Bush caves to protectionist pressure whenever the going gets tough, there's an even larger problem with his approach to trade: Rather than accept the rules of an organized global system, he systematically undermines that system—by pursuing individual deals with individual countries and regions—when it doesn't suit short-term American interests. Bush, in other words, has apparently decided do go down the same unilateralist path in trade negotiations that his administration favors on international security. Over the long term, the result could be to deprive American workers of the benefits of new markets abroad, and American consumers of the benefits of cheaper goods at home.

See Volume 18, Commerce and Trade, Topic 14 Is protectionism good for U.S. business?

The big loser of the Bush divide-and-trade strategy is the World Trade Organization (WTO), the only organization that can guarantee free trade. The administration has announced that, on July 11, it will appeal the trade body's decision that America's steel tariffs are illegal. That appeal has no hope— the steel duties are obviously the kind of protectionism the

A steelworker pours an ingot from molten steel at a mill in Kokomo, Indiana. The steel industry received protection from the U.S. government in the form of tariffs.

WTO is designed to prevent—and its effect will be largely to fan anti-WTO sentiment at home. Already pro-tariff voices have reacted with fury that belies more than economic concerns. The head of the United Steelworkers of America, Leo Gerard, has said that the ruling was "the latest example of unelected trade bureaucrats undermining national sovereignty and long-established provisions of global trade agreements."

The "unelected bureaucrats undermining national sovereignty" meme is a powerful one that unites the anti-globalization left with conservatives who abhor any hint of foreign restraints on American policy. The notion has a gut-level appeal: Somewhere some faceless foreigner is telling us what we can and can't do in America. But to level such claims at the WTO is farcical. The WTO, in one sense, doesn't really exist, at least as an independent actor in its own right. It is an agreement—a set of rules, established by all members—not to hinder trade. The WTO's own "unelected bureaucrats" are simply the arbiters, deciding who has broken those rules. When one member illegally limits trade, as in the steel case, the WTO tells other members they may go ahead with national sanctions, passed by individual governments like those of Japan, South Korea, and the EU, all complainants in the steel case. The WTO itself neither makes nor enforces policies; it is little more than a referee.

> A "meme" is an idea, style, or behavior that spreads from one person to another within a culture.

WTO is like the UN

As a reflection of its members, the WTO is not unlike another international organization created largely by the United States to monitor compliance with global rules written largely by the United States: the United Nations. Could the Bush administration be showing the same disdain for the WTO it has shown for the United Nations? The signs certainly point that way. America is more than happy to pursue a case at the WTO that it thinks it can and should win, such as its current effort to get the EU to accept genetically modified foods. But when it appears that the United States may not get its way at the WTO, the Bush administration takes its ball, goes home, and plays its own game with the smaller kids it knows it can push around. Hence the push for individual trade initiatives with the Middle East, Africa, and Latin America. The United States has far more leverage with any of these alone than it does in a global, rules-based system.

American officials say trade deals with individual countries and regions are a building block, not a stumbling block, to global trade negotiations. Robert Zoellick has written in *The*

> While genetically modified (GM) goods are widely accepted in the United States, countries within the EU remain more cautious about them. In 2003 several African nations rejected food aid from the United States, fearing that it might include GM goods and that trade relations with Europe might be affected as a result.

Economist that America's bilateral and regional details "multiply the chances for success" of global free trade. But other countries aren't buying it. Once a leftist firebrand, Brazil's new president, Luiz Inácio Lula da Silva, has moved closer to neoliberal economic orthodoxy since coming into office, going so far as to make positive sounds about free trade in principle. But Lula hasn't hesitated to criticize American bullying, saying that "if trade is free, it will be free for everybody." He hopes, in turn, to unify the Latin American countries for more negotiating leverage with the United States—an effort that can be seen as little other than the product of years of American arm-twisting over the proposed Free Trade Area of the Americas. Countries in Africa and the Middle East may soon also come to resent Bush's peculiar form of "free" trade.

Luiz Inácio Lula da Silva (1945–) was born in the state of Pernambuco, Brazil. On October 27, 2002, Lula, as he is more popularly known, was elected president under the slogan "for a decent Brazil."

Free trade benefits all

Toughness in trade negotiations is nothing new. Especially in democracies, there will always be pressure to get the "best deal," which is taken to mean exporting as much as possible while protecting your domestic industries from imports. But this isn't free trade in a meaningful economic sense. And, if pushed to its extreme, it quickly devolves into the kind of bitter finger-pointing that prevents important trade deals from being inked. What's particularly maddening about that scenario is that it's so unnecessary: Free trade, done fairly, benefits everyone, including the United States. The agreements policed by the WTO are America's best hope for getting the Europeans and Japanese to abandon some of their most protectionist practices, and to prevent truly unfair dumping of steel or farm products in the United States by developing countries.

If the United States is the world's largest economy, is it inevitable that it often gets its own way in economic agreements?

But by carving up the world into individual regions or countries that America can punish, manipulate, or ignore as it sees fit, George W. Bush undermines the best hope for the real free trade he touted last week in Africa. This is a shame. Global free trade really can help both America and the world's poorest countries. The president should not only say this; he should act as though he believes it.

Summary

Congressman Pete Visclosky clearly believes the WTO is anti-American. Not only that, the organization's actions and decisions are "arbitrary and bias[ed]" against the United States and its workers, favoring instead the countries of—and workers in—the developing world. The WTO decision that the article focuses on is the ruling of March 5, 2002, that U.S. tariffs against the import of cheap foreign steel violate the WTO Safeguards Agreement. The U.S. appeal against this ruling was also rejected. In the view of Visclosky and 60 of his fellow-congressmen, the tariffs (which Visclosky fought for) are "safeguards" for America's domestic steel industry, protection in a market that had been "saturated" by a "flood of illegally dumped steel," causing the bankruptcy of domestic steel companies and the loss of thousands of jobs. The WTO's ruling, therefore, is evidence of its anti-American bias.

Robert Lane Greene, however, derides the idea that the WTO is composed of a group of "unelected bureaucrats" who make decisions about U.S. trade policy, the majority of which are against the interests of working Americans. He argues that the WTO is not an independent actor in its own right. Rather, it is an agreement, a set of rules that have been established and agreed by all of its members, including the United States. Therefore, WTO bureaucrats are actually arbiters or referees—they help resolve disputes between member countries over the trade rules and decide whether retaliatory action can be justified by one against another or whether economic sanctions should be applied. The organization's goal is free trade, a concept to which George W. Bush pays mere lip service. In Greene's opinion it is the United States that is undermining the WTO, not the WTO that is anti-American.

FURTHER INFORMATION:

Books:

Gomory, Ralph E., and William J. Baumol, *Global Trade and Conflicting National Interests.* Cambridge, MA: MIT Press, 2000.

Useful websites:

http://www.aiis.org/201_issues/ ?file=white_paper.htm
American Institute for International Steel site.
http://www.freetrade.org/index.html
Cato Institute Center for Trade Policy Studies site, includes some interesting articles.
http://www.house.gov/visclosky/
Site for Congressman Pete Visclosky.
www.wto.org
World Trade Organization site.

The following debates in the Pro/Con series may also be of interest:

In this volume:
Part 3: International organizations, pages 100–101

In *International Development*:
Part 3: Trade, pages 122–123

In *Commerce and Trade*:
Topic 14 Is protectionism good for U.S. business?

IS THE WORLD TRADE ORGANIZATION ANTI-AMERICAN?

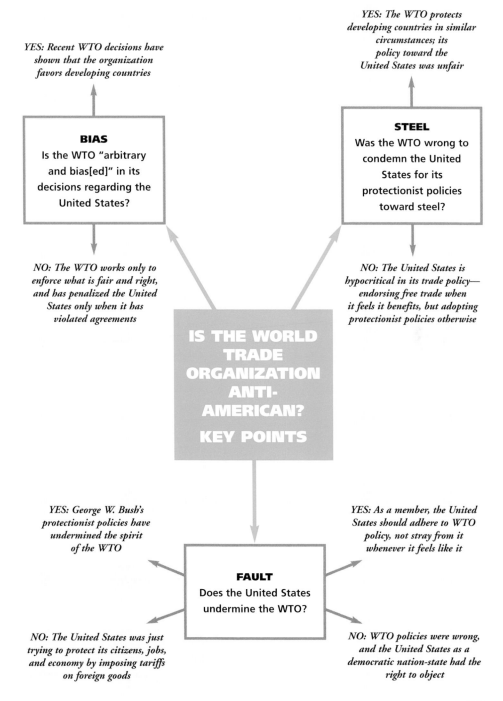

YES: Recent WTO decisions have shown that the organization favors developing countries

YES: The WTO protects developing countries in similar circumstances; its policy toward the United States was unfair

BIAS
Is the WTO "arbitrary and bias[ed]" in its decisions regarding the United States?

STEEL
Was the WTO wrong to condemn the United States for its protectionist policies toward steel?

NO: The WTO works only to enforce what is fair and right, and has penalized the United States only when it has violated agreements

NO: The United States is hypocritical in its trade policy—endorsing free trade when it feels it benefits, but adopting protectionist policies otherwise

IS THE WORLD TRADE ORGANIZATION ANTI-AMERICAN?
KEY POINTS

YES: George W. Bush's protectionist policies have undermined the spirit of the WTO

YES: As a member, the United States should adhere to WTO policy, not stray from it whenever it feels like it

FAULT
Does the United States undermine the WTO?

NO: The United States was just trying to protect its citizens, jobs, and economy by imposing tariffs on foreign goods

NO: WTO policies were wrong, and the United States as a democratic nation-state had the right to object

Topic 12
COULD THE ARAB LEAGUE DO MORE TO PROMOTE PEACE IN THE MIDDLE EAST?

YES
"TEN REASONS WHY ISRAEL SHOULD JOIN THE ARAB LEAGUE"
OPINION, *MIDDLE EAST TIMES*, ISSUE 29, 2002
MOSHE HILLEL EITAN

NO
FROM "A SUSTAINABLE ARAB LEAGUE"
AL-AHRAM WEEKLY ONLINE, ISSUE 646, JULY 10–16, 2003
GAMIL MATTAR

INTRODUCTION

The League of Arab States—usually known as the Arab League—was set up on March 22, 1945. It was established to protect the common economic and political interests of the world's Arab nations. The founding members were Egypt, Iraq, Jordan, Lebanon, Saudi Arabia, Syria, and Yemen. Membership was later extended to Algeria, Bahrain, Comoros, Djibouti, Kuwait, Libya, Mauritania, Morocco, Oman, Qatar, Somalia, South Yemen (later part of Yemen), Sudan, Tunisia, the United Arab Emirates, and the Palestine Liberation Organization (PLO).

The league's charter invests authority in a council representing all members equally. Its central focus—on which the states have generally been in agreement—is Arab opposition to Israel. The league has enforced a blanket boycott of trade against the country and also against foreign firms that have Israeli subsidiaries. This policy caused severe problems after the 1979 peace treaty between Egypt and Israel. The league suspended Egypt and moved its headquarters from Cairo to Tunis. However, in 1989 Egypt's membership was restored, and two years later Cairo became the headquarters again.

Some international observers have accused the league of failing to deal with crucial issues, particularly in its dealings with Israel. Relations between Jews and Arabs—which have always been strained—have deteriorated since the creation of Israel in 1948. A second Palestinian intifada (uprising) in 2002 against Israeli rule reached its climax with the beginning of a series of suicide bombings against civilian targets. This has led many to claim that there seems less prospect of finding a solution to this conflict than ever before.

Meanwhile, Israel's demographics have altered significantly. At the start of the new millennium Palestinians comprised nearly 20 percent of Israel's total population of just over six million. In addition, there are an estimated 2.2 to 2.4 million displaced Palestinians living in refugee camps in neighboring Jordan, Lebanon, and Syria, who, it is widely agreed, would return if given the opportunity. Commentators have predicted that the high Palestinian birthrate and the significant exodus of Israeli Jews—some 10 percent of the population has emigrated since the deterioration of internal security—may result in Arabs being a majority within Israel within less than a generation.

"The deliberate daily violations by Israel of human rights in the occupied Palestinian territories do not serve our endeavors for modernization and reform.... They enhance radicalism and terrorism and feed frustration among people."

—EGYPTIAN PRESIDENT
HOSNI MUBARAK (2004)

This has led some commentators to claim that it might be time for the league to lift its trade embargo, since it is hurting more Arabs and fewer Israelis. If the league was to go one step further and invite Israel to join it, they assert, the economic benefits to both sides might lead to the breakthrough that years of superpower shuttle diplomacy have failed to achieve.

This would be a truly momentous step since most Arab countries do not currently recognize Israel's right to exist.

Also of major concern for the Arab League have been events elsewhere in the Middle East, notably the Persian Gulf War in 1991 and the military actions by the United States and its allies against Iraq in response to the terrorist attacks of September 11, 2001. In June 2003 Amr Moussa, secretary-general of the Arab League, made a controversial statement in which he called on members to adapt their attitudes and policies in the light of the new world order. He told them: "In 1990, when one Arab country [Iraq] invaded another Arab country [Kuwait], the notion of collective Arab security as we knew it during the 1950s and 1960s collapsed." Moussa then exhorted the league to adopt "neo-Arab nationalism." By that he meant that member states should accept that they are now subject to U.S. hegemony and adapt their policies accordingly. He also suggested that political and economic reform was necessary. The alternative, he argued, would be the breakup of the league, which would only damage Arab interests. The ramifications of Moussa's proposal are potentially immense. Instead of tackling the Palestinian question head on, the league would focus on socioeconomic and cultural matters, and thus perhaps approach the old problem from a creative new angle.

Moshe Hillel Eitan, an American-educated lawyer resident in Jerusalem, lists the reasons for inviting Israel to join the league. Gamil Mattar, director the Cairo-based Arab Center for Development and Futuristic Studies, argues that the scheme is undesirable.

TEN REASONS WHY ISRAEL SHOULD JOIN THE ARAB LEAGUE
Moshe Hillel Eitan

On September 11, 2002, the one-year anniversary of the terror attacks in the United States, the Arab world should make a groundbreaking historic decision: offer the State of Israel associate membership in the Arab League. I present ten reasons why this step should be taken:

Systematically listing your main points can give your argument clarity and strength.

• Reducing tension in the Middle East

First, if the Arab League grants admission to the State of Israel, this action would immediately reduce tension in the Middle East and pave the way towards comprehensive peace.

As an Arab League member, Israel would be able to freely engage in direct talks with Syria, Lebanon and other Arab states. This action would transform non-action and non-recognition into solution-oriented problem solving.

The Arab League would be transformed into a progressive forum for peace.

The league has been heavily criticized for failing to do more to solve the Arab–Israeli conflict. Most Arab nations do not recognize the right of Israel to exist. Go to http://www.usatoday.com/news/world/2003-06-02-arabs-israel-glance_x.htm for an outline of the status of Israeli relations with Arab League nations.

• Economic benefit

Second, Israel, as a member of the Arab League, could help boost the economies of Arab countries by paving the way towards an Arab–Israeli Trade Agreement. Products made in Saudi Arabia could be marketed in Tel Aviv.

Furthermore, the Middle East itself could evolve into a stable economic zone of investment in order to attract more foreign investment.

By joining the Arab League, Israel and the Arab world would effectively end the self-destructive economic boycott of Israel. Business and investment would be forever separated from political strife.

Do you believe that it is possible to separate business issues from political ones?

• Diplomatic recognition

Third, this historic act would help to bring about full diplomatic recognition and normalization of relations. The exchange of dialogue at Arab League meetings would be a precursor to an exchange of ambassadors and consuls between Israel and the Arab world.

• Accepting Israel's Arabs

Fourth, nearly 20 percent of Israel's population is made up of Israeli Arab citizens. Accepting Israel into the Arab League would also grant acceptance to Israel's Arab population as well. Logically, the Israeli Arab is a fundamental member of the Arab world. It therefore follows that this population should have a voice in the Arab League. By granting membership to Israel as a whole, both Israeli Jews and Arabs would have a forum in which to discuss political, social, cultural and economic matters.

• Security

Fifth, Israel, as a member of the Arab League, would make possible military and security cooperation throughout the Middle East. Today the region is unfairly known as a haven for terrorists. With a greater degree of cooperation, the region could be transformed into a modern, thriving realm of peace and security.

Only security cooperation between Israel and the Arab world can stabilize the balance of power in the region and build mutual trust.

• War against terrorism

Sixth, the Arab world and Israel could, together, develop a common agenda in the war against terrorism. Terrorism impacts all of us, both Jews and Arabs. No one wants to be a victim of terror.

Instead, the people of the Middle East want a safe and stable region, in which the strong are fair, the weak are stable, and the security is preserved. A joint Arab–Israeli war on terror could help to crush terrorism and vanquish prophets of violence from the region.

• Technology

Seventh, the Arab world could also benefit from Israel's expertise in high technology. From computer software to laptop computers to Internet security programs, Israel is known as one of the world's leaders in the area of high-tech.

As a member of the Arab League, Israel would be able to share its advanced consumer technology with Arab states.

In the near future, Syrian professors in Damascus could be utilizing Israeli software to teach students in their university classrooms.

The term "Israeli Arab" is sensitive. It refers to the political status rather than the ethnicity of Arabs, who are citizens of Israel. The Arab community tends to include the word "Palestinian" in definitions of Arab citizens living in Israel. Go to http://www.icf.org.il/arabs.htm for an article on the Arab population in Israel.

The United States views Iran, Iraq, and Syria as state sponsors of terrorism. In 2000 the government's coordinator for counterterrorism suggested that terrorism in the Middle East was waning. How does this view compare with the state of terrorism in the region today? Go to www.cnn.com to search for recent articles.

President Bashar Al Assad of Syria at the closing session of the Arab Summit, Beirut, 2002. Al Assad has called for the modernization and empowerment of the Arab League.

• Tourism

Eighth, Israel and the Arab League together could develop a joint tourism agenda. Currently, the situation of war, conflict, bloodshed and terrorism prevents large numbers of wealthy tourists from investing in the region.

By accepting Israel as a member of the Arab League, the Arab world would send a message to tourists around the world that the Middle East truly welcomes tourism and leisure investment.

• Peace negotiation

Ninth, the Arab League should initiate Israel as a member in order to spur the development of personal relationships between Arab and Israeli leaders. How can hostile strangers ever make peace?

Does Bashar Al Assad have a personal rapport with Ariel Sharon? Of course not. It is quite obvious that a warm personal relationship can enhance trust, communication and commitment to peace.

By accepting Israel as a member of the Arab League, the Arab world would be effectively indicating that Israel is a permanent state in the Middle East. This act would help to minimize the atmosphere of fear and paranoia in the region.

• Legitimizing the Arab League

Tenth, the Arab League should admit Israel as an associate member for the sake of the legitimacy of the Arab League itself. The Arab League currently lists 'Palestine' as a member, but does not mention 'Israel.' This detracts from the legitimacy of the league itself.

No longer would the Arab League be viewed as a one-sided institution promoting a hostile anti-Israeli agenda. Instead, it would be viewed as a dynamic forum that is committed to peace, security and justice in the Middle East.

The acceptance of Israel into the Arab League would lead to a reinterpretation of both Zionism and Arab nationalism. The very idea of Zionism, for example, need not be viewed as a threat to the Arab world.

Instead, perhaps the Arab world should embrace Zionism as a historic example of self-determination, military success and economic empowerment. Indeed, Zionism could be the engine of growth for the entire Middle East.

The day may come when Arabs throughout the Middle East will consider themselves proud of both Zionism and Arab nationalism. It all begins with one bold idea.

The Charter of the Arab League forbids member states from resorting to force against each other. Critics argue that this did not prevent Iraq's invasion of Kuwait in 1990.

Bashar Al Assad (1965–) is the president of Syria. Ariel Sharon (1928–) is the prime minister of Israel.

"Associate" membership suggests that Israel would have a subordinate position in the league. Do you think Israel should settle for less than full membership?

Zionism began as a movement in the late 19th century to establish a national Jewish homeland. It is now mainly concerned with the development of the modern state of Israel. Arab nationalism is a movement that aims to create a united Arab nation across the Middle East and North Africa. It was strongest in the 1950s and 1960s.

A SUSTAINABLE ARAB LEAGUE
Gamil Mattar

Gamil Mattar is director of the Arab Center for Development and Futuristic Research.

Judging by the language Mattar uses, what opinion do you think he has of Arab intellectuals?

NO

X Some Arab intellectuals are still insisting, not only on reforming the Arab League, but that the reformed league should in turn reform the social, economic and political order in the Arab world. In unleashing their imaginations in this direction, they appear to have overlooked an important fact, to which those familiar with the rules and procedures of the league have repeatedly drawn our attention. The general-secretariat of the Arab League does not have the right to pressure members to reform their domestic affairs. The league does not possess an army for liberating occupied territories, for resisting the American invasion of Iraq or militarily confronting new challenges in the post-Saddam era. Nor does it possess a will independent of the wills of its member nations. The general-secretariat cannot, above all, make a bid to include Israel in the league … By even embarking on such a step the league would forfeit the legitimacy it so needs in these difficult times.

Taking the "Arab" out of the Arab League
Naturally, this is not the first time the Arab League has come under concerted criticism. However, the current campaign differs from its forerunners in intent. If, in the past, critics … were venting dismay and, perhaps, anxiety over the collective fate of the Arabs and their league, today, the thrust of the campaign aims at deriving a new formula for Arab cooperation and Arab identity in which the Arab component of these terms is left out. I am not exaggerating or reading more meaning than exists into the statements and articles issued by the planners and leaders of the campaign. The league, they maintain, should be transformed into an institution whose form, substance, charter, activities and title conforms to the new realities in the region. One of the realities is the growing impact of nations bordering the Arab world, notably Turkey, Iran and Ethiopia. Another is that one of the members of the league has become a major item on a superpower's domestic policy agenda. The issue here is not how accurate these contentions are, but rather that the people who assert them believe they are telling us something new, whereas the questions of neighbouring powers and the

Go to http:// weekly.ahram. org.eg/2003/ 644/re8.htm for a full report of the comments made by Arab League Secretary-General Amr Moussa to which this article refers.

Here the author is referring to Iraq.

hegemony of superpowers have posed themselves in various forms for decades.

Some of the critics have been bolder and more explicit. Among them are those who hold that the true reason behind the insistence on overhauling the Arab League is that we have come to live in an Arab ghetto surrounded on all sides by Israel, which can penetrate or control this ghetto whenever and however it wants. Therefore, they argue, we should take the initiative and invite Israel into the league, after which the league will automatically be transformed into a regional organisation and, as a natural outcome of this, its members will drop the modifier "Arab" out of deference to the sensitivities of the Israelis and other neighbours.

Is it realistic for the league to absorb a former enemy as a member?

Defining Arab identity

Others have been franker yet. After the occupation of Iraq … many Arabs are contemplating abandoning "Arabism." This is the first time I have ever heard of a people discarding their identity before having found a new one. True, there are those who speak of the "new Arab identity" and the secretary-general of the Arab League has come up with the expression, "neo-Arab nationalism". However, I, along with many others, am at a loss as to what [this] means. Perhaps the clearest explanation I have heard is that the "new Arab identity" is derived from the implicit and contractual agreement between a number of Arab states to work directly with Israel without fear of domestic or outside opposition and to bow to the reality of American hegemony and move closer to those nations located on the other side of the political boundaries of the Arab world. It hardly bears mentioning that this succinct explanation still eludes our grasp….

"Arabism" means dedication to Arab interests, culture, or aspirations.

Do you think the author's sarcastic tone adds weight to or detracts from his argument?

What is particularly interesting is that some of the advocates of liberating the Arab League from its identity … indeed, its whole legacy, say that if it wants to survive it must prove its ability to do so in the realm of regional—Middle Eastern, not inter-Arab—cooperation. Others, undoubtedly out of the best intentions, have joined their ranks and presented the secretary-general of the Arab League with another list of demands. One of the more noteworthy proposals called upon him to form a fact-finding committee to investigate the state of human rights and civil freedoms in the Arab world … They also suggested that the general-secretariat produce a report on unemployment in the Arab world, identifying the relevant social discrepancies in member nations, pinpointing governments' shortcomings in addressing the problems and offering appropriate recommendations.

Other writers have suggested that the Arab League be conferred the right to judge the success or failure of foreign policies and performance of its member states in accordance with a set of criteria it devises either independently or in cooperation with organisations or persons with expertise in these matters. There was also that piece of advice given to the secretary-general that he intervene personally, with the weight of the league behind him, to promote the establishment of civil society organisations in its member states and the establishment of federations linking these organisations with their counterparts across the political boundaries of the Arab world. Perhaps the giver of this advice had forgotten that Arab governments had nationalised a good many non-governmental organisations and subjected sectors of civil society to semi-official control. Perhaps he is also unaware that Arab governments reject the UN and U.S. State Department reports on human rights violations in their countries and are extremely unlikely to agree that writing such reports should become [a] function of the Arab League.

Go to Amnesty International's website at www.amnestyusa.org to find out about human rights in the Middle East.

Creating desire for change

One of the toughest challenges that the secretary-general of the Arab League has to contend with stems from the following question: What can he do to make member states want the changes that he wants for the league? In other words, how can he win the support of member states for reforms that would render the Arab League a tool, not for him to wield against the interests of its member nations, but an instrument that member nations can avail themselves of in order to better their domestic circumstances and that will support them in their foreign relations against the forces of hegemony, aggression and occupation? If he is unable to do this, at the very least he should urge member states, or at least most of them, to agree to stay quiet or to put into effect, if only grudgingly, some of the reforms he would like to introduce gradually for the sake of the higher Arab interest.

The Arab League meeting to which Mattar is referring took place in Cairo in June 2003.

In a meeting that was held recently to discuss the challenges before the Arab League, I couldn't help but notice the pessimism and despair in the eyes of some of the participants. The problem, they said, is far greater than the secretary-general trying to convince member states of the need for change, however important that is. His most formidable challenge … will be to hold his ground on keeping the word "Arab" affixed to the institution he is heading. In this regard, more than one participant said that the crucial problem we all face, as people concerned with the future of the league, is the assault on "Arabism" by some Arabs who are totally immersed in the illusions of ultra-realism.… What is under assault is the entire Arab order, from its philosophical and ideological principles and its historical legacy to its institutions and infrastructure.

Facing the reality of U.S. hegemony

When a participant said we will have to prepare for the day when the secretary-general finds himself in front of a delegate from Iraq carrying credentials signed and stamped by the American governor, another participant remarked, "Let's not deceive ourselves. We have two types of members in the league: those who maintain that they control their own fate and those who recognise that their fate is controlled by others." The response reflected the opinion of some, even if they did not voice it openly, that it was pointless to discuss such details when our greater task was to come to terms with the reality that the region was under U.S. hegemony.…

At that point a tone of bitter wit was injected into the meeting. One participant said that delegates and ministers … all speak the same language, whereas if non-Arabs are admitted as observers people will have to be brought in to translate … A second participant countered, sarcastically, that many Arabs who have attended Arab League sessions felt they could have used a translator to interpret what was being said in Arabic. So much of what is said in those meetings is impossible to follow because of the ubiquitous slogans and the emotion-packed oration.…

What most intrigued me in the meetings on the crisis of the Arab order and the Arab League was that appeal by an Arab intellectual to the secretary-general to call upon the Arab Foreign Ministers Council to draw, in addition to the "negative" lists, containing the names of millions of Arabs who would be banned from travel across inter-Arab borders for reasons pertaining to security and terrorism, a "positive" list allowing for the easy and rapid movement across borders, without visas, of millions of other individuals who have something to contribute to inter-Arab cooperation, such as investors, skilled labour, producers and transmitters of knowledge and know-how and all who are keen to promote the political stability and prosperity of the Arab nation.

Certainly, the millions on the second list merit a portion of the attention of Arab foreign ministers, if the desire for domestic political reform and the intention to rescue the Arab people, the Arab order and the Arab League from their crisis are sincere.

Can the United States do anything to reduce its hegemony, or is it just the consequence of its wealth and power?

Summary

In the first article the author sets out exactly what his title promises: He makes his 10 points. The crux of his argument is that for as long as there is no local dialogue between the Arab states and Israel, there can be no real and lasting progress toward peace. If Israel were to join the Arab League, however, the historic adversaries would have to enter practical discussions about day-to-day matters such as trade. Commercial contact would bring the two sides closer together, leading them to diplomatic recognition and greater security. Arabs and Israelis share many goals, not least the end of suicide-bomber attacks and assassinations: They should work together to achieve them through mutual membership of the Arab League.

The author of the second article takes the view that the Arab League is not a suitable vehicle for promoting peace in the Middle East because it is by definition a body that exists solely to promote the interests of Arab states. Peace cannot be achieved by converting institutions and organizations that are definitively Arab into regional ones.

The author rejects calls for the Arab League to monitor human and civil rights, stating that such moves would turn the league into an imitation of the United Nations, many of whose reports Arab League members do not accept anyway. The role of the Arab League is not as a watchdog or monitoring group that can rein members in if they step out of line. At the core of the Arab struggle is the desire for self-determination; the so-called "new Arab identity" may turn Arabs into homogeneous Middle Easterners, but it will not bring peace.

FURTHER INFORMATION:

Books:

Sheehi, Stephen, *Foundations of Modern Arab Identity*. Gainesville, FL: University Press of Florida, 2004.

Shlaim, Avi, *War and Peace in the Middle East: A Concise History*. New York: Penguin, 1995.

Useful websites:

http://www.arableagueonline.org/arableague/index.jsp
Site of the Arab League.
http://english.aljazeera.net
Online version of Aljazeera, the independent news bureau. Comprehensive coverage of Arab world issues.
http://www.middleeastnews.com/ArabLeague.html
Site of Middle East News and World Report, a news and information bureau containing flagged links to the Arab League and its member states.

The following debates in the Pro/Con series may also be of interest:

In this volume:

Topic 6 Has the War on Terrorism reinforced U.S. global leadership?

Topic 7 Can Israel and Palestine ever reach a peace settlement?

Arab–Israeli relations after 1948, pages 98–99

COULD THE ARAB LEAGUE DO MORE TO PROMOTE PEACE IN THE MIDDLE EAST?

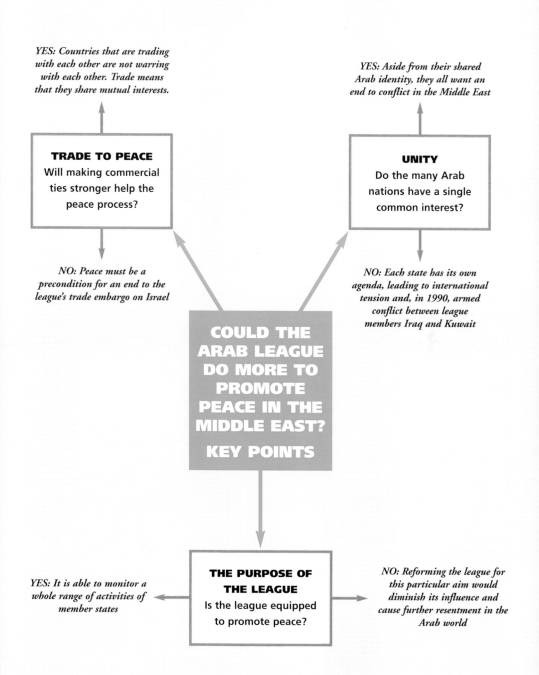

YES: Countries that are trading with each other are not warring with each other. Trade means that they share mutual interests.

YES: Aside from their shared Arab identity, they all want an end to conflict in the Middle East

TRADE TO PEACE
Will making commercial ties stronger help the peace process?

UNITY
Do the many Arab nations have a single common interest?

NO: Peace must be a precondition for an end to the league's trade embargo on Israel

NO: Each state has its own agenda, leading to international tension and, in 1990, armed conflict between league members Iraq and Kuwait

COULD THE ARAB LEAGUE DO MORE TO PROMOTE PEACE IN THE MIDDLE EAST?

KEY POINTS

YES: It is able to monitor a whole range of activities of member states

THE PURPOSE OF THE LEAGUE
Is the league equipped to promote peace?

NO: Reforming the league for this particular aim would diminish its influence and cause further resentment in the Arab world

PART 4
THE UNITED STATES AND THE WORLD

INTRODUCTION

On March 5, 1946, British Prime Minister Winston Churchill, President Harry Truman by his side, stated, "The United States stands ... at the pinnacle of world power.... [W]ith this primacy in power is also joined an awe-inspiring accountability for the future.... Opportunity is here now, clear and shining. To reject it, or to ignore it, or to fritter it away will bring upon us all the long reproaches of the aftertime."

Some critics believe that just as in 1946, the United States today stands at the "pinnacle of world power." The United States is the world's most powerful nation; it is the standard-bearer of democracy, and economically and politically it is one of the most influential voices in international affairs. With this position, however, comes huge responsibility, some observers state, not least to defeat global terrorism, help promote nation-building, end poverty and disease, protect human rights, and help conserve the environment, among other things. But some politicians, among others, believe that the U.S. government's first priority should be to look after its own interests and protect its citizens. They claim that the United States is naturally isolationist, and that it should not intervene in other nations' affairs. Topic 13 discusses this further.

The concern of Americans with their nation's role or purpose in the world economy is as old as the republic, and in fact even antedates the establishment of the state itself. As early as 1630, for example, Massachusetts colonial governor John Winthrop implored his people "to consider that we shall be as a city upon a hill," setting an example for the rest of the world. The Framers also believed that the United States was created not just to promote the freedom and happiness of its own citizens; the new "empire for liberty," as Thomas Jefferson termed it, was also intended to serve the cause of freedom in the world.

Since then many U.S. leaders have sought to combine an attention to the realities of power with a concern for the unique moral responsibility of the United States to promote freedom globally. Some historians argue that just as President Woodrow Wilson led the country into World War I (1914–1918) under the banner of "making the world safe for democracy," President George W. Bush (2001–) has also sought to justify the War on Terrorism and more specifically U.S. military involvement in Iraq by reminding U.S. citizens that "America is a nation with a mission.... This great republic will lead the cause of freedom." There is, however, tension between those who would like to limit the U.S. role largely to that of freedom's exemplar and those who would champion freedom's cause abroad.

Some critics, however, see 20th-century U.S. involvement in the political affairs of countries in such places as Latin America, Southeast Asia, and the Middle East as evidence that U.S. foreign policy is essentially interventionist. They claim that it is driven by the need to impose U.S. economic and political

Pinochet in Chile and that of Jorge Rafael Videla in Argentina. Both these men were accused of committing extreme human rights abuses and of bad governance, and this has also brought America heavy criticism.

For some, better investment in diplomatic missions abroad, staffed by people who speak the local language and have an understanding of the local culture, would go along way to help

---

"[B]y playing a constructive role, we can regain respect and support of the world."
—GEORGE SOROS, *THE AMERICAN PROSPECT*, MAY 27, 2003

---

power on other lands. Others, however, support George W. Bush's stance that "[America has] no desire to dominate, no ambitions of empire." For these people the United States by nature of its position in the world has a divine right to intervene in countries that are neither democratic nor free.

Diplomacy and foreign affairs

Intervention in other countries' affairs has, however, led to criticism and has contributed to America's unpopularity in many nations. For many the U.S. negative image has much to do with its seemingly imperialist economic, military, and political policies.

The United States has in the past provided finance, training, and military support to insurgent groups opposing regimes it has disapproved of. Some of them have gone on to create repressive regimes themselves, sometimes opposed to America. The United States has also supported dictatorships, including the military rule of Augusto

prevent many of the problems that the United States has experienced in the past. It would also, they believe, give other nations a better understanding of what the United States is hoping to achieve in involving itself in the affairs of Latin America, for example. Topic 14 looks at U.S. diplomacy in recent years, specifically whether it contributed to September 11, 2001.

Different governments have, however, defended their security decisions by stating that the end justifies the means. Topic 15 explores this issue by looking at whether the support of dictatorships is ever justifiable. It touches on the U.S. relationship with some former Latin American dictators. Some people believe that America is responsible for many of Latin America's problems through its interventionist and often exploitative policies. They believe it should do more to help Latin American countries develop. Topic 16 examines this issue with regard to the promotion of good governance in the region.

Topic 13
IS THE UNITED STATES NATURALLY ISOLATIONIST?

YES
FROM "AMERICA'S TRADITION OF NONINTERVENTIONISM"
LE QUÉBÉCOIS LIBRE, NO. 133, NOVEMBER 22, 2003
CHRIS LEITHNER

NO
"INTERNATIONALISM VERSUS ISOLATIONISM IN U.S. FOREIGN POLICY"
USIS WASHINGTON FILE, OCTOBER 25, 1999
SAMUEL L. BERGER

INTRODUCTION

Isolationism can be described as an approach to government that advocates nonparticipation in foreign affairs as the best means of serving national interests. It is the opposite of internationalism, which favors cooperation with other nations. At different times in U.S. history politicians have argued that the country should adopt an isolationist approach. The country is now so large, so wealthy, and so powerful, they claim, that it does need to involve itself in wars and other international problems. Protected, they believe, from most possible aggressors by the Atlantic and Pacific oceans, the United States can enjoy the situation envisioned by the Framers, free from the squabbles and tensions of the Old World.

Other politicians and commentators, however, argue that isolationism might seem attractive to many Americans in theory, but practical considerations make it impossible. As the globe's only superpower, and as a nation with economic ties in all parts of the world, the United States cannot simply stand apart from foreign affairs. Some people go further: They regard the United States as having a duty to lead the international community toward democracy and free market economics.

The tendency to isolationism began early in U.S. colonial history, when many settlers moved there to escape religious persecution and war in Europe. Politicians were wary of getting involved in European affairs. In his farewell address George Washington (1732–1799), the first president, warned America to "steer clear of permanent alliances" with European countries.

During the 19th century the United States did indeed largely steer clear of Europe, but it simultaneously began to extend its presence in the western hemisphere. In 1823 President James Monroe (1758–1831) announced the Monroe Doctrine. It stated that the United States would not allow Europe to interfere in the American continent. Successive U.S. governments broadened the doctrine's interpretation. By the beginning of the 20th century the United States had a more assertive role in the region, having acquired Puerto Rico, Guam, and the Philippines from Spain in 1898. In 1904 President Theodore Roosevelt (1858-1919) added a corollary to the Monroe Doctrine that was later used to justify intervention in Cuba, Nicaragua, Mexico, and Haiti.

The United States proclaimed neutrality when World War I broke out in 1914. To many Americans it seemed a distant conflict of tangled European rivalries. Germany's unrestricted submarine warfare and its attempt to form an alliance with Mexico, however, changed public opinion: The United States entered the war in 1917.

"Honest friendship with all nations; entangling alliances with none."

—THOMAS JEFFERSON, 3RD PRESIDENT (1801–1809)

Isolationism became a major issue in the postwar period. President Woodrow Wilson (1856-1924) called for a League of Nations to settle disputes between countries, but the Senate refused to ratify the Treaty of Versailles, which included provisions for the league. Many Americans feared that a league would inevitably drag the United States back into other nations' fights.

In 1920 Warren Harding (1865-1923) won the presidency on a promise of "normalcy" and isolationism. Soon,

however, the Republican administration found itself engaged in international politics to protect U.S. interests. From 1921 to 1922 it hosted the Washington Conference, which sought to limit naval armaments, particularly in Japan. It also instigated the Dawes Plan and the Young Plan, which were intended to help the Germans pay their postwar reparations to the Allies—and the Allies to pay their debts to the United States.

After the Nazi Party came to power in Germany in 1933, many Americans recoiled from the thought of becoming involved in another European conflict. In the late 1930s Congress passed a series of acts to underline U.S. neutrality. After World War II began in 1939, President Franklin D. Roosevelt (1882-1945) relaxed the laws, notably with the 1941 Lend-Lease Act, which permitted the sale of arms to any nation whose existence was deemed vital to U.S. defense. Some commentators, however, assert that the United States might still have stayed out of the war were it not for the Japanese attack on Pearl Harbor in December 1941.

U.S. obligations to international peacekeeping under the 1945 Charter of the United Nations made a return to isolationism unfeasible. At the same time, concerns about the influence of the Soviet Union led the United States to intervene in the affairs of countries that it considered were at risk of becoming communist. Since the end of the Cold War in 1989, however, some people have begun to argue that the United States should be wary of being seen to "meddle" in foreign affairs. Some critics even claim that U.S. interventionism led to the terrorist attacks of September 11, 2001.

The following two articles examine the debate in greater detail.

AMERICA'S TRADITION OF NONINTERVENTIONISM
Chris Leithner

Chris Leithner is a Canadian academic based in Australia. In 2003 he wrote this article for Le Québécois Libre, a Montreal newspaper.

Go to http://www.townhall.com/bookclub/Sowell3.html for a review of Thomas Sowell's book, published in 1996.

For a discussion of interventionism in U.S. foreign policy see Volume 8, U.S. Foreign Policy, Topic 2 Is U.S. foreign policy too interventionist?

What does the author mean by "welfare-warfare state"? Read the article "Bush Swells the State" at http://www.mises.org/fullstory.asp?control=939 to help you reach a definition.

YES

✓ "The notion that a radical is one who hates his country is naïve and usually idiotic. He is, more likely, one who likes his country more than the rest of us, and is thus more disturbed than the rest of us when he sees it debauched. He is not a bad citizen turning to crime; he is a good citizen driven to despair."
—H. L. Mencken (letter to Upton Sinclair, October 14, 1917)

Labels, as Thomas Sowell teaches us in *The Vision of the Anointed*, are both convenient and dangerous. Carefully and dispassionately used, vocabulary helps to transmit complex ideas accurately and efficiently. Employed carelessly, however, terminology creates vagueness, ambiguity and misunderstanding; and utilised malevolently, it can obstruct reasoning, obscure corroborating evidence and thereby set the stage for mistakes—and sometimes catastrophes.

War and related issues

"American Isolationism" is a label that has long been used malevolently by its opponents. Noninterventionism, a less emotive phrase, denotes disapproval, ranging from scepticism to outright opposition, with respect to a cluster of related issues: war (particularly ideological wars and crusades) and other government interventions (alliances, "aid," posting of military personnel, etc.) in foreign lands; the eclipse of the authority of the U.S. Congress to declare war, the concentration of authority … in the Executive and the consequent ability of a President to execute war deceptively and secretly; America's abandonment of republicanism and limited government and embrace of imperialism and a welfare-warfare state; the erosion of civil and political liberties for the sake of "security;" and the linkages between a large military establishment and permanent war economy, industry, government and bureaucracy.

Congressman Howard H. Buffett, (R-Nebraska), the Midwestern campaign manager for "Mr. Republican" Senator

Robert Taft in 1952, was a leading opponent of America's increasingly interventionist policies, foreign and domestic, during the 1930s, 1940s and 1950s. Criticising the proposal of FDR [Roosevelt's] Secretary of the Interior … to build a $165m oil pipeline in Saudi Arabia, Mr. Buffett stated on 24 March 1944 "it would terminate the inspiring period of America's history as a great nation not resorting to intercontinental imperialism. This venture would end the influence exercised by the United States as a government not participating in the exploitation of small lands and countries.… It may be that the American people would rather forego the use of a questionable amount of gasoline at some time in the remote future than follow a foreign policy practically guaranteed to send many of their sons … to die in faraway places in defence of the trade of Standard Oil or the international dreams of our one-world planners."

Congressman Buffett was a staunch anti-Communist who nevertheless questioned the morality as well as the efficacy of America's Cold War crusade. He declared "our Christian ideals cannot be exported to other lands by dollars and guns. Persuasion and example are the methods taught by the Carpenter of Nazareth.… We cannot practice might and force abroad and retain freedom at home. We cannot talk co-operation and practice power politics.…"

The price of interventionism

Patrick J. Buchanan uttered similar sentiments and outlined a stark choice during the 2000 U.S. Presidential campaign. "How can all our meddling not fail to spark some horrible retribution.… Have we not suffered enough—from PanAm 103, to the World Trade Center [bombing of 1993], to the embassy bombings in Nairobi and Dar es Salaam—not to know that interventionism is the incubator of terrorism? Or will it take some cataclysmic atrocity on U.S. soil to awaken our global gamesmen to the going price of empire? America today faces a choice of destinies. We can choose to be a peacemaker of the world, or its policeman who goes about night-sticking troublemakers until we, too, find ourselves in some bloody brawl we cannot handle."

Élite indignation

Yet presently in America, as for most of the past half-century, few things provoke more indignation, ridicule and denunciation from political, academic and journalistic élites (as opposed to consumers and taxpayers) than scepticism towards America's interventionist foreign policy. To be

U.S. geologists discovered oil in Saudi Arabia in the 1930s, but large-scale production did not start until the late 1940s. Today Saudi Arabia is the world's leading producer and exporter of oil.

Has the American people's attitude to war changed since the 1940s? Go to www.google.com, and search for the latest polls.

Patrick J. Buchanan (1938–) was twice a candidate for the Republican presidential nomination. He now works as a journalist. He is the founder of the magazine The American Conservative.

Do you think the roles of peacemaker and policeman are always incompatible?

associated with isolationism is, in privileged quarters, to be cast outside the perimeter of serious conversation….

In praise of internationalism

Charles Lindbergh (1902–1974) made the first solo nonstop flight across the Atlantic. Prior to Pearl Harbor he campaigned against U.S. involvement in World War II (1939–1945). Father Charles E. Coughlin (1891–1979) was known as the "radio priest" because of his weekly broadcasts. During the 1930s his sermons became more political.

During the past couple of years, leading politicians and commentators and prominent organs of mass communication have glorified "internationalism" and denigrated "isolationism." In the first major interview after his election, on CBS' *60 Minutes II*, President George W. Bush stated that "the principal threat facing America is isolationism … America can't go it alone." Robert Kagan wrote in *The Washington Post* (29 January 2002) "Sept. 11th must spur us to launch a new era of American internationalism…." Michael Hirsh, in an article entitled "The Death of a Founding Myth" (*Newsweek/ MSNBC*, January 2002), went further. "The terrorist attacks permanently altered America's self-identity. We must now embrace the global community we ourselves built…. While the isolationists—the Charles Lindberghs, Father Coughlins and Pat Buchanans—tempted millions with their siren's appeal to nativism, the internationalists were always hard at work in quiet places making plans for a more perfect global community. In the end the internationalists have always dominated national policy. Even so, they haven't bragged about their globe-building for fear of reawakening the other half of the American psyche, our berserker nativism."

"Nativism" refers to a policy of favoring native inhabitants over immigrants.

Hirsh is simply wrong: interventionism has not always prevailed; noninterventionism is not nativism; and it is arguable whether the consequences of interventionism have been positive. What is presently derided as "isolationism" was once as prominent as it was respected. Indeed, until the last quarter of the nineteenth century it was unshakeable orthodoxy. Thereafter, and for several reasons, it weakened. During the first half of the twentieth century, most American politicians, academics and journalists implicitly (and in the latter half explicitly) abandoned the Founders' [Framers'] noninterventionism. Today's policy, embraced by "liberal" Democrats, "conservative" Republicans and the bureaucratic behemoth within the Beltway, is worldwide, open-ended interventionism. No matter the place and whatever the "problem," America's diplomacy, money or armed forces … will be brought to bear and find a "solution."

Garet Garrett (1878–1954) was a writer and critic of U.S. empire-building. John T. Flynn (1882–1964) was a journalist who was against interventionism.

This policy, as Garet Garrett warned from the 1920s to 1950s, has transformed the United States from a Republic to an Empire. As John Flynn prophesied from the 1930s to 1950s, and as Congressman Ron Paul (R-Texas) now laments, it has gravely weakened the Constitution and unleashed a

Leviathan welfare-warfare state [that] has oppressed American taxpayers and wasted the lives of its youth.

It is embarrassing for the élites who coined the term "isolationism," and hence rarely mentioned by them, that interventionism plays poorly in Peoria. Most Americans, in other words, historically were and today remain noninterventionists. Polls have shown consistently that Americans generally disdain foreign entanglements and overwhelmingly oppose foreign "aid." As the events of 11 September 2001 illustrated, interventionist policies have also generated the hostility and enmity of people not predisposed to appreciate the peculiarities and finer points of American institutions and history.

> By "Peoria" the author is referring to the traditional or conservative element of Middle America, as represented by the small town of Peoria in Illinois.

Ignorance of the Framers

Steve Bonta's chronicle of America's abandonment of noninterventionism and embrace of interventionism, entitled "Minding Our Own Business," provides excellent reading for Americans and admirers of the United States. It emphasises that America's Founders [Framers] possessed an acute—and prescient—understanding of the dangers of governmental meddling in foreign lands. Bonta shows that the Founders [Framers] espoused *political* noninterventionism. Far from being backward, xenophobic and the like, many possessed a keen interest in foreign languages, history, culture, technical and economic developments. Indeed, several ranked among the best literary, technical and commercial minds of the late-eighteenth century. On cultural, scientific and economic grounds, most (Hamiltonians were perhaps an exception) favoured extensive and unfettered private associations with foreigners.

> Go to http://www. thenewamerican. com/tna/2002/ 03-11-2002/ vo18no05_ minding.htm to read Bonta's article.

> Hamiltonians were supporters of Alexander Hamilton (1755–1804), one of the Framers of the Constitution. For more information on Hamilton go to Volume 2, Government, page 81.

To say that noninterventionism proposes to "turn America's back on the world" is therefore to proclaim one's ignorance of America's Founders [Framers], the principles upon which the Great Republic was based, the long success of those principles and the more recent trials, tribulations and catastrophes that have resulted from their overturn.

Perhaps the greatest tragedy in the wake of 11 September 2001, apart from the lives lost, children orphaned and adults widow(er)ed, is that the citizens of the very country that has one of the noblest histories of political noninterventionism are apparently ignorant of that history. For many Americans and their admirers, Bonta's article and the writings of Garrett, Flynn, and other noninterventionists may confirm a point that Harry Truman put best: "There is nothing new in the world but the history you do not know."

INTERNATIONALISM VERSUS ISOLATIONISM IN U.S. FOREIGN POLICY
Samuel L. Berger

Samuel L. Berger was a national security adviser (1997–2001) to President Bill Clinton. He wrote this article in 1999.

Efforts to limit nuclear weapons testing began in the late 1950s. The Comprehensive Test Ban Treaty (CTBT) was approved by the United Nations in 1996. The United States and some other countries have yet to ratify the treaty although nuclear tests are suspended. The CTBT would ban nuclear explosions and prevent new weapons being developed. Opponents say the treaty is unworkable because the ban cannot be properly verified. Supporters argue that the treaty is in U.S. security interests.

Do you think treaties threaten U.S. sovereignty? Are there alternative ways of reaching international agreement?

NO

We are at a defining and paradoxical point in the debate about America's role in the world.

America's strength and prosperity are unrivaled. Our leadership has never been more needed or in demand. And most Americans understand we must provide it; their pride in our achievements makes them not triumphant but confident in our ability to shape, with others, a world that is more democratic, prosperous and at peace.

Yet our internationalist tradition increasingly is being challenged by a new isolationism that would bury America's head in the sand at the height of our power and prosperity. There are leaders in both parties who reject this view—including many who had legitimate concerns about the Comprehensive Test Ban Treaty, but who wanted more time to have them addressed. But with the Senate's hurried defeat of the Treaty and the meat axe Congress has taken to our foreign affairs budget, we must face the reality that it no longer is a fringe view.

Why the new isolationism is wrong

It's tempting to say that the new isolationism is driven only by partisanship. But that underestimates it. There is a coherence to its view of the world and of our role. Here is what I believe its elements are, and why I believe they are wrong.

First: Any treaty others embrace, we won't join. Proponents of this view are convinced treaties are a threat to our sovereignty and continued superiority. That's what they say about the nuclear Test Ban though we have already stopped testing, though the Treaty helps freeze the global development of nuclear weapons when we enjoy an enormous strategic advantage.

We agree it would be foolish to rely on arms control treaties alone to protect our security. But it would be equally foolish to throw away the tools sound treaties offer: the restraint and deterrence that comes from global rules with global backing.

COMMENTARY: The United States and the UN

The United Nations (UN) owes its existence to the vision of Franklin D. Roosevelt, the 33rd president (1933–1945). At the end of World War II (1939–1945) Roosevelt recognized the need for a global security system that could use collective action to prevent future conflicts. The UN was founded in 1945 as a replacement for the League of Nations, an international organization established at the Paris Peace Conference in 1919 to maintain peace. The league, however, failed in its mission. Some commentators have attributed this to the fact that the United States refused to join the organization (see Volume 13, *U.S. History, Topic 7 Should the United States have supported the League of Nations?*).

As a founding member of the UN, the United States holds a privileged position as one of the five permanent members—along with Britain, China, France, and Russia—of the UN Security Council, which means that it has a veto over all decisions relating to international peace and security. Many experts believe that peace would be impossible without the active involvement of the United States, the sole superpower, in the UN.

Paying UN dues

The UN is funded by contributions from its members. Each country's economic growth is measured over a base period to determine the amount it gives. The United States has been the largest financial contributor since the UN's creation. In 2002 it provided an estimated $3 billion in cash and in kind—for example, food donations—contributions to the UN system.

From the mid-1980s the United States became more discerning about how much money it paid the UN and began to hold back a portion of its annual dues. It criticized the UN for being inefficient and unaccountable. The UN's failure to prevent bloodshed in Bosnia, Somalia, and Rwanda in the 1990s further fueled U.S. disillusionment. Some observers suggest that U.S. dissatisfaction with the UN coincided with a reluctance to take up its responsibilities on the international stage—an attitude that was further reflected in its decision to reduce foreign aid, diplomatic initiatives, and military forces. By the late 1990s the United States owed the UN around $1.5 billion in back dues. In November 1999 Congress and the White House struck a deal stipulating that the United States would pay $926 million in arrears over three years if the UN reformed its huge bureaucracy and cut the U.S. share of its financial burden. The United States risked losing its vote in the UN General Assembly if it failed to make a payment by the end of the year. In 2000 the UN agreed to reduce U.S. dues substantially. The contribution the United States makes to the UN basic budget was cut from 25 to 22 percent. Its obligations to peacekeeping expenses were also set to decrease gradually from 31 percent; in 2002 the United States funded 27 percent of the peacekeeping budget.

The Balkan states —Albania, Bosnia and Herzegovina, Bulgaria, Croatia, Macedonia, Moldova, Romania, Serbia and Montenegro, and Slovenia—occupy the Balkan Peninsula in southeastern Europe.

Since the breakup of former Yugoslavia war has ravaged much of the Balkans. Thousands of U.S. troops have been deployed to keep peace in the region. Go to http://www.usip.org/balkans/ for more information.

Do the wealth and power of the United States make it inevitable that it will always have enemies?

Do you believe wealthier countries should give more foreign aid to countries that embrace democracy?

Second: Burden sharing is a one way street. Proponents of the new isolationism rightly insist that Europeans fund the lion's share of reconstructing the Balkans. But then they balk at doing our part. They oppose American involvement in Africa's wars, but will not help others, like Nigeria, when they take responsibility to act. And they will not pay America's part of the cost of UN peacekeeping missions, even to uphold peace agreements we helped forge. This year, Congress has cut our request for peacekeeping by more than half.

That is dangerous. If we don't support the institutions and arrangements through which other countries share the responsibilities of leadership, we will bear them alone.

Foreign wars

Third: If it's over there, its not our fight. Foreign wars like those in Bosnia and Kosovo may hurt our conscience, but not our interests, and we should let them take their course.

We agree America cannot do everything or be everywhere. But we also cannot afford to do nothing, and be nowhere. The new isolationism of 1999 fails to understand what the old isolationism of 60 years ago failed to understand—that local conflicts can have global consequences.

Relations with China

Fourth: We can't be a great country without a great adversary. Since the Cold War ended, the proponents of this vision have been nostalgic for the good old days when friends were friends and enemies were enemies. For the role of new enemy number one, they nominate China.

We should not look at China through rose colored glasses; neither should we see it through a glass darkly, distorting its strength and ignoring its complexities. We must pursue our national interests vigorously with China, but treating it like an enemy could become a self-fulfilling prophesy.

The cost of defense

Fifth: Billions for defense but hardly a penny for prevention. This year's spending bill for most of our foreign programs, which the President has vetoed, fails to fund a vitally needed expansion in our effort to keep nuclear weapons from the former Soviet Union from falling into the wrong hands. It does not fund our pledge to help relieve the debts of impoverished countries that are finally embracing freedom and reform. Astonishingly, it does not fund our commitments to the Middle East peace process growing out of the

Wye Accords. Meanwhile, the Congress is trying to add $5 billion to the defense budget this year that our military says it doesn't need.

The President has requested the first sustained increase in military spending in a decade. But he has also argued that if we underfund our diplomacy, we will end up overusing our military—precisely the outcome critics say they want to avoid. Those who fear that our military may become overextended should make it their first order of business to restore decent levels of funding to the programs that keep our soldiers out of war.

The challenges ahead

America faces many challenges in the world in the coming year: seizing opportunities for peace from the Middle East, to the Balkans, to Africa; weaving Russia and China more closely into the international system; combating terror and the spread of weapons of mass destruction, from the former Soviet Union to Korea to the Gulf, launching a new global trade round, promoting debt relief, supporting hopeful democratic transitions from Nigeria to Indonesia, and others.

There is room for debate about our approach to all these issues. But we should agree that in an era of growing interdependence, we cannot afford a survivalist foreign policy—which relies on military might alone to protect our security, while neglecting all else.

America must maintain its military and economic power. But we must also maintain our authority, built on the attractiveness of our values, the force of our example, the credibility of our commitments and our willingness to work with and stand by our friends. The President wants to work with Congress to preserve a foreign policy that does just that.

The "Wye Accords" were the agreements toward peace reached at the Middle East summit that took place in Wye Mills, Maryland, in 1998. The peace accord fell apart almost immediately after disagreement over the release of Palestinian prisoners and after Israeli Prime Minister Binyamin Netanyahu made additional demands.

Samuel Berger sums up the crux of his argument in one sentence as he concludes. This is an effective way to underline your case.

Summary

According to Chris Leithner, contemporary U.S. foreign policy amounts to a wholesale rejection of a hallowed tradition of nonintervention in the affairs of other countries. He points out that what is now derided as isolationism was once the dominant, respected approach to international relations, and he contends that most Americans essentially remain noninterventionists. Leithner suggests that interventionism has "generated the hostility and enmity of people" in other parts of the world, citing the terrorist attacks of September 11, 2001, as evidence. He argues that the Framers, who favored noninterventionism, "possessed an acute—and prescient—understanding of the dangers of governmental meddling in foreign lands."

In contrast to Leithner, Samuel Berger, who served as national security adviser to President Clinton, argues that a tradition of internationalism is vital for the United States and the modern challenges it faces. "[W]e cannot afford a survivalist foreign policy—which relies on military might alone to protect our security, while neglecting all else," he warns. Berger cautions that if the United States does not support international institutions, such as the UN, through which countries share the responsibilities of leadership, then it will "bear them alone" at its peril.

FURTHER INFORMATION:

Books:

Bennis, Phyllis, and Noam Chomsky, *Before and After: U.S. Foreign Policy and the September 11th Crisis.* Ithaca, NY: Olive Branch Press, 2002.

Nordlinger, Eric, *Isolationism Reconfigured: American Foreign Policy for a New Century.* Princeton, NJ: Princeton University Press, 1995.

Useful websites:

http://college.hmco.com/history/readerscomp/rcah/html/ah_046200_isolationism.htm
Reader's Companion to American History article on the history of isolationism.
http://www.firstthings.com/ftissues/ft0104/opinion/thistime.html
"Conflicts Foreign and Domestic" by James Nuechterlein.
http://www.gaikoforum.com/p35-42_Hendrickson.pdf
"Imperialism versus Internationalism" by David C. Hendrickson.
http://mondediplo.com/2002/10/09nationalism
"United States: So Proudly We Hail" by Norman Birnbaum.

http://www.theatlanticmonthly.com/issues/2004/04/schwarz.htm
"Clearer Than the Truth" by Benjamin Schwarz.
www.thenewamerican.com
Conservative magazine with articles favoring isolationism.

The following debates in the Pro/Con series may also be of interest:

In this volume:
   Topic 6 Has the War on Terrorism reinforced U.S. global leadership?

   Topic 8 Should the United Nations be disbanded?

In *U.S. Foreign Policy*:
   Topic 2 Is U.S. foreign policy too interventionist?

IS THE UNITED STATES NATURALLY ISOLATIONIST?

YES: The United States faces no direct challenges to its security from its neighbors in the western hemisphere

YES: For much of the first century and a half of its history the United States successfully avoided becoming involved in Europe's "entangling alliances"

GEOGRAPHY
Has geographical location resulted in U.S. isolationism?

A MYTH
Has the United States ever truly been isolationist?

NO: That may have been true historically, but the country has expanded its geographical boundaries and trade markets, and since 1945 U.S. foreign policy has been more interventionist

NO: The view of the United States as isolationist is greatly exaggerated because, while it was trying to avoid involvement in European affairs, it was building an empire in the western hemisphere

IS THE UNITED STATES NATURALLY ISOLATIONIST? KEY POINTS

YES: The United States is rich and powerful enough to follow its own agenda. It should be cautious about making enemies by intervening unnecessarily in foreign affairs.

YES: The United States has been drawn into conflicts to support democracies that are weaker or poorer

AN OUTMODED POLICY
Is isolationism still a feasible strategy for the United States?

RELUCTANT ALLIES
Do other countries continually draw the United States into world politics?

NO: As the world's sole remaining superpower, the United States has a duty to pursue internationalism and act as global policeman

NO: The United States has long intervened in the domestic politics of other countries only to protect its own interests

YES
"BEATING TERROR"
THE WASHINGTON POST, JANUARY 27, 2003
SENATOR RICHARD LUGAR

NO
FROM "DON'T BLAME AMERICA FOR TERRORIST ATROCITY"
THE AGE, SEPTEMBER 28, 2001
TONY PARKINSON

INTRODUCTION

Diplomacy is the art of solving disputes, often between nations, through negotiation. In the words of former Secretary of State Henry Kissinger it "presumes that national interests have a tendency to clash." In the aftermath of Al Qaeda's September 11, 2001, terrorist action against New York and Washington, D.C., some people argued that the attacks reflected the failure of U.S. diplomacy. In particular, they claim that U.S. policies in the Middle East clash with the perceived interests and beliefs of radical Islamic groups. Such policies include the presence of U.S. military personnel on the Arabian peninsula, U.S. relationships with moderate Arab regimes—Egypt and Jordan, for example—that have cracked down on radical Islamists, and U.S. support for Israel.

Half-hearted and poorly funded U.S. attempts at diplomacy—dubbed "diplomacy on a shoestring"—may have led to the failure to reconcile U.S. policies with certain radical groups. This, some believe, encouraged a violent reaction against the United States. At the same time, it may also have prevented the United States from forging alliances with other nations to tackle the threat of Al Qaeda before the attacks took place.

Within the U.S. government diplomacy has traditionally been the special responsibility of the State Department. This department was one of four original cabinet departments created on ratification of the Constitution in 1789. Throughout most of U.S. history it was the principal agent of the executive branch of government responsible for managing U.S. foreign policy.

Since World War II, however, the influence of the State Department over foreign policymaking has declined significantly, and other agencies in the government and the White House have sought to control it instead. The State Department operates a network of several hundred diplomatic and consular posts throughout the world, plus delegations and missions to international organizations. In contrast to other important government institutions involved in foreign policy—most notably, the Defense Department—the State Department has been described as "a bureaucratic pygmy among giants." The State Department's operating budget in 2003 was $11 billion, for example, compared to the Defense Department's budget of over $400 billion. This has led some politicians and diplomats, among others, to argue that the United States is still not placing enough importance on diplomatic rather than military action.

"All war represents a failure of diplomacy."

—TONY BENN (1925–), BRITISH LABOUR POLITICIAN

Some people claim that it was actually the government's use of diplomacy and international law to deal with terrorist groups that resulted in 9/11 (as it is more commonly known). The 9-11 Commission set up to look into the circumstances surrounding the attacks found that Bill Clinton's administration had linked Osama Bin Laden, leader of Al Qaeda, to terrorism as early as 1995. Efforts to have Bin

Laden expelled from Sudan came to a halt after Clinton officials concluded that he had to be indicted before he could be brought to the United States. A year later he left Sudan to set up his base in Afghanistan, after which CIA Director George Tenet worked with Saudia Arabia to persuade Afghanistan's Taliban government to expel Bin Laden. Although Saudi intelligence chief Prince Turki Bin Faisal came to an agreement with Taliban leader Mullah Omar that Bin Laden would be handed over, Omar reneged on the agreement.

When George W. Bush became president, his officials failed to act on the intelligence advice of its counterterrorism adviser, Richard A. Clarke, to take out Al Qaeda targets. The result was, critics claim, that the group was able to plan and carry out the U.S. terrorist action. If this is true, 9/11 can be put down to more than just poor State Department funding.

Some believe that the United States has learned from the mistakes of the past and is trying to build up better diplomatic relationships with other nations, particularly since the War on Terrorism began. In 2003 Ambassador Cofer Black, coordinator for counterterrorism stated, "[I]n my view, diplomacy … is one of our most potent offensive weapons in the war on terrorism. Diplomacy is the instrument of power that builds political will and strengthens international cooperation. Through diplomatic exchanges, we promote counterterrorism cooperation with friendly nations that serve our mutual interests."

The following two articles examine the issue in further detail. Senator Richard Lugar argues that diplomacy let the United States down, but journalist Tony Parkinson disagrees.

BEATING TERROR
Richard Lugar

Richard Lugar is Republican senator from Indiana. He is also chairman of the Senate Foreign Relations Committee. He published this article in January 2003.

YES

In the 16 months since the Sept. 11, 2001, attacks, the United States has taken a number of steps—in the military, security and intelligence areas—that greatly improved its ability to fight the war on terrorism. What it has not done is develop a plan or demonstrate the political will to win the war.

Military action will be necessary to deal with serious and immediate threats to our national security, but the war on terrorism will not be won through attrition—particularly because military action will often breed more terrorists. To win this war, the United States must assign to economic and diplomatic capabilities the same strategic priority we assign to military capabilities. What is still missing from American political discourse is support for the painstaking work of foreign policy and the commitment of resources to vital foreign policy objectives that lack a direct political constituency.

Events since the Cold War

Since the end of the Cold War, our ability and will to exert U.S. leadership outside the confines of a military crisis have been badly eroded by inattention, budget cuts and increasing partisanship. In 2001 the share of the budget devoted to international affairs was a paltry 1.18 percent. We are conducting diplomacy on a shoestring in an era when embassies are prime terrorist targets and we depend on diplomats to build alliances, block visas to potential terrorists and explain the United States worldwide.

A 2001 General Accounting Office report found that significant staffing shortfalls plague the more than 150 diplomatic posts considered to be hardship locations. Many jobs are being filled by Foreign Service officers serving two or three grades higher than their experience warrants. Staffing shortfalls also lead to abbreviated language training. U.S. foreign assistance in constant dollars has declined about 44 percent since its peak during the Reagan presidency. The United States devotes about one-tenth of 1 percent of its GNP to economic assistance.

In 2000 former Secretary of State Lawrence S. Eagleburger published an article in which he stated that the international affairs budget (including the State Department's budget) was in recent times 20 percent less than it had been in the 1970s and 1980s. What effect might this have on U.S. diplomacy? Go to http://www.his.com/~councill/eagleburger.htm to read the article.

The General Accounting Office presented a report in September 2003 that found that the United States was still perceived unfavorably. It concluded that the secretary of state had to develop an integrated policy to improve its image.

Contrary to the media-inspired illusion that foreign policy is determined by a series of decisions and responses to crises, most of the recent failures of U.S. foreign policy have far more to do with our inattention and parsimony between crises. For example, in 2002, amid speculation about terrorists acquiring weapons of mass destruction, inaction by Congress effectively suspended for seven months new U.S. initiatives to secure Russia's immense stockpiles of nuclear, biological and chemical weapons. Congressional conditions also have delayed for years a U.S.–Russian project to eliminate a dangerous proliferation threat: 1.9 million chemical weapons housed at a rickety and vulnerable facility in Russia.

> *"Parsimony" means thrift, or being careful with money.*

Leadership failure

The United States has repeatedly failed to exert the leadership necessary to bring multilateral treaties in line with important U.S. interests.

> *Does it matter if the United States refuses to join agreements ratified by virtually every other nation?*

The result has been problematic agreements such as Kyoto, the Nuclear Test Ban Treaty and the International Criminal Court Treaty [see Volume 22, *International Law*], all of which lack sufficient support in the United States and divide us from our allies. Partisan posturing continues over whether to support these treaties, when the real question is why the United States—occupying a seemingly unrivaled position in the world—cannot achieve agreements that would be supported both at home and overseas.

Meanwhile, between 1995 and 2002 the United States—economic engine of the world—effectively constrained itself from entering into significant new trade agreements by failing to pass trade promotion authority. This monumental political failure hurt U.S. workers and businesses, perplexed allies, ceded markets to competitors and weakened development overseas.

> *The trade promotion authority (TPA) was a trade liberalization agreement discussed by Congress in 2002. It would have allowed the president the ability to negotiate trade agreements, and to submit them to Congress. Go to http://www. heritage.org/ Research/Tradeand ForeignAid/ WM60.cfm for more information.*

Generating international support

In the Iraq crisis, military capability has never been in doubt. If we decide to go to war, we will depose Saddam Hussein's regime. What have been in doubt are factors determined by our diplomatic strength, our alliance relationships and foreign perceptions of the United States. Can we line up the support of the U.N. Security Council? Can we secure basing and overflight rights? Can we generate international support that will mitigate anti-American reactions in the Arab world?

In short, the unknown in our Iraqi policy depends on U.S. foreign policy capabilities. It depends on programs

Would spending more money on foreign policy programs help prevent military conflict in the future?

and personnel that are funded at about $26 billion per year, an amount equal to 6.7 percent of our defense budget.

The Iraq debate in Congress focused on whether the United States should make concessions to world opinion or pursue its perceived national security interests unencumbered by the constraints of the international community. But this was a false choice.

National security decision-making can rarely be separated from the constraints of the international community, if only because our resources and influence are finite. Our security depends not on clever decision-making about when to go it alone but on executing a potent foreign policy that ensures the international community will be with us in a crisis.

Senate Foreign Relations Committee recommendations:

In the coming months, the Senate Foreign Relations Committee will explore five foreign policy campaigns necessary to win the war against terrorism:

- Strengthen U.S. diplomacy

Congress and the president must commit to robust, long-term investments in diplomats, embassy security, and effective foreign policy communications strategies and tools. We also must gear up our foreign assistance programs.

This agreement was named for Senators Richard Lugar and Sam Nunn, who negotiated it in 1991. Its aim was to work jointly with Russia and former Soviet states to reduce the threat posed by the legacy of the Soviet nuclear arsenal. Since then 5,504 warheads have been deactivated, and 423 intercontinental ballistic missiles destroyed.

- Expand and globalize the Nunn–Lugar program

Since 1991 the Nunn–Lugar Cooperative Threat Reduction Program has worked effectively to safeguard and destroy the immense stockpiles of weapons of mass destruction in the former Soviet Union. We need to redouble these efforts and expand the process to all nations where cooperation can be secured.

- Promote trade

Free trade is essential to strengthening our economy, building alliances and spreading the benefits of market economics. Expanding trade in the developing world is essential to building the conditions that dampen terrorist recruitment and political resentment.

- Strengthen and build alliances

The stronger our alliances, the more likely we are to have partners who will share financial burdens and support our efforts against terrorism.

• Reinvigorate our commitment to democracy, the environment, energy and development

The United States must reassert itself as a positive force for democracy and development. This must include improving energy supplies worldwide to free up resources in developing nations and reduce the dependence of the world economy on Persian Gulf oil. International environmental protection is required for successful economic development in many regions. Environmental concerns are linked to the dismantling of weapons, our ability to build alliances and political attitudes toward trade expansion.

Should the United States do more to penalize home-based transnational companies that damage the environment?

On the side of the terrorists

These five campaigns will require not only money but also political leadership from the Bush administration and Congress. We must explain to the American people why these campaigns are as critical to the war on terrorism as our military efforts. Without them we will relegate ourselves to fighting a holding action in which time is on the side of the terrorists.

DON'T BLAME AMERICA FOR TERRORIST ATROCITY
Tony Parkinson

Tony Parkinson is international editor of the Australian newspaper The Age.

NO

On February 26, 2001, the Taliban announced that all pre-Islamic statues in Afghanistan would be destroyed. in March two 1,500-year-old Buddha statues, carved into a mountainside at Bamiyan, were dynamited. The tallest statue stood 175 feet (53 meters) tall and was thought to be the highest in the world. Go to http://www.tamu.edu/anthropology/Buddhas.html to find out about the statues.

Only six months before terrorists brought crashing to earth the twin towers of the World Trade Centre, Taliban chief Mullah Mohammed Omar issued orders for the desecration of the Buddhas of Bamiyan.

Giant statues that had looked benignly over an Afghan valley for 1500 years were reduced to rubble by rocket fire and dynamite.

There was universal, unconditional condemnation from all corners of the world. Nobody went looking for excuses.

Nobody said Buddhism had only itself to blame. Nobody sought to draw obscure linkages to the plight of the Palestinians. Nobody pointed to the shaming and humiliation of Islam by foreign powers as a reason why these extremists would take out their vengeance on the icons of another civilisation.

The destruction of the statues was self-evidently the act of madmen. The same collection of madmen, it seems, who brought terror to the cities of America.

Paying the piper

Yet compare the reactions, particularly from those who argue that innocent civilians trapped in those towers in New York City paid the inevitable price for a history of flawed American policy in the Middle East.

In a time of tragedy, writers such as Noam Chomsky, John Pilger, Robert Fisk and Susan Sontag … have been careful not to indulge in rhetoric that could be confused with smug satisfaction.

But the common underlying theme of their assessments is that America is somehow getting its come-uppance for not paying due regard to the aspirations of the Arab and Islamic worlds.

In exploring why a network of terrorists would be ready to carry out one of the most blood-curdling atrocities in modern times, they ask us to look beyond the more obvious possibility—a psychotic ideology of hatred—and search instead for the "root causes".

This empty niche in Bamiyan, Afghanistan, marks the site of one of the two giant statues of Buddha destroyed by the Taliban in 2001. The Afghan government hopes to restore the Buddhas in the future.

The United States is more powerful than other nation in the world. Do you think that other people have a right to question U.S. foreign policy?

We are asked to see these events in the context of a long history of grievance against the West. We are asked to put U.S. foreign policy in the dock alongside Osama Bin Laden. We are asked to look for excuses.

But the real dangers arise if Arab and Islamic leaders resort to this dangerous cop-out, in which they can deflect proper scrutiny and escape accountability for what is happening in their midst.

A clash of civilizations

In statements released since the September 11 attacks, Osama Bin Laden and the Taliban leader, Mullah Mohammed Omar, have cast this episode as a defining moment in what they characterise as a civilisational struggle between Islam and the West. In seeking to mobilise the support of the Arab and Islamic masses, they cite U.S. backing for Israel as the core violation against which all acts of violence and terror and perfidy must be judged.

It is a seductive cry. The denial of a Palestinian homeland is seen by many Muslims, from the wealthiest Saudi businessman through to impoverished street hawkers in East Java, as a religious and cultural affront.

But as an excuse to wage a war of terror on America? Not even close.

A megalomaniac is someone who has a mania for great or grandiose things or power.

Like a long line of megalomaniacs before them, Bin Laden and the Taliban are seeking to use the suffering of the Palestinian people as a human shield for their extremism.

It is a transparent strategy, which ought not be given credence—neither by fellow Muslims nor by the West's so-called enlightened left. They might consider taking a cue from Yasser Arafat's anxious efforts to resurrect peace talks with Israel. Having learnt from his miscalculations in the 1991 Gulf War, this is not a cause that the Palestinian leader wants to be identified with.

The truth about double-dealing

The United States has been accused of intervening only in regions in which its economic interests are threatened. See Volume 13, U.S. History, Topic 15 Was the Persian Gulf War a war about oil?

For the truth is, whatever double-dealing characterised U.S. policies in the Middle East and Afghanistan in the Cold War years, the accusation of one-sided intervention in the politics of the region simply does not stand up to rigorous analysis.

Where was the U.S. during the Suez crisis? Supporting Egypt's Nasser against Britain, France and Israel.

Where was the U.S. when Iraq invaded tiny Kuwait, in August, 1990? Mobilising the biggest military operation ever assembled in defence of an Arab nation.

Moreover, it was the activism of an American president in 1991 that gave rise to the Madrid peace conference, and created the first serious dialogue between Israel and the Palestinians since 1948. True, America provides massive funds to Israel, but it is also extremely generous in providing aid and soft credit to Egypt and Jordan.

And where was the U.S. in 1980 when Saddam Hussein sent six army divisions into neighboring Iran, starting an eight-year war that cost as many as 1.5 million lives, created a massive refugee crisis, brought missile attacks on civilian targets, the large-scale deployment of unarmed boy soldiers, and the first use since World War 1 of nerve gases as weapons of war?

At the time war began, the U.S. had diplomatic relations with neither of the Islamic nations, and adopted a posture of "relative neutrality". Only in 1982, when Iran had driven back Saddam's forces did the U.S. begin to tilt in Baghdad's direction.

Even then, it surreptitiously sold arms to Iran, and its assistance to Iraq was largely confined to intelligence data, protection of "friendly" oil tankers and the supply, ironically enough, of four Boeing airliners.

Often overlooked, these aspects of Middle East history show why it is fanciful to point a finger of accusation at the U.S. as the culprit for the woes of the region.

It shouldn't take the rap. Nor should it be expected take the hits.

George H.W. Bush (1989–1993) and James Baker (1989–1992), his secretary of state, were instrumental in bringing about the Madrid peace conference, held in October 1991. See http://216.239.59.104/search?q=cache:yYwMQfpnhuUJ:www.fas.org/man/crs/IB82008.pdf+George+H.W.+Bush+instrumental+Madrid+conference&hl=en&start=5&ie=UTF-8 for an article on U.S.–Israeli relations.

Summary

The preceding articles examine the controversial question of whether the U.S. policy of "diplomacy on a shoestring" was responsible for the September 11, 2001, terrorist attacks against the United States.

In the first Richard Lugar, a U.S. senator, asserts that this might be the case. After all, he says, "most of the recent failures of U.S. foreign policy have far more to do with our inattention and parsimony between crises." According to Lugar, the State Department is woefully underfunded in comparison to the Defense Department, even though the United States now depends more than ever on what he calls "diplomatic strength" to help it build essential international support for its policies. In sharp contrast to Lugar, journalist Tony Parkinson refuses to look for any "root causes" of anti-Americanism in the Middle East. "It is fanciful to point a finger of accusation at the United States as the culprit for the woes of the region," he concludes, when in fact September 11 was simply the result of what he calls "a psychotic ideology of hatred." Whereas Lugar suggests that many foreign policy crises could be averted through diplomatic strength, Parkinson argues that no amount of U.S. diplomacy could have alleviated the kind of hatred of the United States that was revealed in the New York and Washington, D.C., attacks.

FURTHER INFORMATION:

Books:

Bacevich, Andrew J., *American Empire: The Realities and Consequences of U.S. Diplomacy.* Cambridge, MA: Harvard, University Press, 2003.

Useful websites:

http://66.102.11.104/search?q=cache:s 13S6nkdCkJ:www.afsa.org/fsj/jul03/lugar.pdf+ Diplomacy+on+a+shoestring&hl=en&start=2&ie= UTF-8text
Richard Lugar article on strengthening diplomacy in the War on Terrorism.
http://www.fas.org/man/crs/IB82008.pdf
Congress Research Service report on Israeli–U.S. relations, October 2003.
http://www.govexec.com/dailyfed/0403/041003 cdam2.htm
Article by Margo MacFarland on 2003 budget increases to combat shortfalls in diplomatic funding.
http://www.publicdiplomacy.org/21.htm
The General Accounting Office's 2003 report on U.S. diplomacy since September, 2003.

The following debates in the Pro/Con series may also be of interest:

In this volume:
Topic 13 Is the United States naturally isolationist?

In *U.S. Foreign Policy*:
Part 1: The United States' position in the World?

September 11, 2001, pages 176–177

Topic 16 Should the United States take more responsibility for promoting peace in the Middle East?

DID "DIPLOMACY ON A SHOESTRING" CONTRIBUTE TO SEPTEMBER 11, 2001?

YES: Diplomats could have countered negative Muslim perceptions of Americans and U.S. foreign policy

YES: A 2003 report said that diplomats who were better trained in local customs and languages would help promote better understanding

PUBLIC IMAGE
Could diplomats have done more to promote the United States abroad?

TRAINING
Did diplomatic missions suffer from inadequately trained staff?

NO: Diplomats were constrained by factors such as lack of trained personnel, inadequate security, and budget cuts

NO: September 11 did not result from inadequately trained personnel. U.S. interventionist policy, globalization, and resentment of the Americanization of culture were also contributing factors.

DID "DIPLOMACY ON A SHOESTRING" CONTRIBUTE TO SEPTEMBER 11, 2001?

KEY POINTS

YES: No nation can be truly isolationist in the modern world. It is important to pursue diplomatic relations with different nations, and that requires investment.

YES: Good diplomatic relations can help preserve world peace. It is thus as, if not more, important to fund foreign missions and to train people properly.

INVESTMENT
Is investment in diplomacy as important as investment in the military?

NO: The world is rife with conflict, and it is important to be prepared

NO: The War on Terrorism shows how much a well-trained and funded military is necessary

Topic 15

IS IT JUSTIFIABLE FOR THE UNITED STATES TO SUPPORT DICTATORSHIPS?

YES

"WHEN THERE'S NO GOOD GUY"
USA TODAY, NOVEMBER 13, 2002
DINESH D'SOUZA

NO

FROM "TAINTED LEGACY: DANCING WITH DICTATORS"
AMNESTY NOW, FALL 2003
WILLIAM F. SCHULZ

INTRODUCTION

In the last one hundred or so years U.S. foreign policy has had a significant effect on world politics. The United States has helped many nations achieve freedom and democracy, but its conduct and policies have on occasion come under scrutiny. There are, critics argue, numerous examples of the United States forming alliances with and giving support to dictatorships in order to achieve a certain political or economic goal. These regimes have often been repressive and had poor human rights records. Critics believe that there can be no possible justification for U.S. support of such governments. Others, however, claim that history shows that the end justifies the means—whether it be in supporting dictators, such as former Chilean President General Augusto Pinochet (1974-1990) to stop the spread of communism in Latin America, or forming alliances with the military regime in Pakistan to help the aims of the War on Terrorism.

Once an isolationist power, the United States began to intervene increasingly in international affairs after the end of World War II in 1945. After the war the United States and the Soviet Union emerged as the two world superpowers. International affairs became defined by the constant state of tension between these countries, which came to be known as the Cold War (1946-1991).

Postwar U.S. foreign policy was based on the principle of "containment" to stop the global growth of communism. Containment policies differed according to the region: In eastern Europe the United States built up its military strength by setting up bases. In other nations, such as the many newly independent countries in Asia, Africa, and Latin America, the containment strategy was far more subtle. The United States often used foreign aid, sanctions, counterinsurgency, and covert paramilitary forces to promote relationships with what it considered "friendly" regimes—governments sympathetic to U.S. interests.

Several presidents supported containment policies. In 1947 President Harry S. Truman (1945-1953) gave $300 million in military and economic aid to Greece and Turkey, which were both under threat from communist insurgents. Truman's attitude, known as the Truman Doctrine, formed part of the U.S. policy to fight communism. Presidents John F. Kennedy (1961-1963), Gerald Ford (1974-1977), and Ronald Reagan (1981-1989) also all pursued covert and overt policies to stop communism.

> *"The United States will never survive as a happy and fertile oasis of liberty surrounded by a cruel desert of dictatorship."*
> —FRANKLIN D. ROOSEVELT, RADIO BROADCAST (1941)

Declassified State Department documents reveal that in 1976 Henry Kissinger, the secretary of state, met with Admiral Cesar Augusto Guzzetti, the foreign minister of the Argentine government. General Jorge Rafael Videla's military dictatorship had been accused of human rights abuses, but Guzzetti claimed that his government had been dismantling terrorist groups and dealing with subversives in what came to be known as the "Dirty War." An internal State Department

report, however, issued just a week before the meeting stated: "The most spectacular aspect of the counterterrorist drive has been the murderous exploits of the extra-legal, right-wing goon squads.... [T]he rightwingers are responsible for abducting and/or murdering hundreds of 'leftist security risks,' including political exiles from neighboring countries, foreign nationals, politicians, students, journalists, and priests." The U.S. government, some claim, turned a blind eye to these deaths.

Although President Jimmy Carter (1977-1981) argued that the United States should only be allies with countries that respected human rights, for many people communism remained the main priority. They believed that U.S. military and economic support of dictatorships was preferable to a communist-led government, even if that regime had killed thousands of people during its rule. Some people believe that this view led to hypocritical U.S. policy: Ronald Reagan, for example, terminated aid programs, imposed a trade embargo, and supported guerillas against the elected Marxist government of Nicaragua while giving economic and military aid to the equally repressive governments of South Korea, the Philippines, and Zaire.

After the Cold War ended, the United States continued to have relations with dictatorships, particularly in areas of political, military, or economic importance. This has inevitably led, critics argue, to great resentment toward the United States and a rise in anti-U.S. feeling.

Dinesh D'Souza and William F. Schulz further examine whether U.S. support of dictatorships can be justified.

WHEN THERE'S NO GOOD GUY
Dinesh D'Souza

Dinesh D'Souza is Robert and Karen Rishwain Fellow at the Hoover Institution, Stanford University, and the author of What's So Great about America (2002).

YES

Critics of President Bush's policy toward Iraq often raise the same questions: Isn't it ironic that we're trying to get rid of Saddam Hussein when we once supported him? Doesn't history show that you cannot impose democracy at the point of a bayonet? Isn't it hypocritical for the United States to condemn Saddam as a dictator when it supports many unelected regimes?

These criticisms of American foreign policy are not justified, however, and provide no basis for opposing a U.S.-led military campaign to liberate Iraq. A brutal dictator such as Saddam has no inherent right to rule. His support for terrorism, his willingness to use chemical and biological weapons, and his attempt to acquire nuclear weapons all make him an imminent danger to world peace and security.

What do you think the writer means by the phrase "inherent right to rule"? Might this apply to monarchs? Should anyone have an inherent right to rule?

What's the difference with this dictator?

"But why should America get rid of this dictator while it continues to support dictators elsewhere in the world?" the critics of an Iraq invasion ask. For decades, these critics say, U.S. leaders have sung paeans to democracy and human rights while backing dictatorships such as Anastasio Somoza in Nicaragua, Augusto Pinochet in Chile, the shah of Iran, and Ferdinand Marcos in the Philippines. Even now, they point out, the United States is allied with such despots as General Pervez Musharaff in Pakistan, Hosni Mubarak in Egypt, and the members of the royal family in Saudi Arabia.

Some commentators believe that good U.S.–Pakistan relations are wrong, since Pakistan may have links with terrorist groups. President Musharraf, however, has blamed two assassination attempts (December 2003) on Al Qaeda.

First consider the longtime U.S. support for Somoza, Marcos, Pinochet, and the shah. In each case, the United States eventually turned against the dictatorial regime and actively aided in its ouster. In Chile and the Philippines, the results were favorable: Democratic governments that have so far endured replaced the Pinochet and Marcos regimes. But in Nicaragua and Iran, one form of tyranny gave way to another. Somoza was replaced by the Sandinistas, who suspended civil liberties and set up a Marxist-style dictatorship. In Iran, a harsh theocracy presided over by the Ayatollah Khomeini replaced the shah.

These outcomes highlight a crucial doctrine of foreign policy: the principle of the lesser evil. In the real world, as

Pakistani leader General Pervez Musharraf shakes hands with U.S. President George W. Bush in November 2001 as they reaffirm the bilateral relationship between their countries.

Dictator Saddam Hussein ruled Iraq from 1979 until 2003. Following the invasion of Iraq, he was captured by U.S. troops in December 2003. An interim government of Iraqis was established on June 28, 2004, and Hussein was put on trial in Iraq. The interim government's powers will expire in January 2005, when elections for a National Assembly will be held.

opposed to the philosophy seminar, the choice is often not between the good guy and the bad guy but between the bad guy and the really bad guy. In such a situation, a country is justified in allying with a bad guy to oppose a regime that is even more terrible. The classic example of this occurred in World War II. The United States allied with a very bad man, Josef Stalin, to defeat someone who then posed a greater threat—Adolf Hitler.

Although it's impossible to say who would succeed Saddam, the United States can be confident that his replacement will be less barbarous and less dangerous. So the United States will avoid the problem that it had in Iran, where the shah's flawed dictatorship was replaced by an even worse regime.

Fighting the Cold War

Once the principle of the lesser evil is taken into account, then U.S. alliances with dictators such as Marcos and Pinochet become defensible. These were measures taken to fight the Cold War. If one accepts what today is an almost universal consensus—that the Soviet Union was an "evil empire"—then America was right to attach more importance to the fact that Marcos and Pinochet were reliably anti-Soviet than to the fact that they were autocratic thugs.

But, the critics respond, the Cold War is over. Why back such tyrannical regimes in the Middle East as the royal family in Saudi Arabia or Pakistan's Musharaff? Again, applying the principle of the lesser evil, what is the alternative? Are there viable democratic forces in Pakistan or Saudi Arabia to replace the existing despots? Or is the alternative to Musharaff the forces of radical fundamentalism, the Osama Bin Laden folk? In that case, America's support for Musharaff is fully warranted.

Osama Bin Laden is the head of the fundamentalist Islamic terrorist organization Al Qaeda (the base). Bin Laden is believed to have been behind many terrorist attacks against Americans, including the attack on the United States on September 11, 2001, and also the 1998 bombing of U.S. embassies in Africa and the 2000 attack on the USS Cole in Yemen. See http://news.bbc.co.uk/1/hi/world/south _asia/155236.stm for more information.

Critics of U.S. intervention abroad frequently miss the point that foreign policy is a practical enterprise. Those who condemn the United States for once backing Bin Laden and Saddam are blind to the fact that situations change and, therefore, that policies must be devised to deal with a particular situation at a given time. It is foolish to hold the United States culpable for "inconsistently" changing its policy when the underlying situation that justified the original policy has also changed.

By this reasoning, America was justified during the 1980s in providing weapons to the mujahideen, even if this group included Bin Laden, to drive the Soviet Union out of Afghanistan. Similarly, there was nothing wrong with

America's supporting Saddam in the late 1970s and early 1980s, when the greatest threat in the region came from Iran. Obviously Bin Laden and Hussein are much greater threats today, and we know things about them now that were not known at the time we supported them. This new situation justifies the Bush administration's current policy of attempting to neutralize the threat posed by both men.

But, as the critics continually emphasize, does violence really solve problems? Actually, yes. Violence helped to end the regimes of Hitler and Benito Mussolini. The atomic bombs the United States dropped on Hiroshima and Nagasaki, however controversial their use, solved the big problem of an unyielding Japan. Violence proved equally effective against the Taliban. "You can't impose democracy at the point of a bayonet" is another shibboleth. At the end of World War II, America imposed democracy in just that manner on Japan and Germany, and the result has proved resoundingly successful in both countries.

The problem with critics of U.S. force is that they are never willing to give bayonets a chance.

Do you think the author's argument is true? Is violence ever justifiable? See Volume 13, U.S. History, Topic 10 Was it necessary to drop the atomic bomb?

TAINTED LEGACY: DANCING WITH DICTATORS
William F. Schulz

Dr. William F. Schulz is the director of the human rights organization Amnesty International USA. He is a regular contributor to international newspapers and journals.

NO

X "Washington has much to learn from Algeria on ways to fight terrorism," said William Burns, assistant secretary of state for Near Eastern and Northern African Affairs in December 2002. In 1992 the Algerian government declared an election null and void because Islamists were poised to win it. If the Islamists had been allowed to assume power peacefully and forced to cope with the challenges of governing one of the world's poorest and most fractious countries, it is entirely conceivable that, as in Iran today, the extremists might have split into factions, a viable opposition have arisen naturally, and the radicals eventually driven from power. (Islamists are very good at mounting protests but have an abysmal record at actually running countries.) Instead, tens of thousands of people, many of them civilians, were killed by the Algerian government over the next decade in the name of restoring "order." Algerian militants were responsible for manifest atrocities as well, but the government's response to terrorism is hardly one that the United States ought to emulate.

Yet since the events of September 2001, the United States, never a purist when it has come to aligning itself with human rights-abusing regimes, has appeared even less cognizant of the bitter fruit such alliances yield, even less willing than in past years to challenge repressive rulers as long as they were on the right side in the War on Terrorism. And one authoritarian government after another, taking their cue from President Bush's declaration of all-out war on all terrorists everywhere, has used that war as an excuse to further erode human rights.

Dancing with dictators

Robert Mugabe's notoriously repressive regime in Zimbabwe, for example, has expelled foreign journalists who have reported critically on his rule. "We would like them [the journalists] to know," a government spokesperson explained, "that we agree with President Bush that anyone who in any way finances, harbors, or defends terrorists is himself a

Robert Mugabe (1924–) became president of Zimbabwe (formerly Rhodesia) in 1980. Over the years his policies have become increasingly repressive, and his treatment of white farmers has been criticized. He has been ruthless in his dealings with critics, including journalists and opposition politicians.

terrorist. We, too, will not make any difference between terrorists and their friends and supporters." Burma (Myanmar), one of the world's most brutal dictatorships, was quick to enroll in the antiterrorist club, declaring [that] it "has been subject to terrorism in the past," no doubt including at the hands of its great democracy advocate, Daw Aung San Suu Kyi.

Aung San Suu Kyi (1945–) is one of the world's leading civil rights activists. Since 1988 she has led the nonviolent protest for Burma (Myanmar) to become a democracy. She has been under house arrest off and on since 1990. Her supporters have been repressed.

China has in effect extracted a quid pro quo from Washington, saying shortly after 9/11, "The United States has asked China to provide assistance against terrorism. China, by the same token, has reasons to ask Washington to give its support and understanding in the fight against terrorism and separatism," which is Chinese code language for those who, usually nonviolently, seek independence for Tibet and the Muslim province of Xinjiang. President Megawati Sukarnoputri of Indonesia has used the threat of terrorism as an excuse for that country's abusive crackdown in the provinces of Aceh and Irian Jaya. Under cover of fighting terrorism, even Australia is refusing entry to political asylum seekers and holding them in deplorable conditions on Christmas Island, 1,400 miles from Darwin.

The United States has continued to speak out against some of these regimes—notably, those less central to the war, like Zimbabwe and Burma—but has far too often given new found allies a "pass." Washington is eager, for instance, to resume military contacts with Indonesia that had been severed because of human rights abuses committed by the Indonesian military in the past and, even more tellingly, has argued in court against a lawsuit that seeks to hold ExxonMobil responsible for rape, torture, and murder committed by that military in conjunction with its protection of ExxonMobil assets in the province of Aceh. Though the State Department was not required to take a position one way or the other on the lawsuit, it chose to do so because "initiatives in the ongoing war against Al Qaeda" could be "imperiled … if Indonesia … curtailed cooperation in response to perceived disrespect for its sovereign interests."

On June 20, 2001, a Washington-based labor rights organization, the International Labor Rights Fund (ILRF), brought a lawsuit against the U.S-owned oil company ExxonMobile on behalf of 11 villagers in the Indonesian province of Aceh.

Malaysia and its outspokenly anti-Semitic prime minister, Mahathir bin Mohammad, have long been objects of criticism by both private human rights groups and the State Department, but in May 2002 the U.S. attitude toward this enemy of democracy changed markedly when President Bush received him at the White House and was effusive in his praise of Malaysia's support for antiterrorism efforts.

Nor was the president reticent in December 2001 to embrace President Nursultan Nazarbayev of Kazakhstan,

In April 2000
President Nursultan
Nazarbayev
admitted that the
torture and
mistreatment of
suspects and
detainees by law
enforcement
officers were
widespread.

Is it any business
of the U.S.
government how
Russia treats
Russian citizens?
Would the United
States stand for
interference in its
own domestic
affairs?

despite his government's continuing harassment and torture of its Uighur minority and Nazarbayev himself being suspected by the Justice Department of having extorted millions of dollars from American oil companies. "We … reiterate our mutual commitments to advance the rule of law and promote freedom of religion and other universal human rights," the two presidents said in their joint statement, though critics might be excused from the cynical observation that this friendship was founded more upon U.S. desire to secure access to an airbase in Kazakhstan than a sudden discovery that the two both loved human rights. (Not surprisingly, within the following six months some 20 newspapers in Kazakhstan were shut down and opposition leaders beaten.) But perhaps the most dramatic reversal of field had to do with Russia, whose brutality in Chechnya candidate Bush had regularly decried. "Russia cannot learn the lessons of democracy from the textbook of tyranny," he said during the 2000 presidential campaign, and he had vowed no cooperation without "civilized self-restraint from Moscow"—strong language which in his May, 2002 trip to Russia had warped into "We will work to help end fighting and achieve a political settlement in Chechnya," his sole comment on the matter.

A legitimate foreign policy goal?

It goes without saying that gaining the cooperation of other governments to fight terrorism is a legitimate foreign policy goal. But what the United States seems to forget with great regularity is that by identifying itself with those who abuse human rights—particularly when the rights being abused are those of Uighur Muslims in China, Acehnese Muslims in Indonesia, Uighur Muslims in Kazakhstan, and Muslims in Chechnya—we invite the conclusions that U.S. rhetoric about democracy and freedom is no more than that, and that the war on terror is in fact a war on Islam.

And one thing more: We seed a new generation of terrorists. In Uzbekistan, to take one of the most egregious cases, the United States has cultivated a military alliance with a government that is renowned for the grotesque nature of its human rights record: people detained without access to lawyers, families, or medical assistance; widespread torture; regular reports of deaths in custody; no dissent; no real elections. "Needless to say," explains one informed observer, "U.S. military aid for antiterrorist activities in countries like Uzbekistan will invariably provide their leaders with resources that can be turned indiscriminately against their

Should the United
States be held
criminally
responsible by the
international courts
if the weapons it
supplies to certain
countries are used
in the suppression
of minority groups?

own populations. And that, paradoxically … will end up driving the discontented toward the only political alternatives that are radical enough to put up a fight."

Jeffrey Goldfarb, who teaches democracy to foreign students all over the world, reports that, more and more, those students (from South Africa to Ukraine to Indonesia), potentially our strongest allies, are turning against the United States. They see the war on terrorism "being used as a cover by dictators around the world to justify crackdowns on democracy advocates…. Suddenly the strategic resources of … dictatorships are more important than the lives of human rights activists. Suddenly the defense of the American way of life and our democracy seems predicated upon a lack of concern for the democratic rights of people in less advantaged countries."

Can the United States do anything to make sure that dictators do not use the War on Terrorism to restrict civil rights further?

Why does it have to be like this?

It doesn't have to be this way. How much wiser it would be to look to some of our great human rights successes for guidance. In 1987 when the United States was closely identified with an autocratic regime in South Korea, anti-American demonstrations were commonplace among pro-democracy advocates, in spite of the sacrifice American soldiers had made in the Korean War. Gradually that changed. And what made the difference? "The antipathy declined as the United States was no longer seen as supporting repressive military regimes in Korea," said the U.S. ambassador, Thomas C. Hubbard. "Korea is an example of how democratic currents can dissipate heat and anger."

Of course no parallel is perfect: Korea was relatively prosperous; it was not threatened by terrorism; and American influence was pervasive. And that support for Korean strongmen still grates: When two 14-year-old South Korean girls were run over and killed by an American armored vehicle in 2002, it unleashed an outpouring of resentment attributed at least in part to lingering indignation at the past U.S. alliance with South Korean dictators. But there is still a lesson to be learned here: It does matter what company you keep. The United States would fare far better fighting terrorism if it fought more consistently for human rights.…

Summary

For years the U.S. government has been criticized for following a highly interventionist foreign policy that has involved the covert and overt support of dictatorships to strengthen U.S. economic and political interests abroad. The two preceding articles represent opposing views on the issue of whether such policies can be justifiable. In the first political analyst Dinesh D'Souza argues that the United States correctly bases its foreign policy on the "principle of the lesser evil." D'Souza claims that in the real world the choice is between "the bad guy and the really bad guy," and in such a situation a country is justified in supporting a tyrannical regime. He also argues that violence can, and should, be used to impose democracy on enemy states.

Amnesty International USA director William F. Schulz, on the other hand, argues that the U.S. administration is often not fully aware of the consequences of its actions. He claims that the United States is perceived as helping nations that repress Muslim populations, for example. This, he argues, angers Muslims, who interpret U.S. policy as oppressive to Islam. Schulz also highlights the paradox by which the United States, the leading voice for democracy, often helps suppress it through its support of nations that commit human rights abuses. Schulz argues that it does not have to be that way. He concludes that there are other, more benign options available to the United States in responding to political change in the world.

FURTHER INFORMATION:

Books:

Carter, Ralph G., *Contemporary Cases in U.S. Foreign Policy: From Terrorism to Trade*. Washington, D.C.: Congressional Quarterly, 2001.

Litwak, Robert S., *Rogue States and U.S. Foreign Policy: Containment after the Cold War*. Baltimore, MD: Johns Hopkins University Press, 2000.

 Useful websites:

http://www.cato.org/cgi-bin/scripts/printtech.cgi/pubs/pas/pa058.html
Cato Institute policy brief on the United States and Third World dictatorships.
http://www.informationclearinghouse.info/article5664.htm
Article analyzing whether the United States practices double standards.
http://times.hankooki.com/page/opinion/200211/kt20021 12916093812870.htm
Korean Times article on U.S. relationship to dictatorships.

The following debates in the Pro/Con series may also be of interest:

In this volume:
Topic 1 Is liberal democracy the only viable political system?

Topic 13 Is the United States naturally isolationist?

In *U.S. Foreign Policy*:
Topic 2 Is U.S. foreign policy too interventionist?

September 11, 2001, pages 176–177

IS IT JUSTIFIABLE FOR THE UNITED STATES TO SUPPORT DICTATORSHIPS?

YES: Dictatorship and democracy are incompatible and work against each other

YES: Sometimes the good of the country must come before individual rights. Such alliances are only made when necessary.

HYPOCRITICAL
Is it hypocritical for the United States to claim to defend democracy and still support dictators?

HUMAN RIGHTS
Can the United States justify supporting regimes with bad human rights records?

NO: In the past, especially during the Cold War, the United States had to form alliances with certain dictatorships to counterbalance the threat from the Soviet Union and China

NO: The United States cannot claim on one hand to support democracy and place sanctions against certain regimes, but support others that behave in the same way just because they are of use

IS IT JUSTIFIABLE FOR THE UNITED STATES TO SUPPORT DICTATORSHIPS?

KEY POINTS

YES: The U.S. government is a democratically elected body; it always acts in the best interests of its citizens even if it does not appear so at the time

YES: Sometimes governments have to "dance with the devil" to ensure that both world peace and world order are protected

THE END
Does the end justify the means?

NO: The events of September 11, 2001, have shown that ill-conceived U.S. foreign policy can have serious consequences

NO: Historically the United States has allowed business interests to dictate its relations with dictatorships

Topic 16

SHOULD THE UNITED STATES DO MORE TO PROMOTE GOOD GOVERNANCE IN LATIN AMERICA?

YES

"U.S. MUST ABANDON ITS ANACHRONISTIC FOREIGN POLICY"
THE MIAMI HERALD, DECEMBER 15, 2003
ABRAHAM F. LOWENTHAL

NO

FROM "SUCCESS STORY IN LATIN AMERICA"
THE WORLD & I, MARCH 2004
MARK HOLSTON

INTRODUCTION

The word "governance" refers to the way in which a government exercises its power in managing the social and economic resources of a country. In international terms "good governance" is the exercise of power that is fair, effective, transparent, and accountable. Its proponents believe it is desirable because it improves political stability, reduces poverty and corruption, and boosts economic performance. National and international bodies increasingly grant aid to developing nations on the proviso that they introduce reforms to promote good governance. Some critics, however, argue that good governance is an ideal that is impossible to attain. They say that it is therefore unfair to make aid to poorer countries conditional on its accomplishment.

Discussions about good governance often include Latin America. The region suffers from sliding economic growth,

poverty, unemployment, unequal income distribution, crime, a thriving drug trade, and declining natural resources. Many commentators believe that the United States should do more to help its southern neighbors achieve good governance.

Some critics, however, say that Latin America's problems actually stem from its relationship with the United States, and thus the latter should recognize its moral duty to support the region. Critics claim that the United States has exploited Latin America for resources such as coffee, bananas, sugar, and oil, and has negotiated trade agreements that favor U.S. businesses. In addition, U.S. farmers receive subsidies that allow them to sell their produce in Latin America at low prices that leave the region's farmers unable to compete. The Free Trade Area of the Americas (FTAA), scheduled for completion by

2005, will create the world's largest free-trade zone by eliminating tariffs from 34 countries. Again, critics claim that the FTAA will privilege large U.S. corporations and will limit the ability of smaller nations to protect their citizens. They argue that fair trade agreements would do far more to tackle poverty within the region.

> *"The deepest root cause of development failure … is a lack of good governance."*
> —LARRY DIAMOND,
> POLITICAL SCIENTIST (2003)

Other commentators believe that the United States should promote good governance in Latin America for reasons of self-preservation rather than obligation. They argue that the region's problems threaten U.S. national security and the economy. Past U.S. governments have not hesitated to intervene in Latin America when they have perceived their interests to be under threat. For example, in 1973 the CIA was involved in a plot in Chile to destabilize the democratically elected government of Marxist Salvador Allende (1908–1973). Allende had nationalized many industries in which U.S. businesses had invested. Augusto Pinochet (1915–), who overthrew Allende in a coup in 1973, welcomed the return of U.S. investment, but his regime committed many human rights violations. Some critics use this example to argue that U.S. interference in Latin America's affairs has worked to the detriment of ordinary people throughout the region.

Other critics claim that the United States is an unreliable partner for Latin America. In 2000 George W. Bush pledged to "look south … as a fundamental commitment of my presidency." But since the terrorist attacks of September 11, 2001, Latin America has trailed behind the War on Terrorism as a foreign-policy priority. The exception is Colombia: By 2003, under the antidrug program Plan Colombia, it had become the largest recipient of U.S. military and economic aid outside of Afghanistan and the Middle East. However, critics of the program insist that it has done little good: Violence has increased, with paramilitary groups continuing to kidnap and kill civilians; security forces have been involved in human rights abuses; and the number of internal refugees has risen sharply.

Despite the fact that Latin American countries have shown commitment to good governance by signing the Inter-American Convention Against Corruption and the Inter-American Democratic Charter, many democracies remain unstable. Some critics suggest that even if the United States did more to help its southern neighbors, good governance is simply not achievable throughout the region. They claim that the capacity and willingness for reform in each country vary greatly. Some also say that corruption is endemic in Latin America and has actually been fueled by attempts at economic reform. For example, privatization has encouraged insider trading. Other critics counter that corruption still exists in advanced democracies, but it can be managed through better regulatory laws.

The following articles by Abraham F. Lowenthal and Mark Holston examine these issues further.

U.S. MUST ABANDON ITS ANACHRONISTIC FOREIGN POLICY
Abraham F. Lowenthal

Abraham F. Lowenthal is a professor of international relations at the University of California. He is also the author of several books on Latin America and inter-American relations. He wrote this piece for the Miami Herald in December 2003.

At a special Summit of the Americas in Mexico in January 2004, 34 leaders signed a declaration pledging support for setting up the FTAA in 2005. However, at the insistence of Venezuela and Brazil, which both have strong reservations about the FTAA, no specific deadline was agreed.

YES

When President Bush took office in January 2001, he was largely devoid of foreign-policy experience and temperamentally and ideologically committed to reducing U.S. activism abroad.

The one foreign-policy priority that the new administration emphasized was to improve U.S. relations with Mexico and, more generally, with the countries of Latin America and the Caribbean. Unfortunately, Bush's earlier focus on Latin America has all but disappeared in the sea-change in foreign policy that occurred after Sept. 11. Promising discussions with Mexico about significant cooperation on immigration and energy was indefinitely postponed, if not aborted.

Also, the high-profile commitment to seek a Free Trade of the Americas Agreement by 2005 was politely gutted at the recent Miami conference [held in November 2003]. The assembled representatives resoundingly adopted what might be called the NANSOFTPA: the Non-Agreement for Not So Free Trade for Part of the Americas.

The exception: Colombia

The only Latin American country that has been able to capture Washington's attention during the past two years is Colombia, largely because that country's president [Alvaro Uribe] and its ambassador to the United States have been able to portray Colombia's violence as a case of international terrorism. The fact that Colombia's terrorists are almost entirely home-grown and locally focused has been obscured, as Washington's "war on terror" button has been successfully pushed.

What is worse, the administration's approach to Latin America and the Caribbean has largely reverted to discredited patterns of the past.

- U.S. officials continue to talk about free trade while increasing the level of protection for items of interest to several Latin American nations, and they insist on domestic agricultural subsidies that undercut South American exports.

Backed by U.S. military aid, President Uribe of Colombia has launched a fresh offensive against the guerrilla fighters of the Revolutionary Armed Forces of Colombia (FARC), pictured above.

- They express satisfaction with Latin America's turn toward democracy while ignoring the serious erosion of democratic governance in many nations.
- The administration's apparent response to expanding poverty and worsening inequities in the region is to complain about corruption and champion the rule of law.
- When pressed to pay more attention to Latin America's growing economic and social crisis, U.S. officials resort to the old slogans of a "special relationship" and an "inter-American community"—lofty phrases that have little positive resonance in today's Latin America.

Over the years, Latin Americans have come to regard such invocations as empty if not cynical. Like the United States and others, Latin American countries pursue their own interests and make a variety of alliances to realize them; they no longer respond to Pan-American rhetoric by obediently following the U.S. lead. That Brazil sided with India, China and other developing countries at the recent Cancún trade talks would not have been so surprising to U.S. officials if they had been taking Latin American countries seriously.

Future importance of Latin America

Despite our current inattention, the fact is that Latin America's future will matter a great deal to the United States in the medium and longer term, perhaps more than what occurs today in the Persian Gulf, South Asia or the Middle East. Latin America is important to the United States for five main reasons:

- A prolonged recession in Latin America would sharply curtail U.S. exports in the region where they have grown most in the past decade. It is already severely reducing the earnings of several major U.S. banks and corporations.
- Latin America—especially Mexico, Venezuela and Colombia—provides a large share of U.S. energy imports. Severe instability in Latin America could greatly intensify energy insecurity in the United States.
- Latin American cooperation is required to deal with tough issues—the narcotics trade, global warming, environmental protection, contagious diseases—that the United States cannot resolve by itself.
- Conditions in Latin America will determine the scope and pace of immigration to the United States, legal and illegal. Economic and political disasters in Latin America and the Caribbean will put intense pressure on U.S. borders.

World trade talks broke down in Cancún, Mexico, in September 2003 after four days of discussions. The main area of disagreement was the subsidies that rich nations pay their farmers. Developing nations want these subsidies reduced in order to stop agricultural goods being exported at artificially low prices that destroy their own markets.

In early 2004 President George W. Bush proposed changing U.S. immigration laws to allow illegal immigrants to be employed as temporary workers in jobs that U.S. companies are unable to fill with Americans. This move was welcomed by President Vicente Fox of Mexico. It is estimated that 30 percent of the Mexican population relies on money sent home from relatives working in the United States Do you think that the author should also consider how important immigrants are to the U.S. economy?

• Our closest neighbors—linked ever more closely to the United States by the fast-growing Latin American and Caribbean diasporas in this country—are an important testing ground of our core values and ideals: democratic governance, the protection of individual human rights and the benefits of free-market competition. If democratic governance and market economies collapse in Latin America, Washington's preferred world order will be seriously threatened.

The kind of society for which we are fighting in Iraq could well be destroyed without a shot in Latin America, heretofore the best Third World candidate for successful transition to the political and economic order we prefer. It is high time we refocus attention on our closest neighbors.

Do you think that the author is justified in labeling the whole of Latin America as part of the "Third World"?

SUCCESS STORY IN LATIN AMERICA
Mark Holston

The U.S.–Chile Free Trade Agreement—the first such arrangement between the United States and a South American country—came into force at the beginning of 2004. It faced opposition from some Chilean politicians, who expressed concern over the future of jobs. Others argued the deal would undermine regional trade.

The "Pacific Rim" refers to countries that border the Pacific Ocean.

Augusto Pinochet Ugarte (1915–) was president of Chile between 1974 and 1990. More than 3,000 people were killed or vanished during his rule. In 1998 he was arrested while being treated in a London hospital. After a legal battle to extradite him to Spain to face trial for the torture of Spanish citizens, he was allowed to return to Chile in 2000. See Volume 22, International Law, pages 34–35, for more information.

NO

By most outward appearances, Chile is an oasis of political stability and economic progress in a region noted for social upheaval and grinding poverty. While neighboring Bolivia and Peru teeter on the brink of anarchy and Brazil and Argentina attempt to get their economic houses in order after bouts of political ills, Chile seems to be on an even course.

Its ports bustle with a steady flow of exports and imports. Such primary Chilean exports as timber, salmon, copper, and wine are in increasing demand around the world. The recently signed free-trade agreement between Washington and Santiago, as well as separate Chilean trade pacts with the European Union, Mercosur (the South American free-trade zone that encompasses Brazil, Argentina, Paraguay, and Uruguay), and a growing number of Pacific Rim trading partners, bodes well for the country's economic future. In recent months, the Chilean peso has rebounded in strength against the U.S. dollar—a rare occurrence in Latin American nations.

On the home front, there are many equally positive signs. Chile's cities are well scrubbed and booming with new construction. The country's infrastructure is impressive; its primary highways are the most modern in all of Latin America, and while other countries in the region are cutting back on their railway systems, Chile is investing in new rolling stock and expanding passenger service. University campuses brim with students eager to finish their degrees and enter the country's professional workforce....

Grappling with the past

Although often proclaimed as being a Latin American miracle, with a robust economy, strong democratic traditions, and a highly educated and culturally sophisticated populace, the country remains haunted by events that unfolded three decades ago and produced 17 years of often harsh military rule under Gen. Augusto Pinochet....

Momentous political and social events that began building in the 1960s, feeding on Cold War paranoia and economic crisis, culminated in the military coup of September 11, 1973.

The putsch overthrew the government of Salvador Allende, the world's first democratically elected Marxist head of state. The takeover ended a long tradition of nonintervention by the military, considered at the time the most professional in all of Latin America....

The degree of U.S. involvement in fomenting the coup is still hotly debated ... When all else fails, critics of U.S. policy fall back on the often-cited quote by then-U.S. Secretary of State Henry Kissinger, who openly questioned why the United States should stand by and "let a country go communist due to the irresponsibility of its own people."

"Along with many observers, I don't think the coup was justified at any time," comments Paul Drake, dean of the social sciences department and professor at University of California San Diego (UCSD) ... "It derailed one of the longest and strongest democracies in Latin America, unleashed massive human rights violations, and left the nation polarized still today.... [T]he opposition and the United States saw Allende through a distorted Cold War lens, which produced a tragedy. As [U.S. Secretary of State] Colin Powell said recently about Washington's role there, 'It is not a part of American history that we are proud of.'" ...

Do you agree with Kissinger that the United States has a right to intervene in another country's affairs if it does not approve of that country's government— even one that has been elected democratically?

Chile's place in the world

Chile may have been lashed by the same economic storms that put a damper on growth in virtually every corner of the world in recent years, but its political stability and successful trade policies have made it a success story at a time when most other developing countries' economies have faltered.

The consensus of a growing number of foreign and domestic observers is that Chile is on the right path and that coming years should lead to an upswing in growth and prosperity. The country's role as host nation of the 2004 summit of the Asia–Pacific Economic Cooperation (APEC) group will provide Chile a rare opportunity for President Ricardo Lagos to show off what his country has accomplished....

APEC is an intergovernmental organization of 21 states that aims to promote economic growth, cooperation, and trade in the Asia–Pacific region.

Soledad Alvear, Chile's foreign minister, terms the APEC gathering "the most important foreign policy event that our country has ever organized." She adds that Chile is "not a wealthy or powerful country but a small nation that has risen above the adversity of a challenging and far-off setting in—as many would call it—the furthermost corner of the world." ...

Despite problems posed by its geographic isolation, in terms of both economic and social progress, Chile ranks high among developing nations. Between 1987 and 2000, for

According to the World Bank, the average life expectancy in Chile in 2000 was 73 years for men and 79 years for women. Compare to the United States, with 74 years for men and 80 years for women and to an average of 67 years for men and 74 years for women in Latin America and the Caribbean as a whole.

instance, the number of Chileans living in poverty dropped from an estimated 45 percent of the population to around 21 percent. In the last decade, the government's budget for social programs has increased by over 100 percent. In recent years, both the literacy and life expectancy rates have increased while the infant mortality count has fallen. These and other quality-of-life measurements compare favorably to those of the United States and other developed nations. Further, the United Nations and other entities consistently rank Chile in the upper echelon of nations best prepared to compete in the global economy.

"The democratic governments of the last 15 years have produced higher growth rates, lower poverty, and lower unemployment than the military dictatorship that preceded them," states UCSD's Drake. "However, unemployment has been creeping up, though not to levels seen under the military, since 1998, due to the international recession. As a result, unemployment is the most vexing current issue facing the government. Nevertheless, Chile still has the most successful economy in Latin America. The legacy from the military government was a free-market economic orientation, which the democracy has maintained."

The website of the UN Economic Commission for Latin America and the Caribbean (www.eclac.cl) provides a useful overview of the economies of Latin America.

The country's gross domestic product more than doubled in the last decade, and growth produced gains of around 3 percent even during the international economic downturn of 2001. Many observers believe that economic growth will increase to 5 or 6 percent in coming years. Inflation, which traditionally hinders economic development in many Latin American nations, has been cut in Chile from 27 percent in 1990 to only 3 percent in 2001.

Independent-minded U.S. partner

"Many of the linkages we historically had with the United States were broken, but now they're starting to be established again," comments Miguel Angel López, a professor of political science at the University of Chile. "The free-trade agreement with the United States, signed in early September by President Bush, is a very good development for the country. But relations with the United States remain complex, exacerbated by the Nixon administration's efforts to undermine Allende and its support after the 1973 coup of the Pinochet military regime."

The National Security Archive at George Washington University (www.gwu.edu/~nsarchiv/) has compiled a collection of declassified government records that relate to the attempts of the Nixon administration to overthrow Allende.

Since then, the relationship has been a roller-coaster affair, as successive administrations have altered their attitude toward Chile based on a variety of national and international factors....

Tomás Chuaqui, director of the Institute of Political Science at the Catholic University of Chile, believes that although Chile is today charting an independent course in international relations, it is a country the United States can count on in a somewhat unsettled part of the globe. "The relationship is quite strong," he comments, "and not likely to change in the immediate future. And it's not based only on trade; it's also political. Chile is a very stable country politically in the region, so the United States looks at Chile as a good ally to have in this part of Latin America. There's a lot more uncertainty in many countries in the region than there is in Chile. One of the reasons for the relationship is that Chile has demonstrated stability and economic strength."

Important differences remain

Although the national interests of Chile and the United States are increasingly aligned, noted differences of opinion remain. In its role as a member of the UN Security Council, Chile voiced strong opposition to U.S. plans to invade Iraq. The war in Iraq remains very unpopular in Chile, and there are lingering concerns about Washington's long-term commitment to Latin American issues....

"The main problem with the United States really doesn't have anything to do with Chile in particular," he adds. "It has more to do with the United States as a hegemonic power in general and [the perception of] its unwillingness to become an equal partner with anyone in the international arena."

Like many of his countrymen, Chuaqui believed the terrorist attack on the United States would produce a change of heart in Washington. "When the other September 11 [Chile's 1973 coup also happened on the same date] happened," he says, "one of the impressions I and many other Chileans had was that this finally signified that there can be no hegemonic power in the world any longer. The weakest power can harm the most powerful. That means that even the most powerful entity requires the assistance of the weaker powers around the world. The first impression we had was that the United States was going to move in that direction. That seems not to have happened."

The recently signed trade agreement, however, is widely perceived in Chile to be a high-water mark in relations between the two countries. Building on the pact's potential for improved economic ties should bring the national interests of the two nations closer together and may help pave the way for improved understanding and cooperation on other issues of mutual concern.

In May 2003 Chile announced that it would be replacing its ambassador to the United Nations, Juan Gabriel Valdès, with Heraldo Muñoz. This was perceived to be a move to appease the United States and to facilitate the signing of the U.S.–Chile Free Trade Agreement. Valdès had been critical of the U.S. decision to go to war against Iraq in the spring of 2003.

Do you agree that the United States has appeared in a stronger rather than a weaker position on the world stage since the terrorist attacks of September 11, 2001? See Topic 6 Has the War on Terrorism reinforced U.S. global leadership?

Summary

Abraham F. Lowenthal, author of the first article, argues that the United States needs to refocus its foreign policy on its nearest neighbors, Latin America. He says that since the terrorist attacks of September 11, 2001, U.S. attention has shifted away from the region, with the exception of Colombia. Lowenthal accuses the U.S. government of returning to "discredited patterns of the past" in its approach to Latin America. The United States has, he says, ignored the breakdown of democracy in many nations and has failed to respond to the region's growing economic and social crisis. He warns that Latin America's future matters more to U.S. interests than what happens in the Middle East or elsewhere. Lowenthal concludes that there is much at stake in the region for the United States in terms of its economy and the promotion of democracy.

In the second article Mark Holston outlines Chile's newfound political stability and economic progress. But he says that the Chilean population remains politically divided over the legacy of the military coup of 1973, which replaced the democratically elected government of Salvador Allende with the dictatorship of General Augusto Pinochet. He reports that there is still controversy over the role that the United States played in Allende's downfall. Holston considers the growth that Chile has witnessed since democracy was restored, which has made it the most successful economy in Latin America. Although the country has become a reliable ally of the United States, Holston points out that some Chileans question U.S. commitment to the region. He believes, however, that the new Free Trade Agreement between the two nations will bring them closer together.

FURTHER INFORMATION:

Books:
Domínguez, Jorge I., and Michael Shifter (eds.), *Constructing Democratic Governance in Latin America* (2nd edition). Baltimore, MD: Johns Hopkins University Press, 2003.
Skidmore, Thomas E., and Peter H. Smith, *Modern Latin America* (5th edition). New York: Oxford University Press, 2001.

Useful websites:
www.ftaa-alca.org/
Official site of the Free Trade Area of the Americas.
http://www.usaid.gov/our_work/democracy_and_governance/regions/lac/
Paper on democracy and governance in Latin America and the Caribbean from the U.S. Agency for International Development.

The following debates in the Pro/Con series may also be of interest:

In this volume:
Topic 15 Is it justifiable for the United States to support dictatorships?

In *U.S. Foreign Policy*:
Has the United States exploited Latin America?

In *International Law*:

Augusto Pinochet: Patriot or war criminal? pages 34–35

SHOULD THE UNITED STATES DO MORE TO PROMOTE GOOD GOVERNANCE IN LATIN AMERICA?

YES: Latin America remains important to the United States. Plan Colombia is an example of its continuing commitment to the region.

YES: Latin America has already progressed from a region of military dictatorships to a community of democracies. It is committed to good governance.

9/11
Are U.S.–Latin American relations still strong since September 11, 2001?

IDEAL VS. REALITY
Is good governance attainable in Latin America?

NO: The War on Terrorism has become the U.S. top priority. Unless it refocuses on Latin America, the region will pursue its own interests and alliances.

SHOULD THE UNITED STATES DO MORE TO PROMOTE GOOD GOVERNANCE IN LATIN AMERICA?

KEY POINTS

NO: Corruption is prevalent in the region. Political support for reform is tentative and is undermined by poverty, lawlessness, and drug trafficking.

YES: It is in U.S. security and economic interests that Latin America embrace democratic governance. The United States needs to erase its history of supporting undemocratic dictatorships in the region.

YES: The FTAA will open new markets to Latin America, boost economic growth, and attract investment in the region

DEMOCRACY
Should the United States do more to promote democracy in Latin American countries?

FREE TRADE
Will the Free Trade Area of the Americas (FTAA) aid good governance in Latin America?

NO: Democracy is not suitable for all nations. Latin America should be allowed to find its own political path. The United States has intervened too much in the region in the past.

NO: The FTAA is primarily in the interests of large U.S. corporations. It will increase unemployment and have a negative effect on smaller economies.

213

GLOSSARY

absolutism a system of government based on a ruler who has unrestricted power.

Al Qaeda literally "the base." It is an international Islamic terrorist network founded in 1988 by Osama Bin Laden and his associates.

anti-Semitism hatred or hostility toward Jewish people.

Arab League an alliance of Arab nations formed in 1945 to protect the common economic and political interests of Arabs.

capitalism an economic system in which private individuals and firms control the production and distribution of goods and services, and make profits in return for the investment of capital, or money.

civil rights rights guaranteed to individuals by certain laws.

Cold War the period of tension between the United States and the Soviet Union, and their respective allies. The Cold War lasted from 1945 until the breakup of the Soviet Union in 1991.

communism a political ideology based on the writings of Karl Marx (1818–1883). It advocates common ownership achieved through the overthrow of capitalism by revolutionary means.

containment the policy of preventing the expansion of a hostile power or ideology.

coup d'etat a sudden, often violent overthrow or alteration of government.

crimes against humanity defined by Article 1 of the Rome Statute, these crimes include murder, enslavement, torture, and rape committed as part of a systematic attack against any civilian population.

democracy a system of government based on the rule of the majority of the population. Citizens elect representatives to carry out their wishes in government.

Democratic Party one of the two major political parties in the United States. Dating from 1792, it has traditionally represented organized labor, minorities, and progressive reformers.

developing countries poor nations that are undergoing economic modernization through the development of an industrial and commercial base.

dictatorship a government ruled by a person or small group of people that exerts absolute power. *See also* absolutism.

diplomacy the art and practice of carrying out negotiations between nations.

ethnic cleansing action intended to remove or extinguish an ethnic group from a country or region. *See also* genocide.

European Union (EU) economic grouping of western European countries that evolved in 1993 from the European Community (EC). A combined European economic community first begun in 1958.

foreign aid financial assistance given by rich nations, humanitarian organizations, or financial institutions to countries in need.

free trade international trade that is not subject to restrictions or barriers.

General Agreement on Tariffs and Trade (GATT) the organization formed in 1948 to agree on the easing of trade restrictions on countries. *See also* WTO.

Geneva Accord an agreement negotiated by the Israeli peace movement and moderate Palestinians in 2003. It would create a Palestinian state including Gaza, most of the West Bank, and the Arab areas of Jerusalem.

genocide action intended to destroy or kill an entire national or ethnic group. *See also* ethnic cleansing.

globalization the worldwide expansion of private corporations and the culture from which they originate.

Hamas a Palestinian fundamentalist organization formed in 1987. It has carried out numerous terrorist attacks on Israelis. *See also* terrorism.

human rights the rights people have irrespective of citizenship, nationality, race, ethnicity, language, sex, sexuality, or abilities, enforceable when they are codified as covenants or treaties.

International Criminal Court (ICC) an independent permanent court established in 1998, the ICC has jurisdiction over persons committing serious crimes in the international community. By 2004, 139 nations had signed up to its establishment, and 94 states had ratified it.

International Monetary Fund (IMF) an organization formed in 1945 to promote international monetary cooperation and economic growth.

internment detention without charge. *See also* human rights.

Intifada a term used to describe the uprising of Palestinian Arabs in the Gaza Strip and West Bank, beginning in late 1987, in protest against Israeli occupation of these territories.

isolationism the theory that a country's interests are best served by minimal involvement in foreign affairs and alliances.

national sovereignty the freedom of a country to conduct its internal affairs without external interference.

North American Free Trade Agreement (NAFTA) an accord between Canada, Mexico, and the United States that established a free trade zone in North America from 1994.

North Atlantic Treaty Organization (NATO) a military alliance of 26 European and North American nations, including the United States, Germany, Spain, and the UK. NATO's role is to safeguard the freedom and security of its members.

Palestine Liberation Organization (PLO) the coordinating council for Palestinian organizations founded at the first Arab summit in 1964.

preemptive war the use of military force in response to an imminent threat.

Republican Party one of the two major U.S. political parties. Founded in 1854, it stands for limited government and low taxes. *See also* democracy, Democratic Party.

"Roadmap to peace" a document published in 2003 outlining internationally endorsed provisions for Israeli–Palestinian peace.

Security Council UN executive organ whose main responsibility is to preserve peace. *See also* United Nations.

suicide bomber a person who detonates a bomb to kill others regardless of the fact that the explosion will kill him- or herself.

Taliban an Islamic fundamentalist political group that emerged in Afghanistan in the mid-1990s following the withdrawal of occupying Soviet troops.

terrorism the unlawful use or threat of violence by a person or organized group against people or property with the intention of intimidating or coercing societies or governments, often for ideological or political reasons.

transnational corporation (TNC) an enterprise that operates in a number of different countries and that has production facilities outside its home country.

United Nations (UN) an international organization founded in 1945 to maintain world peace and to foster international cooperation in solving problems.

USA PATRIOT Act (2001) introduced after the terrorist action of September 11,2001, this law allowed the arrest and detainment of immigrants, and extended the powers of the Military Order to allow tribunals to try noncitizens who have been charged with terrorism. *See also* terrorism.

War on Terrorism (the War on Terror) the effort of the United States and its allies to neutralize international terrorist groups and axis-of-evil nations.

World Trade Organization (WTO) founded in 1995, the WTO monitors trade policies and disputes, and enforces the GATT agreements. *See also* GATT.

Acknowledgments

1. Is Liberal Democracy the Only Viable Political System?

Yes: "History Is Still Going Our Way" by Francis Fukuyama, *The Wall Street Journal*, October 5, 2001. Reprinted from *The Wall Street Journal*, copyright © 2001, Dow Jones & Company, Inc. All rights reserved.
No: "The End of the End of History" by Fareed Zakaria, *Newsweek*, September 24, 2001. Copyright © 2001, *Newsweek*, Inc. All rights reserved. Reprinted by permission.

2. Is the Nation-State Consistent with the Idea of Globalization?

Yes: "Will the Nation-State Survive Globalization?" by Martin Wolf. Reprinted by permission of *FOREIGN AFFAIRS*, Vol. 80, No. 1, January/February 2001. Copyright © 2001 by the Council of Foreign Relations. Used by permission.
No: "The Age of Sovereignty Has Come to an End" by Llewellyn D. Howell. Reprinted from the *USA TODAY Magazine*, September 1998. Copyright © 1998 by the Society for the Advancement of Education, Inc. Used by permission.

3. Do Religion-Based Politics Undermine Democracy?

Yes: From "Then: Violence—Now: Genocide" by Priya Lal, *Clamor Magazine*, Issue 23, November/December 2003. Copyright © 2003. Reprinted by permission of *Clamor Magazine* and Priya Lal.
No: "Secularism Is No Answer for the Muslim World" by Amir Butler, *The Age*, October 28, 2003. Copyright © 2003. Reprinted by permission of Amir Butler and The Age.

4. Is Democracy under Threat in Russia?

Yes: "The Era of Liberalism versus Communism in Russia Is Over" by Michael McFaul, Carnegie Endowment for International Peace, Russian and Eurasian Affairs Program, 2003. Reprinted by permission of the publisher, Washington, D.C.: Carnegie Endowment for International Peace (www.ceip.org).
No: "The Awful Truth" by Jonathan Steele, *The Guardian*, December 10, 2003. Copyright © *The Guardian*, 2003. Reprinted by permission.

5. Can Violence Bring about Effective Political Change?

Yes: From "I am Prepared to Die" by Nelson Mandela, April 20, 1964. Reprinted by permission of the Africna National Congress (http://www.anc.org.za/ancdocs/history/rivonia.html). Public Domain.

No: "The Theatre of Good and Evil" by Eduardo Galeano, translated by Justin Podur, *La Jornada*, September 21, 2001 (http://www.progressiveaustin.org/galeano.htm).

6. Has the War on Terrorism Reinforced U.S. Global Leadership?

Yes: "Lawmaker Praises International Cooperation in War on Terrorism," State Department press release, December 12, 2001. Public Domain.
No: From "This War on Terrorism Is Bogus" by Michael Meacher, *The Guardian*, September 6, 2003. Copyright © Michael Meacher, 2003. Reprinted by permission.

7. Can Israel and Palestine Ever Reach a Peace Settlement?

Yes: "Geneva Accord: Open Forum," Americans for Peace Now, the Foundation for Middle East Peace, and the American Task Force on Palestine, Washington, D.C., December 3, 2003. Copyright © 2003. Reprinted by permission of The American Task Force on Palestine (www.americantaskforce.org), an organization dedicated to articulating the U.S. interests of establishing a Palestinian state alongside Israel living in peace and security.
No: "Striking Accord," from *The Economist* online, December 4, 2003. Copyright © 2003. Reprinted by permission.

8. Should the United Nations Be Disbanded?

Yes: "The Time is Now: The United Nations—Irrelevant and Dangerous" by Tom DeWeese, March 28, 2003, American Policy Center. Copyright © 2003. Reprinted by permission of the American Policy Center.
No: "President Bush Meets with UN Secretary General Kofi Annan: Remarks by the President and UN Secretary General Kofi Annan in Photo Opportunity," Office of the Press Secretary, The Oval Office, February 3, 2004. Public Domain.

9. Is NATO Still Needed in the Post-Cold War World?

Yes: From "Speech by Nato Secretary General: Winston Churchill Lecture" by Lord Robertson, www.nato.int, London, November 24, 2003. Copyright © 2003. Reprinted by permission.
No: "Advice for Bush on NATO: End It, Don't Extend It" by Libertarian Party online (www.lp.org), November 21, 2002. Public Domain.

10. Is a United States of Europe Possible?

Yes: "A United States of Europe?" Reprinted from June 5, 2000 issue of *BusinessWeek* by special permission, copyright © 2000 by The McGraw-Hill Companies, Inc.

No: "Giscard Unveils Draft for 'United Europe'" by Ian Black, *The Guardian*, October 29, 2002. Copyright © *The Guardian*, 2002. Reprinted by permission.

11. Is the World Trade Organization Anti-American?

Yes: "Visclosky Calls on President to Reject WTO Ruling on Steel Safeguards" Press Release, November 10, 2003, (http://www.house.gov/apps/list/press/in01_visclosky/wto031110.html). Public Domain.

No: "Lone Sharks" by Robert Lane Greene, *New Republic*, July 17, 2003. Reprinted by permission of THE NEW REPUBLIC, copyright © 2003, *The New Republic*, LLC.

12. Could the Arab League Do More to Promote Peace in the Middle East?

Yes: Moshe Hillel Eitan, "Ten reasons why Israel should join the Arab League" by Moshe Hillel Eitan, Opinion, *Middle East Times*, Issue 29, 2002. Copyright © 2002. Reprinted by permission of Moshe Hillel Eitan and the *Middle East Times*.

No: "A Sustainable Arab League" by Gamil Mattar, *Al-Ahram Weekly* online: July 10–16, 2003 (http://weekly.ahram.org.eg/2003/646/op13.htm).

13. Is the United States Naturally Isolationist?

Yes: "America's Tradition of Non-interventionism" by Chris Leithner, *Le Québécois libre* (www.quebecoislibre.org), November 22, 2003. Copyright © 2003. Reprinted by permission.

No: "Internationalism in U.S. Foreign Policy" by Samuel L. Berger, USIS Washington File, October 25, 1999 (http://www.fas.org/news/usa/1999/10/991021-usa-usia11.htm). Adapted from his address to the Council on Foreign Relations in New York City on October 21. Public Domain. There are no republication restrictions.

14. Did "Diplomacy on a Shoestring" Contribute to September 11, 2001?

Yes: "Beating Terror" by Richard Lugar. This byliner by Senator Lugar (Republican-Indiana) first appeared in the *Washington Post*, January 27, 2003, and is in the public domain. No republication restrictions.

No: From "Don't Blame America for Terrorist atrocity?" by Tony Parkinson, *The Age*, September 28, 2001. Copyright © 2001. Reprinted by permission of Tony Parkinson and The Age.

15. Is It Justifiable for the United States to Support Dictatorships?

YES: "When There's No Good Guy" by Dinesh D'Souza, *Hoover Digest*, no. 1, 2003, Winter Issue. Originally appeared in *USA Today*, November 13, 2002. Copyright © Dinesh D'Souza, 2002. Used by permission.

No: From "Tainted Legacy: Dancing with Dictators" by William F. Schulz, *Amnesty Now*, Fall 2003. Copyright © Nation Books 2003. Reprinted by permission of Amnesty International USA, 322 Eighth Avenue, New York, NY 10001, USA.

16. Should the United States Do More to Promote Good Governance in Latin America?

Yes: "U.S. Must Abandon Its Anachronistic Foreign Policy" by Abraham F. Lowenthal, *Miami Herald* online, December 15, 2003. Copyright © 2003 by *Miami Herald*. Reprinted with permission of *Miami Herald* in the format Textbook via Copyright Clearance Center.

No: "Success Story in Latin America" by Mark Holston. This article appeared in the MARCH 2004 issue and is reprinted with permission from *The World &* I, a publication of The Washington Times Corporation, copyright © 2004.

The Brown Reference Group plc has made every effort to contact and acknowledge the creators and copyright holders of all extracts reproduced in this volume. We apologize for any omissions. Any person who wishes to be credited in further volumes should contact The Brown Reference Group plc in writing: The Brown Reference Group plc, 8 Chapel Place, Rivington Street, London EC2A 3DQ, U.K.

Picture credits

Cover: Corbis: Clive Newton; Military Picture Library
Corbis: Francois Carrel/Montage Magazine 185, Thomas Hartwell 156, Reuters 205, Charles E Rotkin 147; **Corbis Saba:** David Butow 143; **Corbis Sygma:** Ilyas Dean 18, Juha Roininen 6/7; **Mary Evans Picture Library:** 41; **NASA:** 69; **PA Photos:** EPA 110; **Photos.com:** 58/59; **Rex Features:** Action Press 109, 121, Hussein Hussein 98/99, Marco Marianella 49, Ron Sachs 77, 193, Sipa Press 54, 93, 133; **Topham Picturepoint:** UPPA 129, 138/139

SET INDEX

Page numbers in **bold** refer to
volume numbers; those in *italics* refer
to picture captions.

A

Abacha, Sani 14:24–25; 15:197,
  198; 22:152, *153*, 154
Abbas, Mahmoud 19:99
abduction, parent-child abduction
  disputes 22:72–83
Abington Township v. Schempp
  (1963) 16:151
abortion 1:188–201; 7:148;
  11:144
  contraceptives as cause of
    20:90, 98, 99
  do fetuses have rights? 15:140–51
  legalizing the abortion pill
    RU-486 10:9, 48–59
  a religious issue? 20:74–85
  violent protest 7:141, 142–50;
    15:101
  see also Roe v. Wade
Abzug, Bella 13:64
accountability 3:68–69; 16:11
Aceh 19:197
acetylcholine 17:140
Acheson, Dean 13:144, 149
acid rain 4:86–87, 110, 138–39
ACT-UP (AIDS Coalition to Unleash
  Power) 10:41
acupuncture 5:66; 10:88, 92, 97
Adam and Eve 20:14–15, 71, 130
Adams, John 2:103; 7:20
  and the judiciary 21:42, 53, 75
  and women's rights 13:68
address, terms of 12:78, 82
Adolescent Family Life Act (AFLA;
  1981) 11:127
adoptions
  gay couples as parents
    11:16–17, 40–43, 44, 48–49,
    62–73
  single-parent 11:48, 56–59, 60
  transcultural 11:82, 84, 85
  transracial 11:49, 74–85
  United States 11:57
adultery, should be a criminal
  offense? 20:110–11
Advani, Lal Krishna 19:38
advertising 3:203, 205; 6:88–99
  body image and 6:74–77, 82
  business ethics and 3:171, 198–209
  controversial 23:199
  negative 3:199
  objective journalism and 6:87,
    126–37
  political 6:87, 138–49
  tobacco 3:171; 6:87, 104,
    112–23, 125
  to children 6:86–87, 100–111
affirmative action 1:9, 72–85; 13:161
  and black colleges 16:193, 201
  and income 23:65, 75
Afghanistan
  aid for 14:77
  drugs and terrorism 8:152–53
  human rights abuses 15:70
  Mujahideen "freedom fighters"
    19:70

NATO and 19:119
pre-Islamic statues destroyed
  19:184, *185*
prisoners of war from 9:179,
  180–87; 22:196–99
  see also Guantánamo Bay
refugees from 15:94–97, 98
Soviet invasion of 13:206; 15:94
  and U.S. sanctions 15:191
treatment of women 13:67; 15:70
U.S. foreign policy and 8:25, 43;
  13:202, 206; 15:191; 19:75
War on Terrorism 8:166–67,
  184–85, 190–91; 14:79;
    19:18–19, 82–83; 22:31, 202
  see also Taliban
AFL-CIO 8:67; 18:51; 24:166
  and equal pay for women
    11:189, 190–93, 198
Africa
  carbon tax and 23:160
  customs and monetary unions
    18:65
  drug prices 18:37
  famine 23:209
  famine and hunger 14:*81*, 191
  foreign aid for 8:115–16
  good governance 14:40–43, 44
  human rights abuses in 15:69
  privatization in 3:44
  reparations to 1:179–81
  tax policies in 23:160–61
  Third World debt 3:158, 161; 18:94
African Americans
  black Greek-letter societies 16:180
  the civil rights movement and
    13:152–63
  the Constitution and 7:64–65
  and corporal punishment
    11:120–21
  and crime 9:8
  and illegal drugs 7:69; 9:129–30
  income disparity 23:64, 65,
    66–69, 74
  prejudice against 11:23
  in prisons 7:67–69
  racial profiling of 9:126
  sentencing of 21:126, 127, 128–31
  should black universities be
    phased out? 16:190–201
  single mothers 11:53–54
  and transracial adoption
    11:74–75, 80–82
  Tulia trial 11:23
  see also civil rights; segregation;
    slaves/slavery
African, Caribbean, and Pacific
  Group of States (ACP) 14:40
African National Congress (ANC),
  and violence 19:63, 64–67, 72
African Virtual University (AVU)
  23:183
Agnew, Spiro 2:206, 208
agriculture *see* farming
Aguillard v. Edwards (1987) 16:143
aid, foreign 4:38, 39; 8:112–23;
  23:153, 163
  should rich countries donate a
    set percentage of GNP to?
    14:74–85
  see also relief bodies

aid agencies 14:199
AIDS *see* HIV/AIDS
AIDS Prevention for Adolescents
  in School 11:132
Aid to Dependent Children
  (ADC) 7:83
Aid to Families with Dependent
  Children (AFDC) 23:115
air pollution 4:139
  "pay to pollute" systems 4:86–97
  see also acid rain; global warming
aircraft
  computer-aided design 17:205
airlines
  and the unions 18:50
airport security 13:210
Alaska
  national parks 4:63
  native peoples 15:178, 179,
    180–87, 188
Albania, minority schools in
  15:42–43
Albigenses 20:157
alcohol
  advertising 6:104–5
  and hazing 16:188–89
  and Prohibition 13:74–85
  and sexual violence on campus
    16:179–81
  taxing 23:103–4
Alexander the Great 20:131
Algeria
  human rights abuses 15:71
  terrorism 8:165
  government response to 19:196
Allende, Salvador 8:125; 19:70,
  203, 209, 212
Allen, Florence Ellinwood 21:103
Allport, Gordon 11:28
al-Masri, Abu Hamza 20:31, 48, *49*, 50
Alpha Delta Pi 16:180
Alpha Earners 23:83–84, 86
Alpha Phi Alpha 16:180
Al Qaeda 8:23, 25, 111, 153, 179,
  190–91; 9:214; 13:202, 203, 210
  prisoners of war 9:179, 180–88;
    15:63, 79, 81, 167, 172–73,
    209, 211; 22:196–99
Alzheimer's disease 10:80; 17:140
  therapy for 17:182–83
Amazon.com 3:48, 49, 54–55, 57, 58
Amazon rain forest, and capitalism
  3:23, 24–25, 32
Amber Alert network 21:95
American Airlines
  and the unions 18:50
American Arts Alliance 12:35,
  36–39
American Association for the
  Advancement of Science
  17:161
American Association of Retired
  People (AARP) 1:18
American Bar Association (ABA)
  21:25, 74–79, 84, 85, 118, 146
  and Criminal Justice Standards
    21:170
  and Moral Code of Judicial
    Conduct 21:119–21
American Cancer Society (ACS)
  17:122